IMAGES *of America*

ALONG THE CONNECTICUT RIVER

FAIRLEE/WEST FAIRLEE, ORFORD, BRADFORD, PIERMONT, NEWBURY, AND HAVERHILL

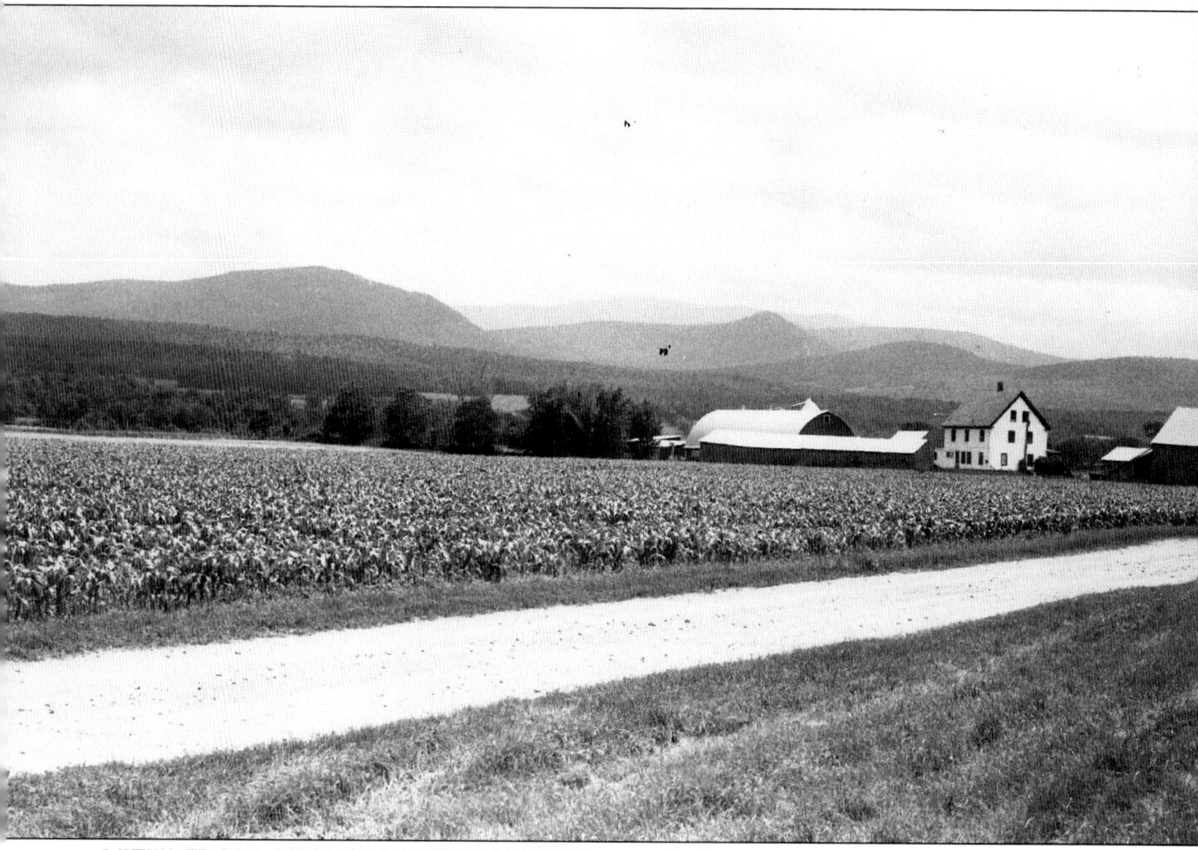

VIEW FROM ABOVE NORTH HAVERHILL. Black Mountain is on the left, the pointed peak is Sugar Loaf, and behind them is Mount Moosilauke. The farms belong to the Elms and McDanolds families.

COVER IMAGE: SIGHTSEERS AND THEIR BICYCLES AT LAKE MOREY.

IMAGES
of America

ALONG THE CONNECTICUT RIVER

FAIRLEE/WEST FAIRLEE, ORFORD, BRADFORD, PIERMONT, NEWBURY, AND HAVERHILL

Compiled by local historical societies:
Bradford: Phyllis Lavelle (chairman), Eris Eastman, Diane Smarro
Fairlee: Fairlee Historical Society
West Fairlee: Milton White
Orford: Laura Verry, Carl Schmidt, Barbara Mack
Piermont: Lloyd Hall, Helga Mueller, Joe Medlicott
Haverhill: Katharine Blaisdell
Newbury: Joseph Marsar

ARCADIA
PUBLISHING

ISBN 978-0-7385-8978-7

Published by Arcadia Publishing
Charleston, South Carolina

Printed in the United States of America

For all general information contact Arcadia Publishing at:
Telephone 843-853-2070
Fax 843-853-0044
E-mail sales@arcadiapublishing.com
For customer service and orders:
Toll-Free 1-888-313-2665

Visit us on the Internet at www.arcadiapublishing.com

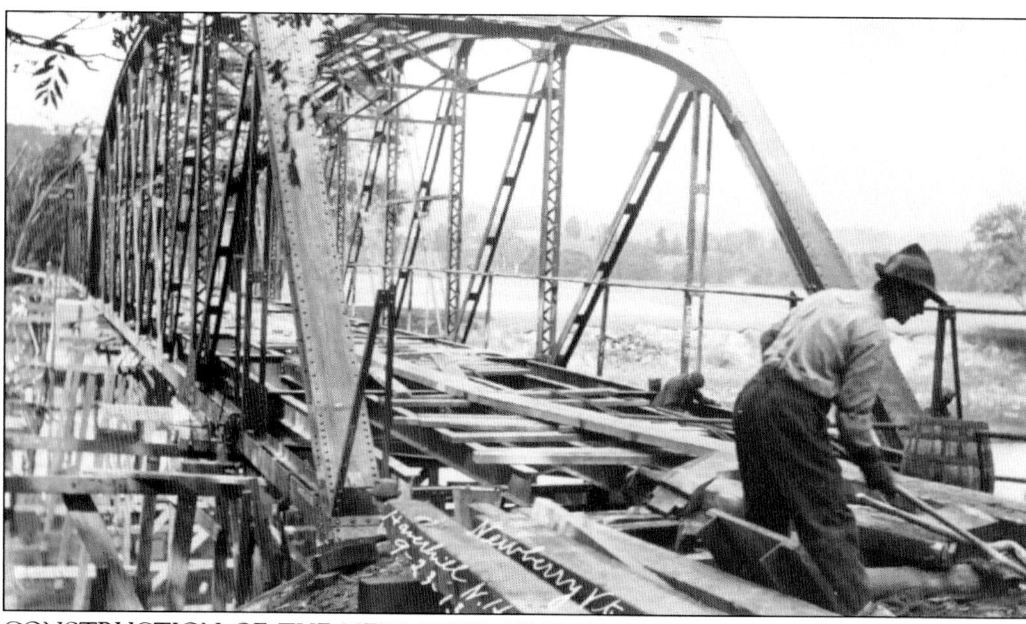

CONSTRUCTION OF THE NEW STEEL BRIDGE IN 1913. This bridge extended from below North Haverhill to below Newbury village, replacing the divided-lane covered bridge that had been damaged in a flood that year.

Contents

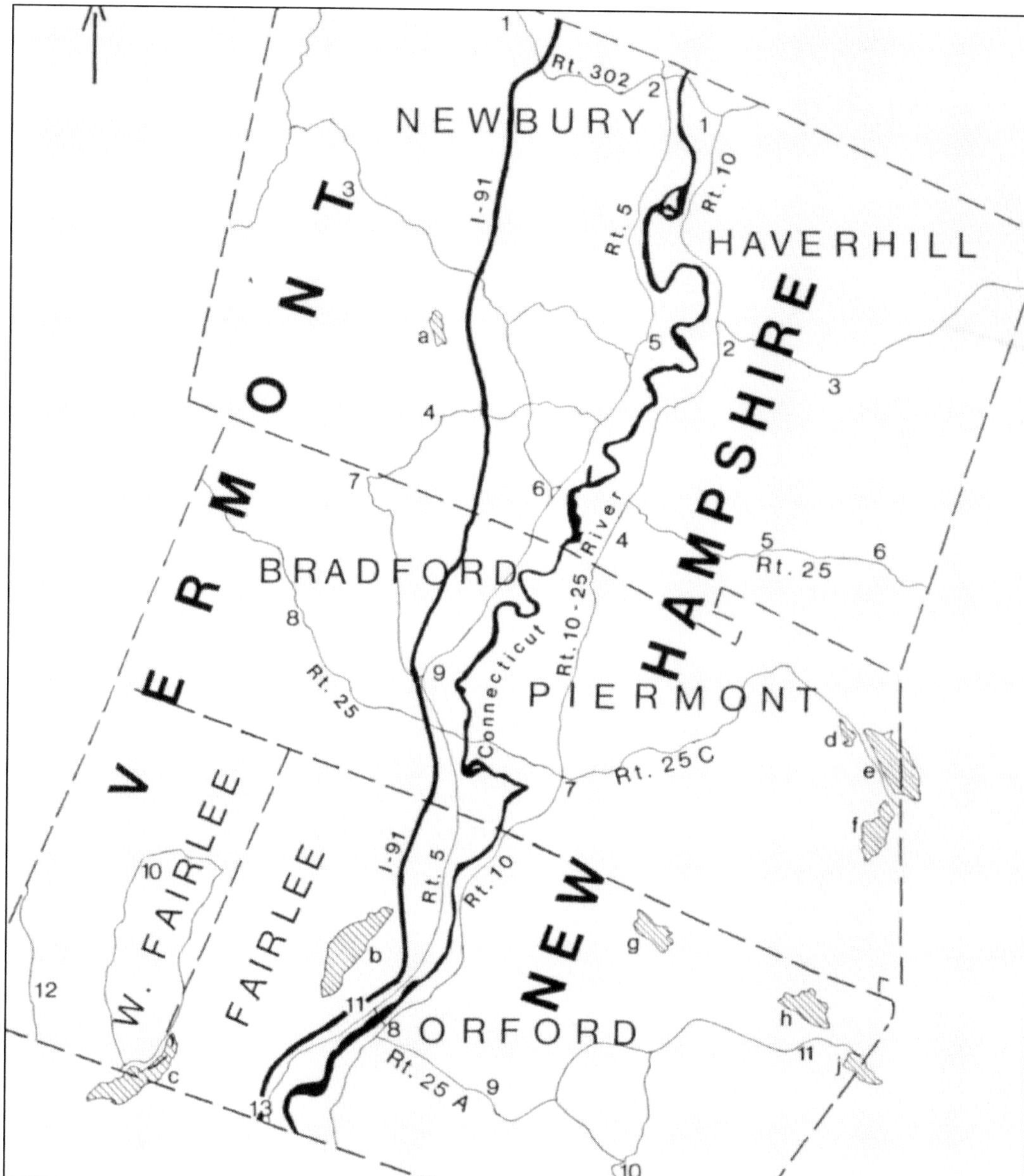

VERMONT

1 Boltonville
2 Wells River
3 Newbury Center
4 West Newbury
5 Newbury
6 South Newbury
7 Goshen
8 Bradford Center
9 Bradford
10 West Fairlee Center
11 Fairlee
12 West Fairlee
13 Ely

NEW HAMPSHIRE

1 Woodsville
2 North Haverhill
3 Center Haverhill
4 Haverhill
5 Pike
6 East Haverhill
7 Piermont
8 Orford
9 Orfordville
10 Gilmans Corner

LAKES AND PONDS

a Hall's Lake
b Lake Morey
c Lake Fairlee
d Lake Katherine
e Lake Tarleton
f Lake Armington
g Indian Pond
h Upper Baker Pond
j Lower Baker Pond

Introduction

Looking at maps of Vermont and New Hampshire together, the towns pictured in this book are right in the center, facing each other across the Connecticut River. They sometimes are called "twin towns" or "sister towns," connected by bridges and closely associated in their history and daily life: Orford, New Hampshire, with Fairlee and West Fairlee, Vermont; Piermont with Bradford; and Haverhill Corner and North Haverhill villages with Newbury.

The most closely connected have been Woodsville, the largest village in the town of Haverhill, and Wells River, in the town of Newbury. They were connected by a double-decker bridge with a railway on the top and a highway underneath. Together they made up the largest railroad center in the North Country for many years.

Settlement of this area occurred after the French and Indian War. Orford and Fairlee were the first to be chartered in 1761. A group of men founded Haverhill and Newbury on the same day in 1763. Next came Piermont in 1764, then Bradford in 1770. The town of West Fairlee separated from Fairlee in 1797. Many of the early settlers of these towns followed the Connecticut River north from Massachusetts and Connecticut, along rough paths on foot or horseback. Some came via the river itself, on the ice in winter, or by canoe or boat in summer, portaging around the many waterfalls. Still other settlers came up from Portsmouth or the Merrimack River area, following old Indian trails up river valleys and over the hills. The settlers of Haverhill and Newbury brought their town names with them, from hometowns in eastern Massachusetts.

Through the years, these early footpaths were improved to become passable for wagons, then for stagecoaches, and finally for automobiles. Clearing the land for farming led to the logging industry, and eventually to such developments as the paper mill in Wells River, the mill for hardwood furniture stock in North Haverhill, and the plywood mill in Bradford. For many years there were log drives down the Connecticut and Ammonoosuc Rivers. After the rivers were blocked by power dams, the logs and their products were transported by rail. Now these logs are transported mostly by truck. The tourist industry in this area was aided by the railroads, and later by the interstate highways. Fairlee was one of the first lake communities in New England. Some of the unique features of each of these towns along the river have been captured on film and preserved for future generations. Working together, modern-day "friends across the river" have compiled this collection, providing readers with glimpses into the lively past of this beautiful area.

Acknowledgments

Under the chairmanship of Phyllis Lavelle of Bradford, this book was compiled by representatives of the historical societies of Newbury, Bradford, Fairlee, and West Fairlee, Vermont; and Haverhill, Piermont, and Orford, New Hampshire; along with the Orford Social Library and the Orford Free Library.

We are grateful to these societies and libraries for the use of photographs and information, and we give our thanks to the many other individuals who have shared and cooperated in this project.

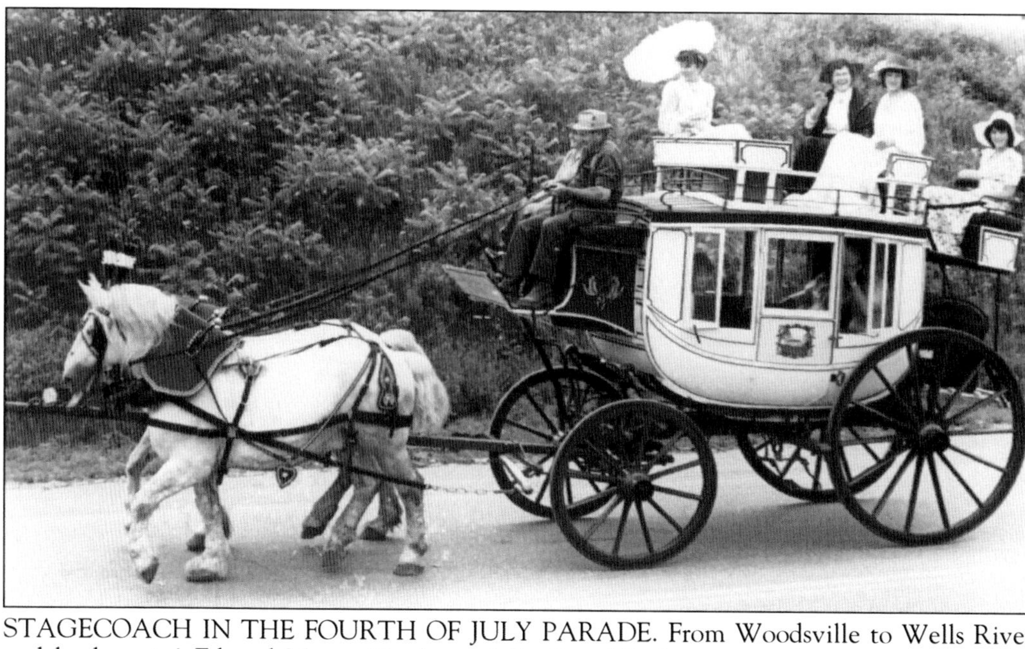

STAGECOACH IN THE FOURTH OF JULY PARADE. From Woodsville to Wells River and back again! Ed and Marge Cowles and family of Bath are topside passengers in their Concord coach, with Francis Brady of Columbia, New Hampshire, driving his horses. (*Journal Opinion* photograph.)

One

Fairlee and West Fairlee

VERMONT
Orange County
First Settled: 1761
Chartered: 1761
Split into two towns in 1797
Population in 1990: Fairlee, 883; West Fairlee, 680
Area: Fairlee,18 square miles; West Fairlee, 23 square miles
Principal Settlements: Fairlee and Ely (South Fairlee); West Fairlee

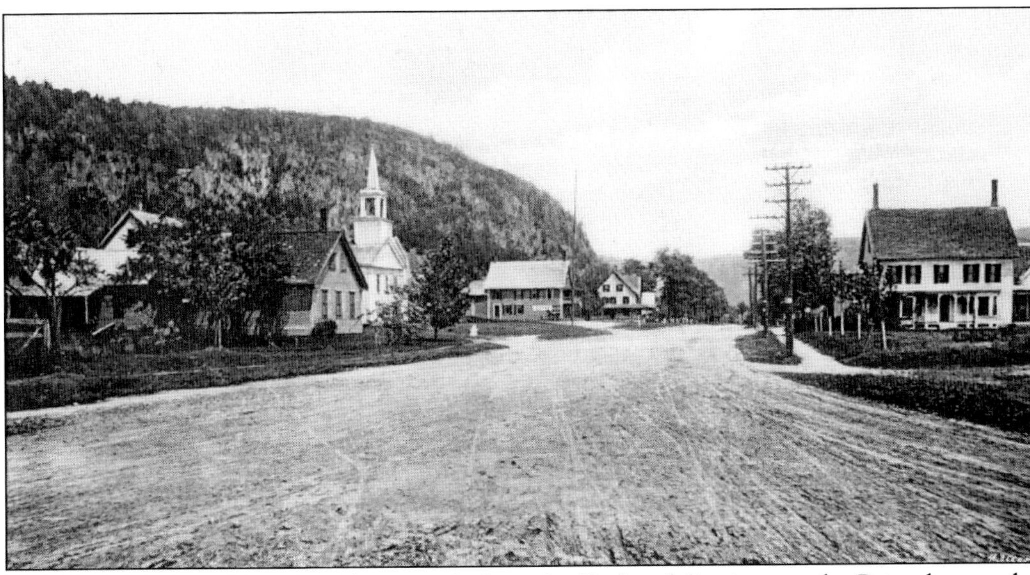

MAIN STREET, C. 1890. Looking north from the Railroad Station are the Paine house, the Union Meetinghouse, Daniell's Opera House (behind tree), Abbott's Drug Store, Church's Tavern, and the Byers house (on the right). The Fairlee Palisades overlook Main Street. Fairlee is fortunate to have two lakes, Lake Morey and a small part of Lake Fairlee, along with the lovely Connecticut River. Lake Morey has one of the oldest lake communities in Vermont, dating back to 1880. Only a few farms now remain in this once-lively farming community. In 1972, Interstate Highway 91 was built through the center of town.

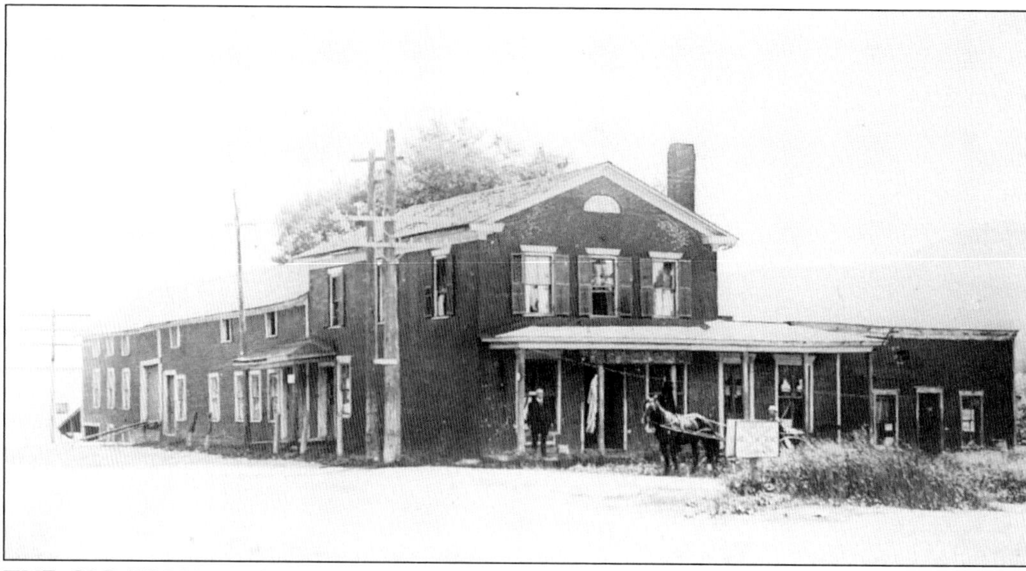

THE OLD BRICK STORE, C. 1900. This old store, which has since burned, stood on the corner of Main and Bridge Streets. The structure was built in 1883 by Silas Read for his pipe and pump-making operation, and it became a general store under Herbert Warren, Hethrington & Bailey, and Lee Andrews, who built the Colby Block. In 1914, John Munn opened a garage here, followed by successive owners Walter Kenyon, Ray Coffin Sr., and Stanley Farnham. Eventually the building became a gift and candle shop.

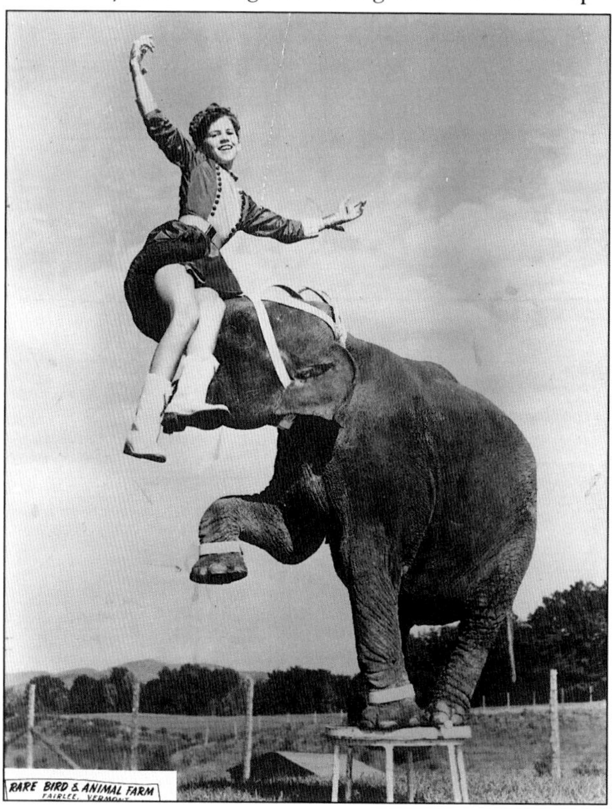

QUEENIE, THE WATER-SKIING ELEPHANT, AND TRAINER ELISABETH GREEN, 1960s. This duo performed for the public here on the Connecticut River in the summer, and in Florida in the winter. Bill Green's Rare Bird and Animal Farm was a tourist attraction from 1955 to 1968. From 1968 to 1970 it was owned by Ted and Virginia Vietje, and was called the Fairlee Rare Bird and Animal Farm.

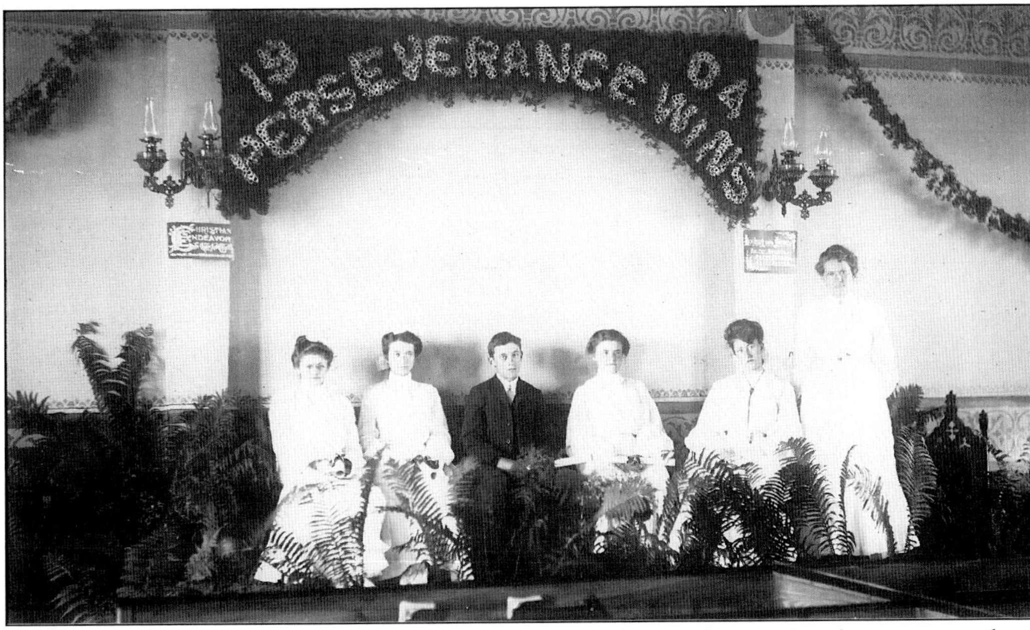

SILVER LEAF GRANGE #254, 1904. The Grange was chartered in 1898 with twenty members, and met in the Union Meetinghouse until the building burned in 1912. Young people pictured are, from left to right: Rose Renfrew, Gertrude Merrill, Harrison Paine, Charlotte Bragg, Inez George, and Rosalene Davis Ordway.

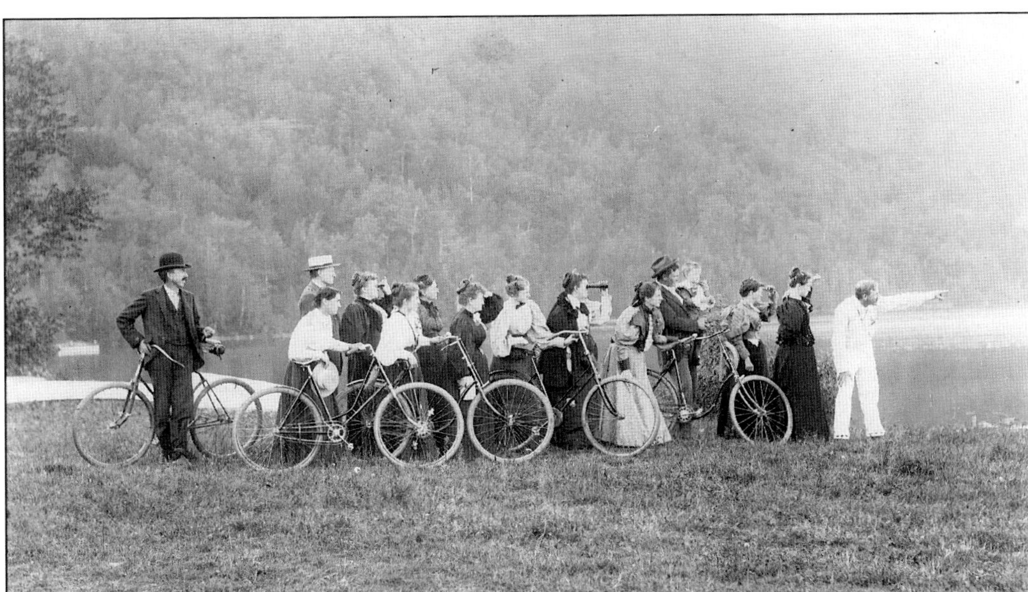

MOREY LAKE, 1896. "The Sea Serpent they said they saw, was never seen." Viewers were: W. Langmark, Helen Bittenger, Joseph Poor, Mrs. J. Poor, Mrs. Barclay, May Burbeck, Mrs. Buzzell, Louise Poor, Mrs. Jewett, Frances Buzzell, Harry Morrison, Sammie Morrison, Mrs. Morrison, Nellie Underhill, and S. M. Weeks.

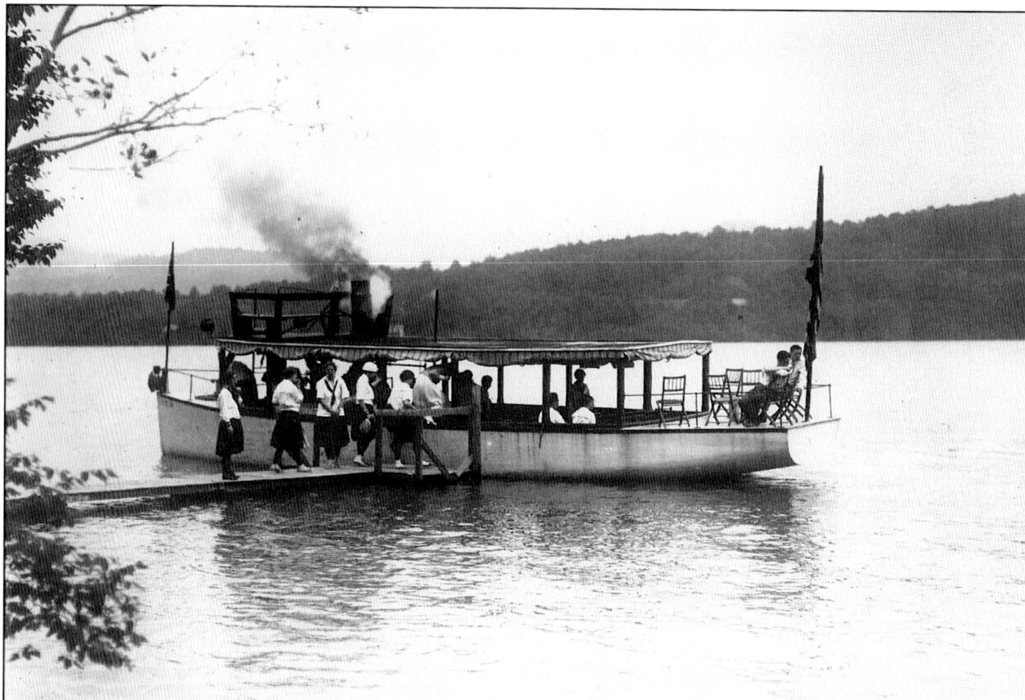

THE STEAMBOAT *GYPSY* (1898–1915). This boat was built and run by "Captain" Ed Lucas, and it was used for giving trips around Lake Morey. With a capacity of only fifty, it soon became too small and was sold to a Mr. Tibbetts on Lake Fairlee. Notice the Aloha Camp girls boarding.

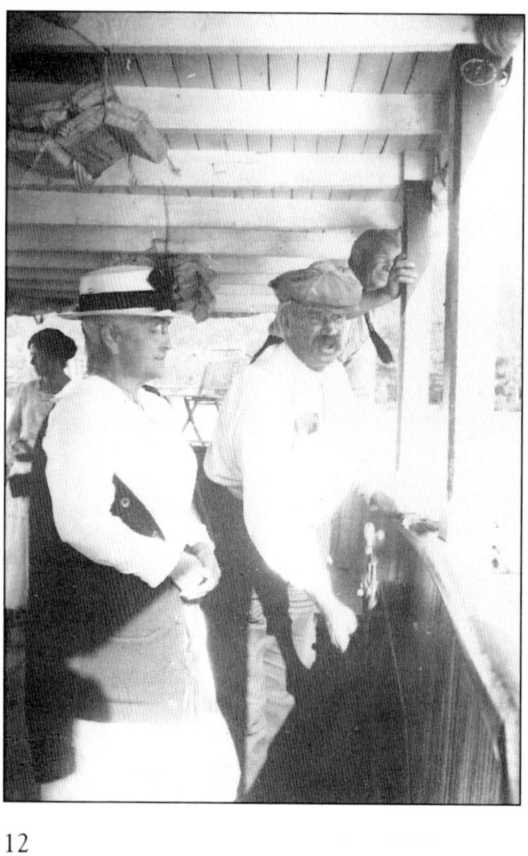

EDGAR O. LUCAS, 1930s. Lucas was the self-appointed captain of several tour steamboats on Lake Morey. "Captain" Lucas and his wife, Amy, bought an excursion boat called *The Pearl* which had been shipped from Boston via railroad. Needing a larger boat, he bought the *Gypsy*, then built the *Misitwalkit*.

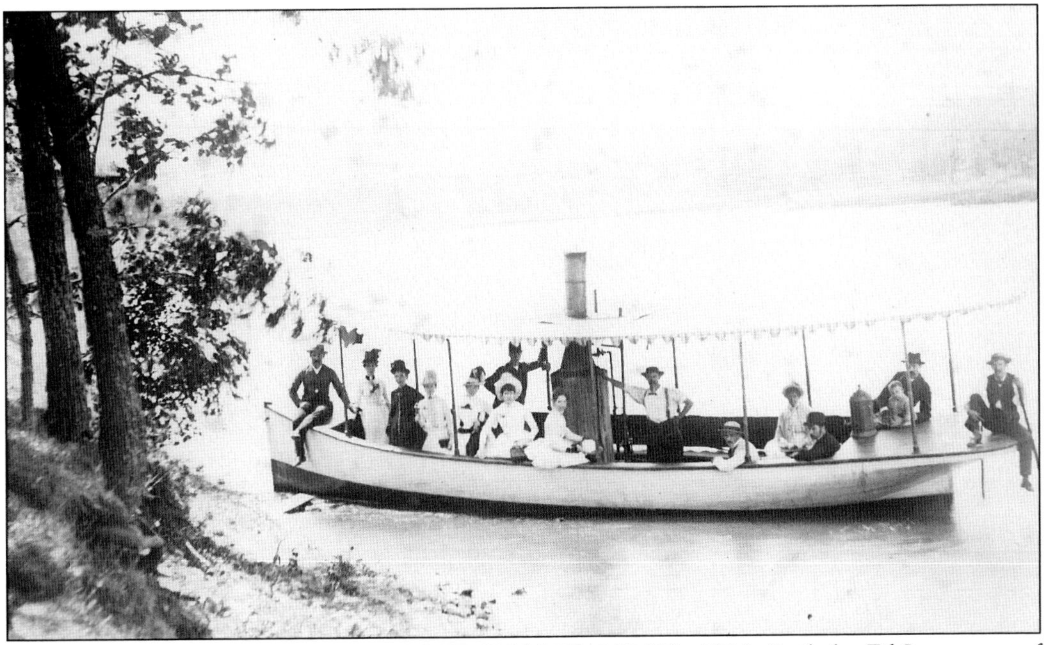

THE *MISITWALKIT* (IF YOU MISS IT, YOU WALK IT), 1918. Built by Ed Lucas out of cypress, this vessel was 45 feet long, and it carried 150 passengers. It ran from 1915 until 1930, when improved roads and cars made it obsolete. At first it had a wood-fired engine, which was later converted to gasoline. It had a regular route and cost 25¢ per ticket for passengers. The highlight of each trip was the blowing of the whistle at the foot of Echo Mountain to hear the echoes.

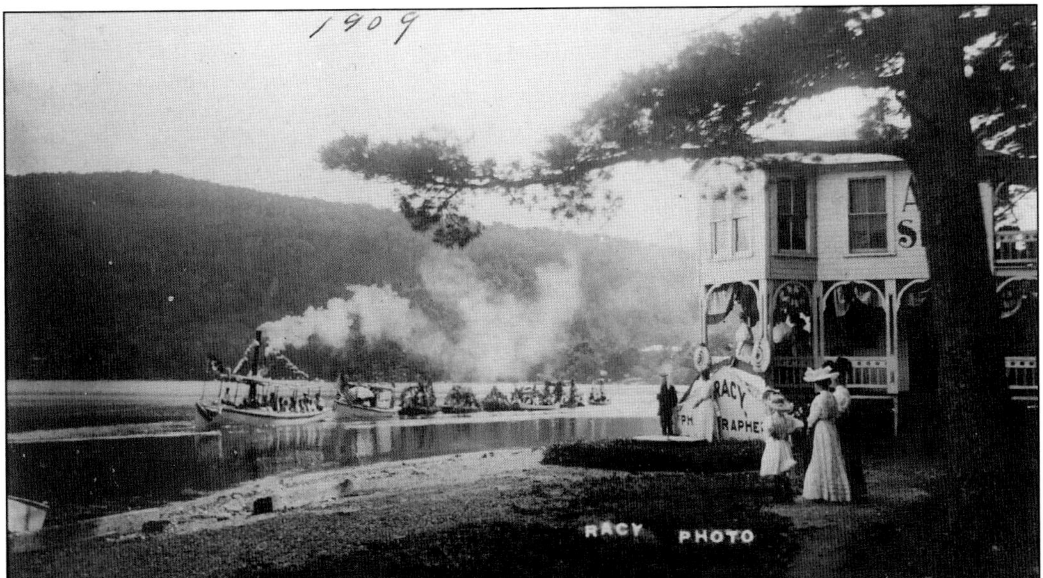

"THE REGATTA"—A LAKE MOREY TRADITION IN THE EARLY 1900s. On the Fourth of July, all available boats were decorated, lined up, and paraded around the lake for awards. Above, Bracy's cottage (now burned) occupied Pine Point. Charles F. Bracy was a fine photographer and this photograph is a good example of his work.

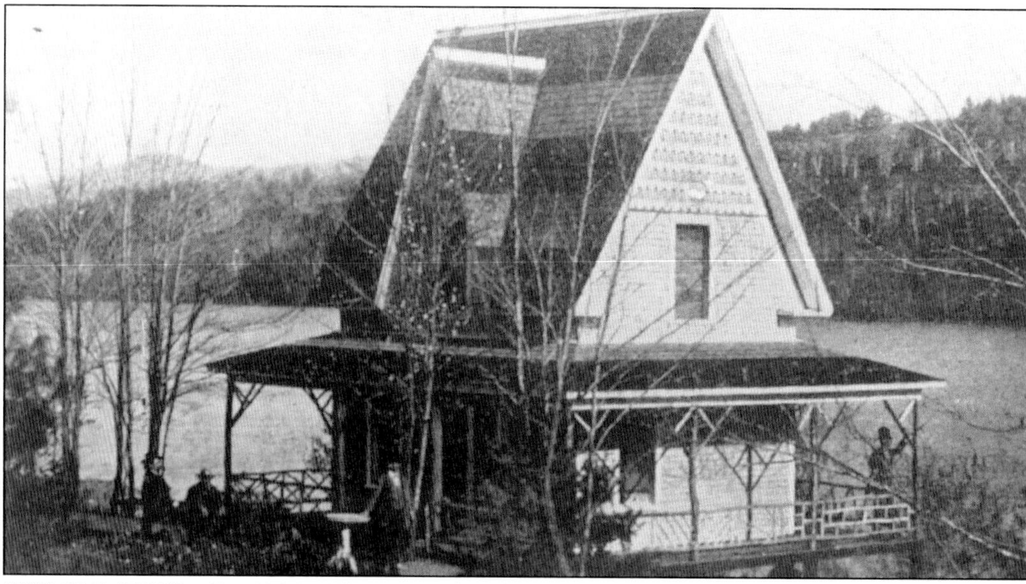

"BIRCHMERE", C. 1900. This was the first cottage built on Lake Morey. In 1888, A. W. Kinney, a Chicago artist, built it near lovely Glen Falls. It was later owned by Adj. Gen. William H. Gilmore.

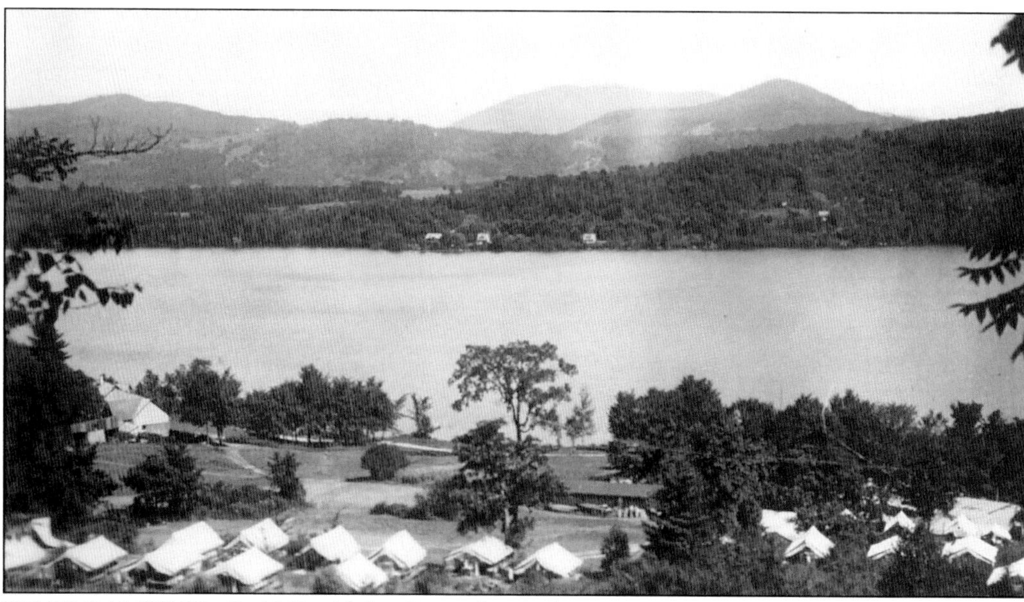

TENT CAMPING, C. 1930. Aloha Camp for Girls was opened in 1905 by Rev. E. L. Gulick. Now owned by the Aloha Foundation, the facility includes Aloha Camp, Lanakila Camp for Boys, the Hulbert Outdoor Center, and Aloha Hive (on Lake Fairlee). Aloha and Lanakila are the only remaining camps on Lake Morey.

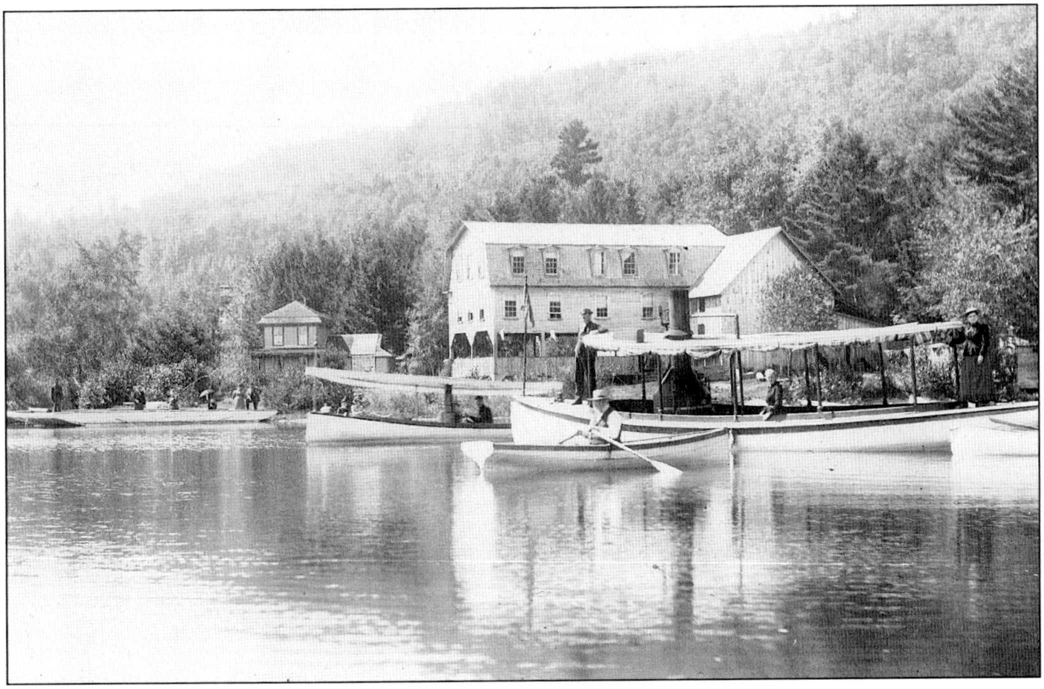

GLEN FALLS HOUSE, C. 1900. In 1888, George Spear built a thirty-room hotel at Middlepoint. In 1912, it burned to the ground after an Independence Day celebration. Four lives were lost.The injured were taken to the hospital in Hanover by train. Sadly, the hotel was never rebuilt. Gluckhauf cottage is to the left of center in this picture. It was the second cottage built on Lake Morey, and it is now owned by the Breetz family.

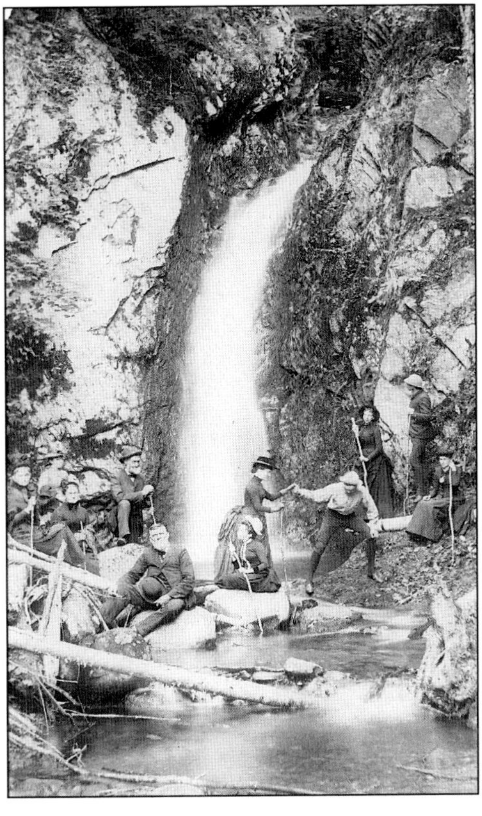

GLEN FALLS, 1910. This was once a favorite hiking and picnicking spot before it was damaged by the 1936 hurricane. At one time, the falls had a bridge spanning the top. It is now on private property, and is not open to the public.

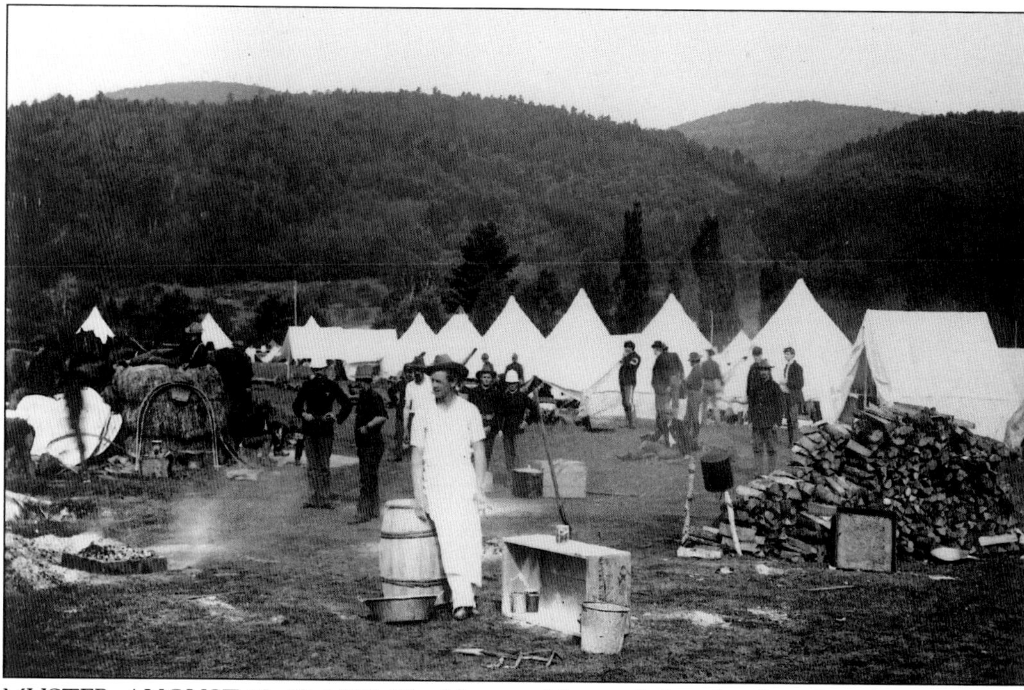

MUSTER, AUGUST 12–17, 1895. The Vermont National Guard gathered on the Lake Morey Inn Golf Course for this historic event. Fairlee's Major-General William H. Gihnore arranged a "Muster," which was the scene of the first combined maneuvers of the infantry, cavalry, and artillery of the Vermont National Guard. Cannonballs fired from this spot have been found on Terry Hill, over a mile away.

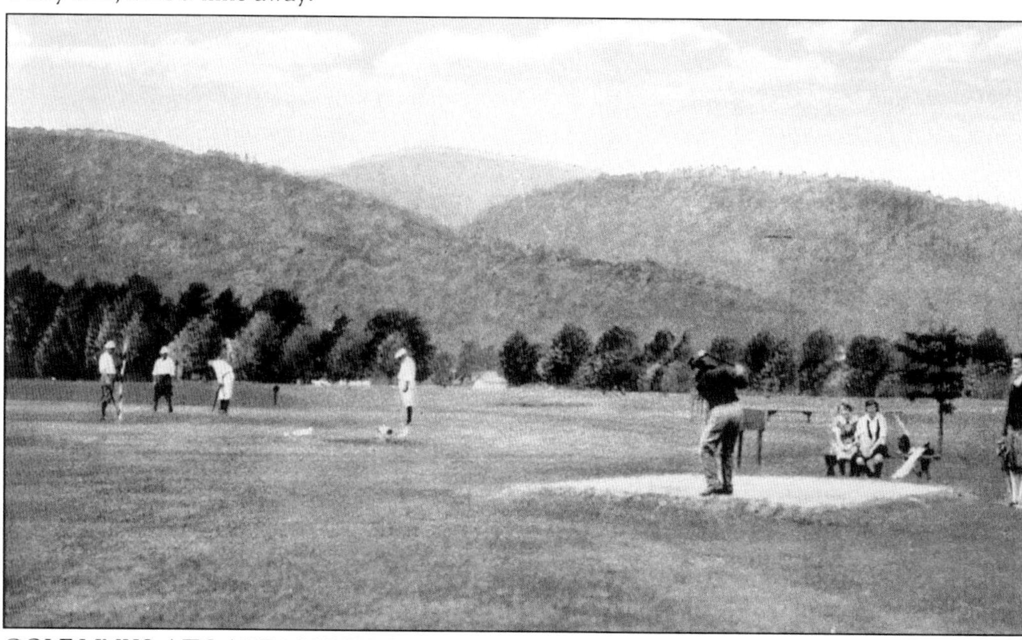

GOLF LINKS AT LAKE MOREY CLUB, 1930s. This fine, eighteen-hole golf course annually hosts the Vermont Open Golf Tournament. This is the fourth tee. Compare this with the above photograph—it seems to be the same location.

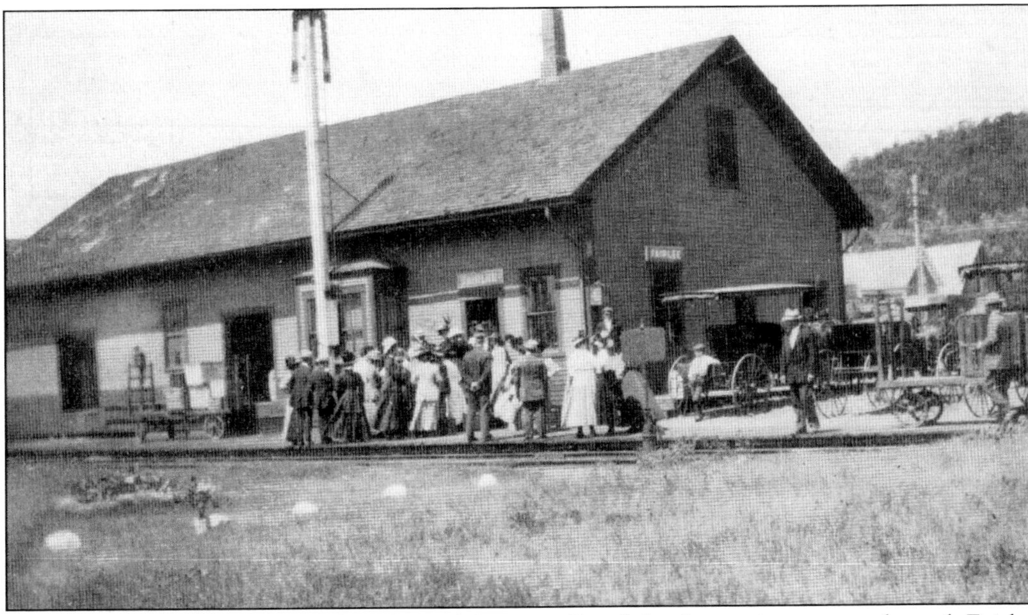

FAIRLEE DEPOT, C. 1910. The "Green Mountain Boy," the first train to come through Fairlee on the tracks of the Connecticut and Paassumpsic Railroad, arrived on October 10, 1848. Here a crowd gathers at the depot to greet visitors, campers, and tourists.

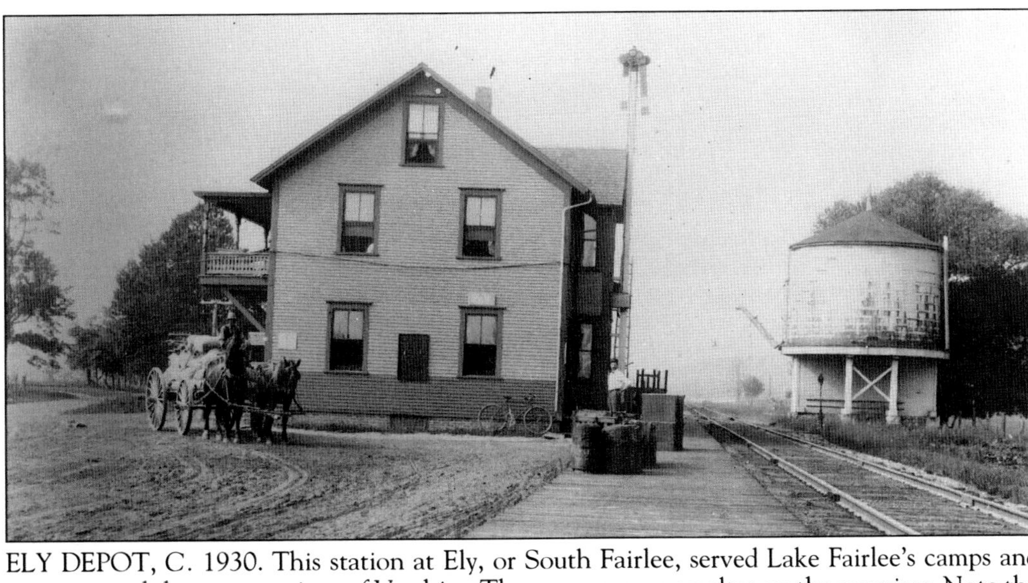

ELY DEPOT, C. 1930. This station at Ely, or South Fairlee, served Lake Fairlee's camps and cottages, and the copper mines of Vershire. There was even a smelter on the premises. Note the large water tower where steam locomotives replenished their water. This building is now on the Historic Register. E. E. Whitcomb is driving the wagon.

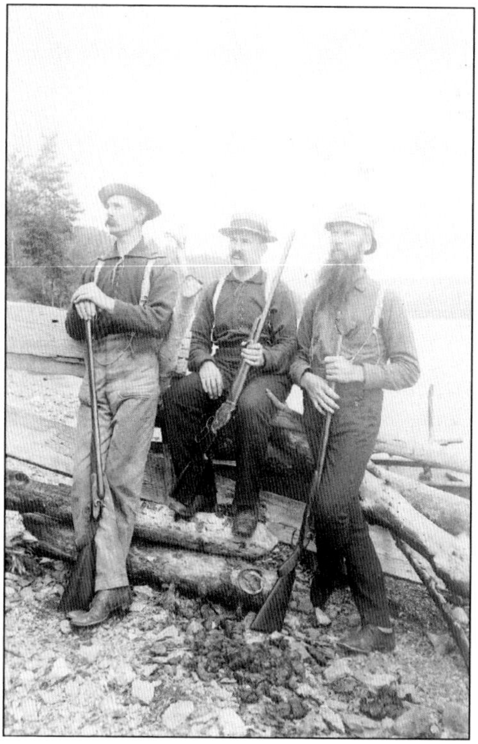

HUNTING, 1870s. This sport has been a major pastime over the years. On the right is Gustav L. Winship, builder of Aloha Camp's main building and the town bandstand. The man in the center is holding a 86 Winchester, and the others have double-barreled shotguns.

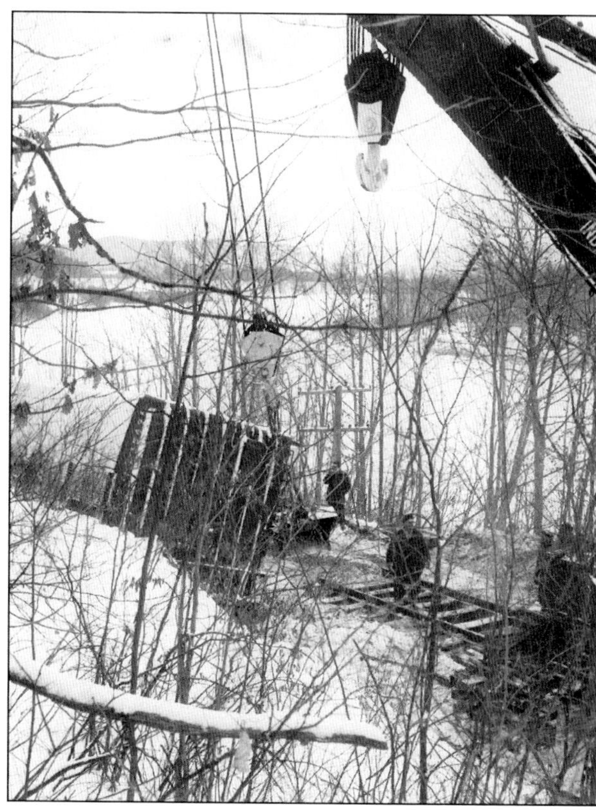

TRAIN WRECK, 1960s. Fairlee has had several train wrecks over the years, but the most memorable occurred when cars of frozen peas, strawberries, and beer overturned. As thrifty Vermonters, many people snowmobiled down and "rescued" the booty. That winter, strawberry shortcake was on the menu and beer sales plummeted.

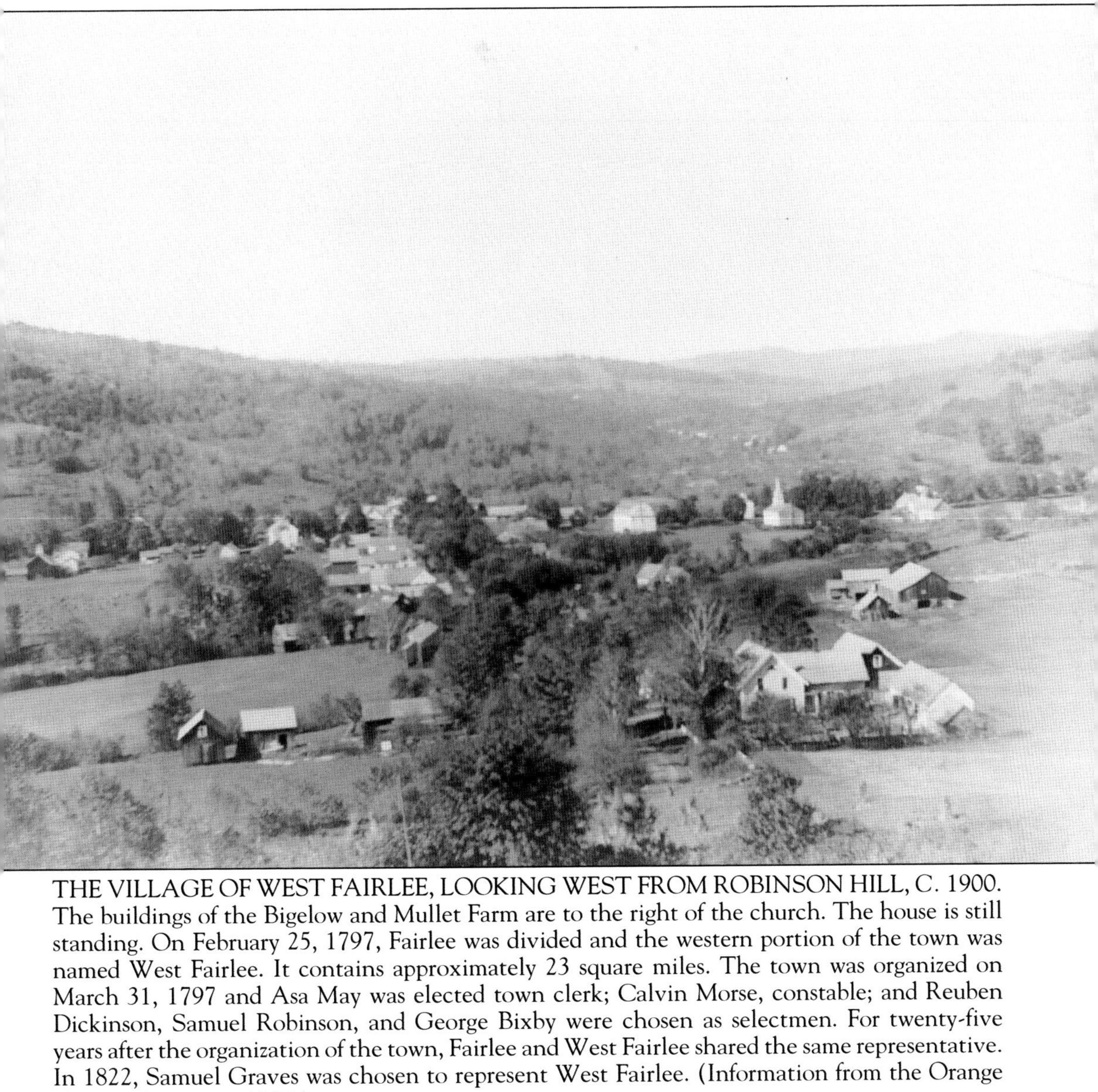

THE VILLAGE OF WEST FAIRLEE, LOOKING WEST FROM ROBINSON HILL, C. 1900. The buildings of the Bigelow and Mullet Farm are to the right of the church. The house is still standing. On February 25, 1797, Fairlee was divided and the western portion of the town was named West Fairlee. It contains approximately 23 square miles. The town was organized on March 31, 1797 and Asa May was elected town clerk; Calvin Morse, constable; and Reuben Dickinson, Samuel Robinson, and George Bixby were chosen as selectmen. For twenty-five years after the organization of the town, Fairlee and West Fairlee shared the same representative. In 1822, Samuel Graves was chosen to represent West Fairlee. (Information from the Orange County Gazetteer, 1888.)

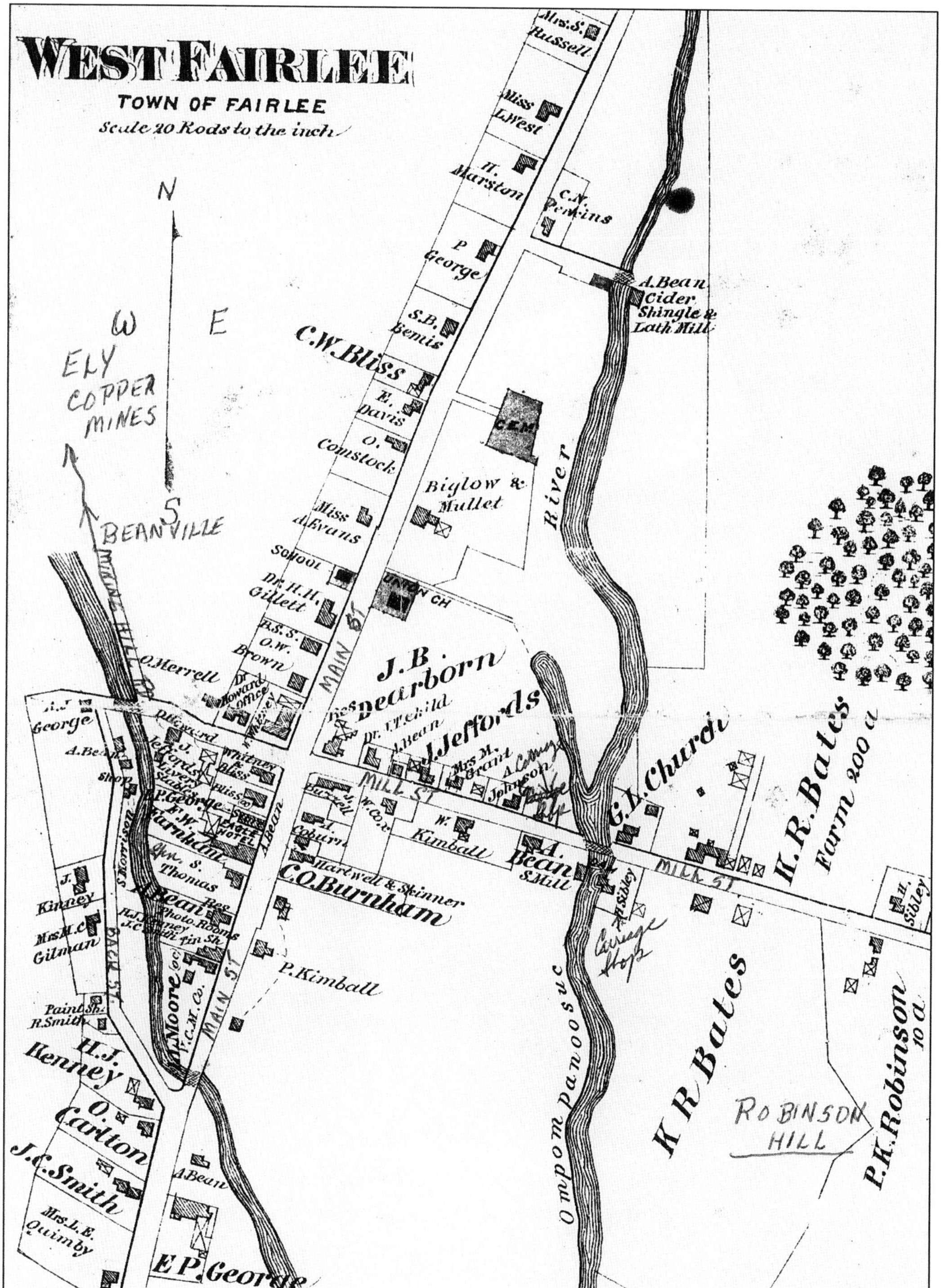

MAP OF WEST FAIRLEE, ABOUT 1880. The J. B. Dearborn house is the present home of Roy Southworth. The school is now the site of the West Fairlee Fire Station. The Eagle Hotel is now the site of Eastman's Garage.

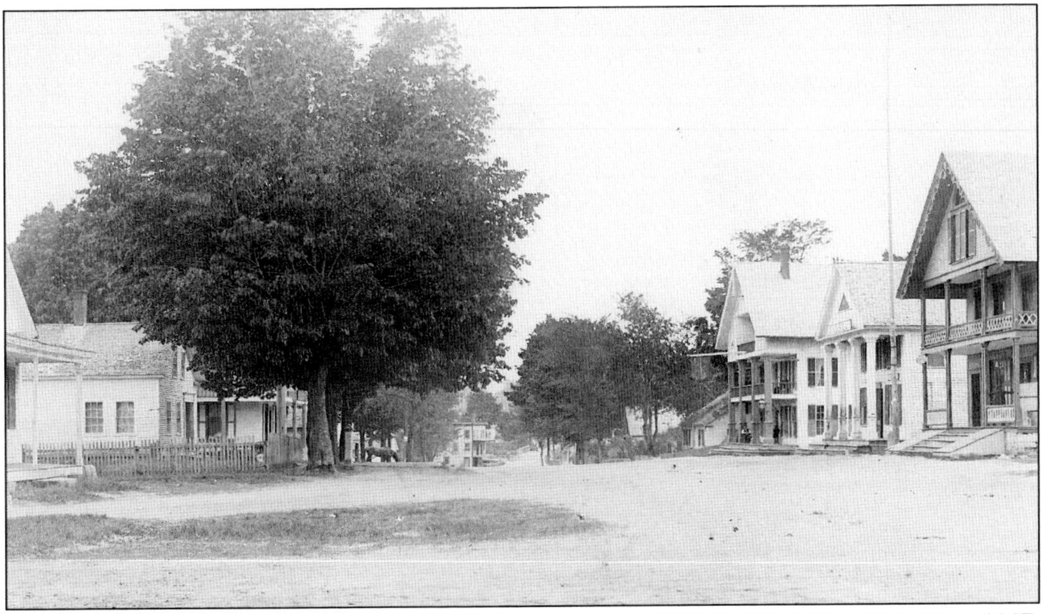

MAIN STREET, LOOKING SOUTH FROM THE CORNER OF MILL STREET AND MINING HILL ROAD, C. 1890. The buildings on the right side of this photograph are, from left to right: the Eagle Hotel, the E. P. George Store and the C. W. Bliss Store. The C. W. Coburn Store is on the left side of Main Street in the center of the photograph.

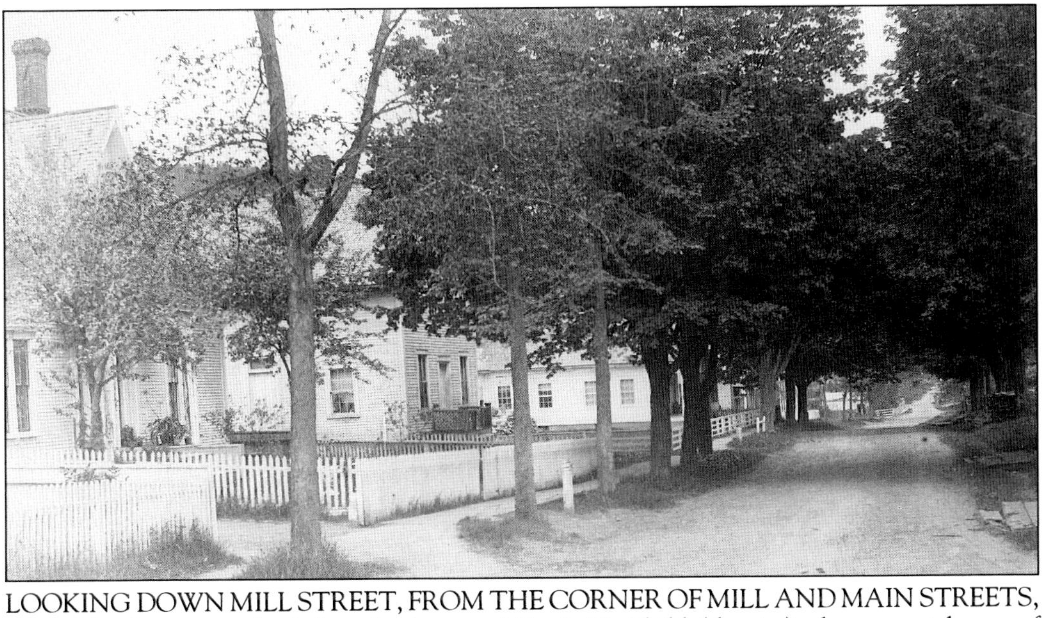

LOOKING DOWN MILL STREET, FROM THE CORNER OF MILL AND MAIN STREETS, 1890. The house on the left is the home of Dr. J. T. Child (dentist), the present home of Nicholas Turkevitch.

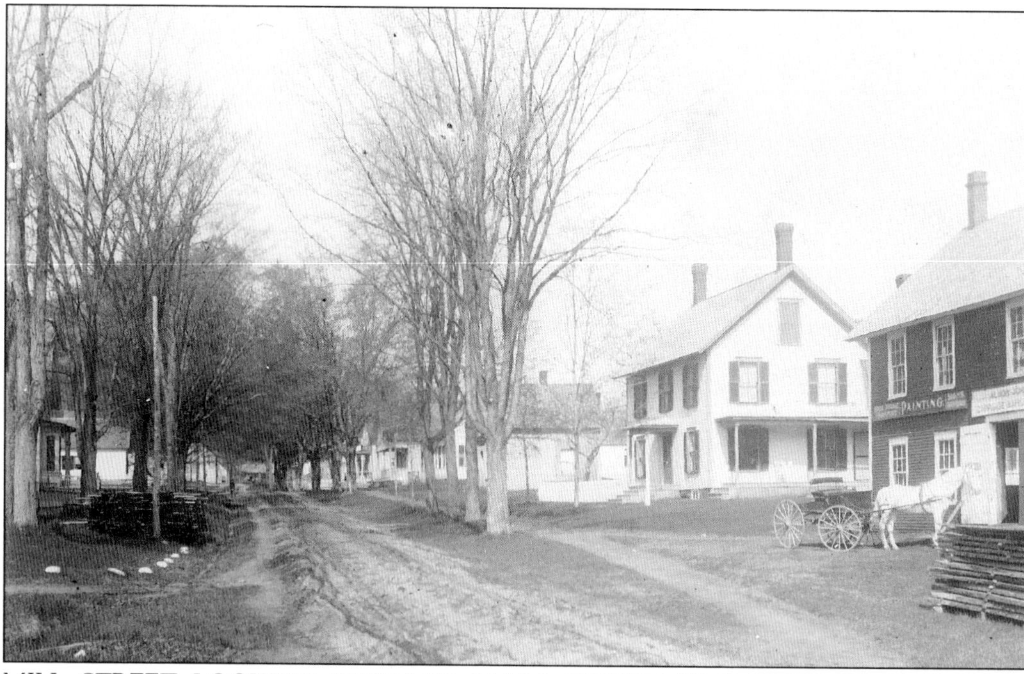

MILL STREET LOOKING TOWARD MAIN STREET FROM THE BRIDGE, 1860s. Almon Johnson's Carriage Shop is on the right. His home is next to the shop.

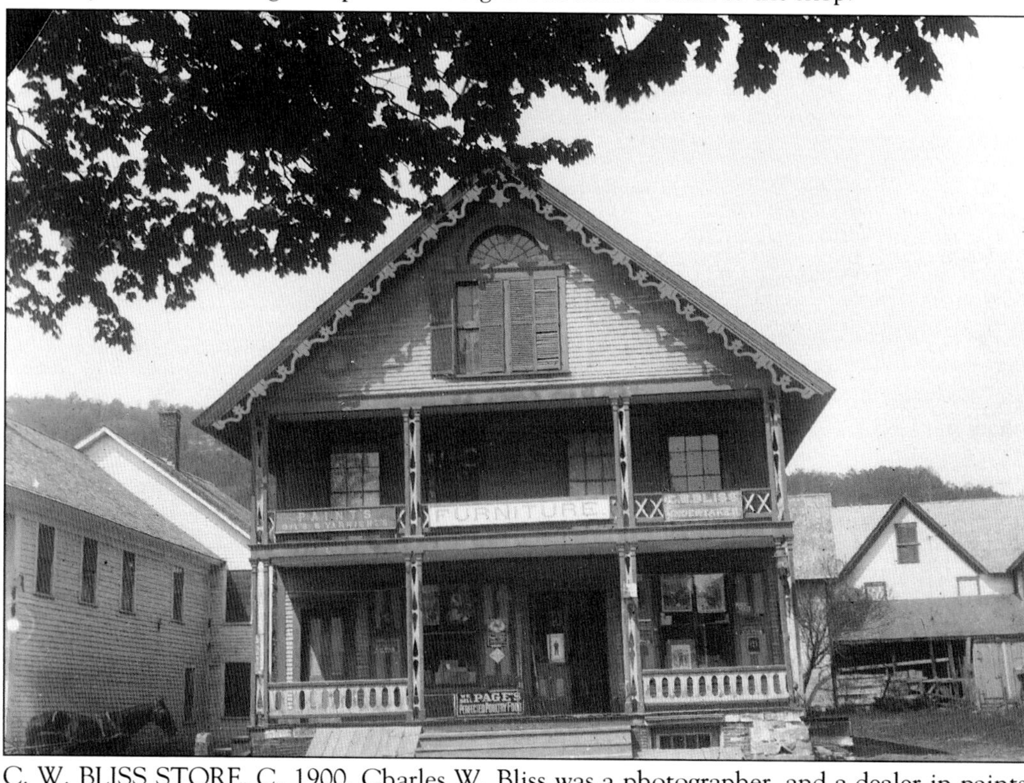

C. W. BLISS STORE, C. 1900. Charles W. Bliss was a photographer, and a dealer in paints, oils, glass, furniture, coffins, and undertaker materials. This building burned in the 1908 fire.

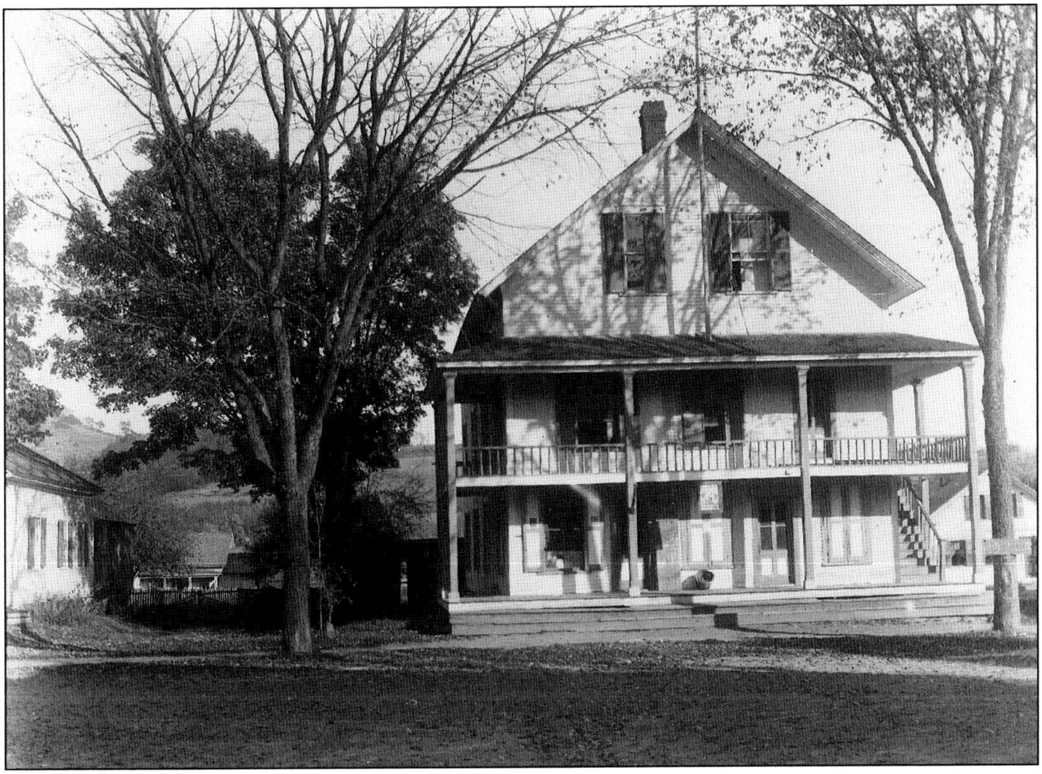

STEVENS' STORE, C. 1900. Stevens was a dealer in watches, clocks, jewelry, spectacles, and violins. The store was located across from the Eagle Hotel and is no longer standing.

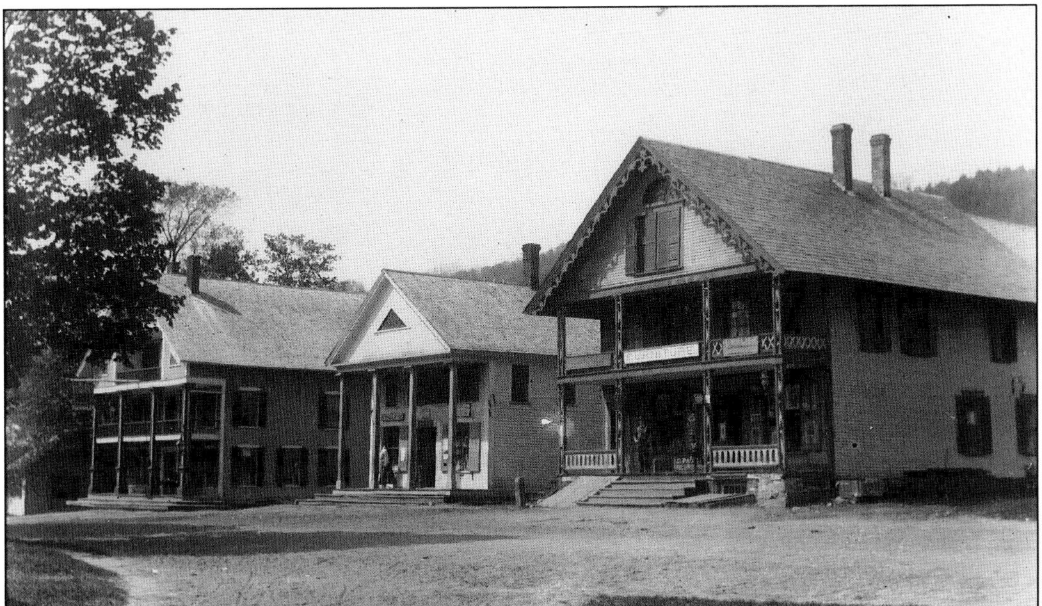

MAIN STREET, C. 1900. From left to right: the Eagle Hotel, the E. P. George Store, and the C. W. Bliss Store. Presently these sites are: Eastman's Garage, the Eastman home, and the U.S. Post Office.

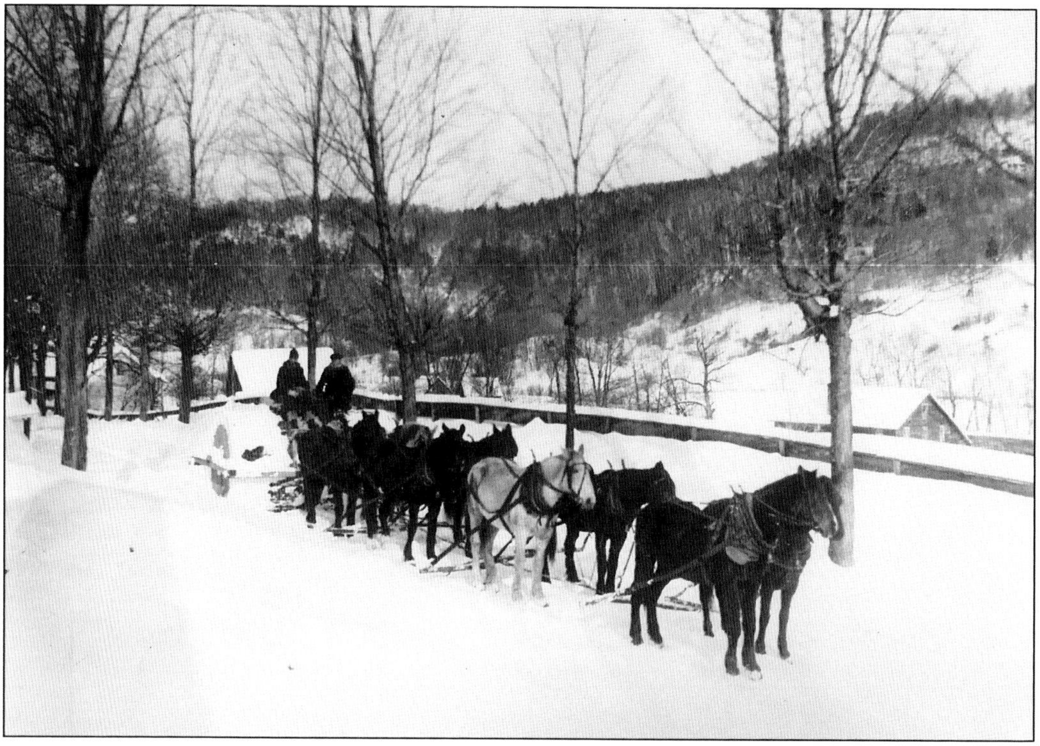

SNOW ROLLING IN WEST FAIRLEE, 1915. Seldon George and Lewis Lackey are on the roller.

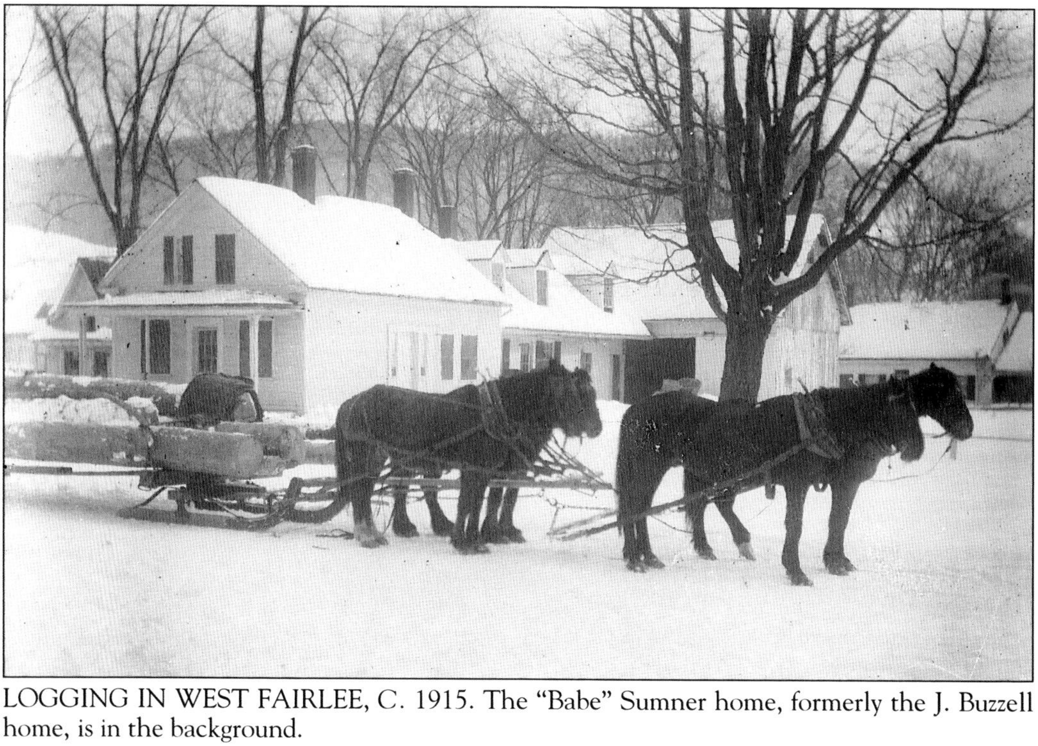

LOGGING IN WEST FAIRLEE, C. 1915. The "Babe" Sumner home, formerly the J. Buzzell home, is in the background.

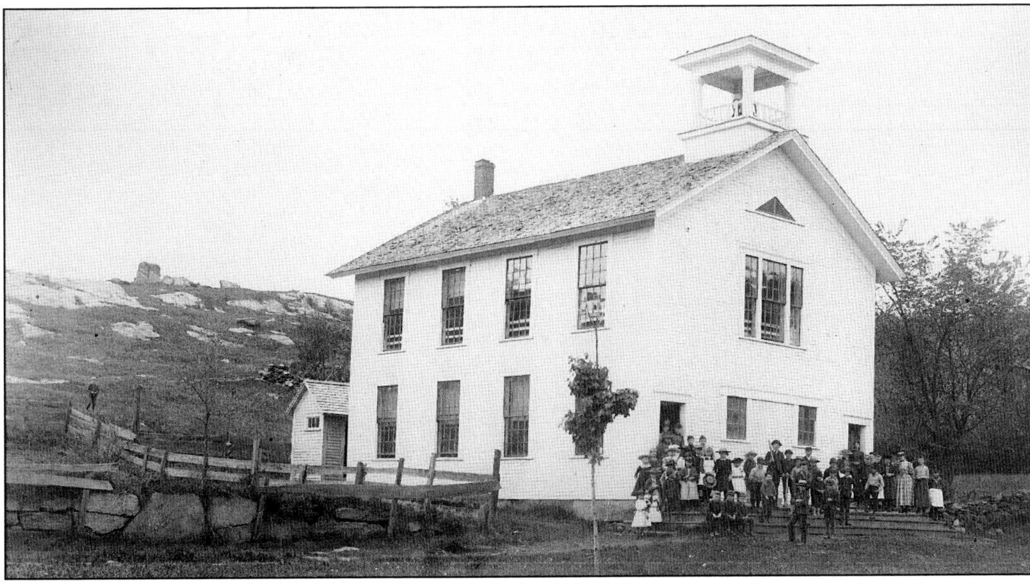

WEST FAIRLEE VILLAGE SCHOOL, 1890. In 1886, the town had seven school districts and seven schools. The present fire station was built on this site.

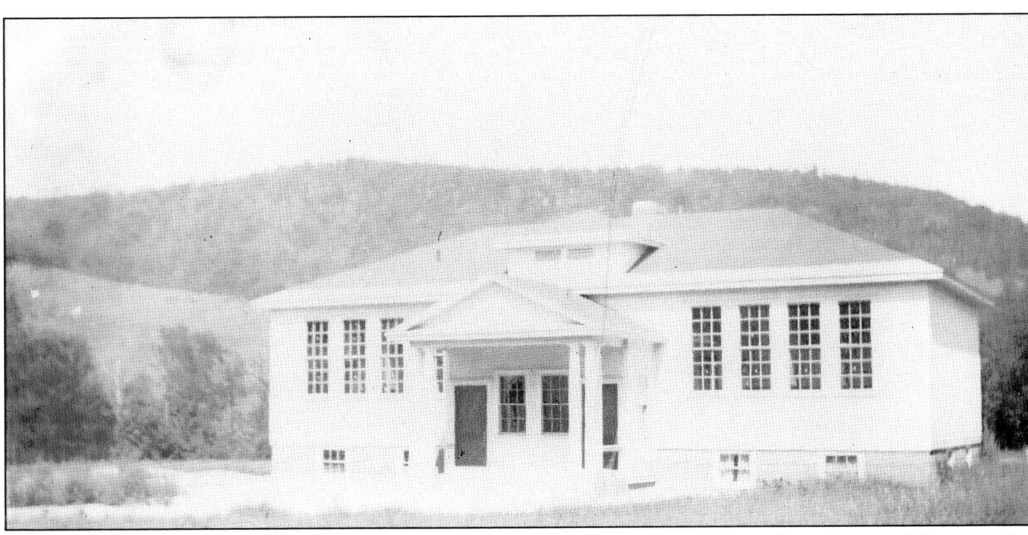

WEST FAIRLEE VILLAGE SCHOOL, C. 1940. Built in 1935 with a later addition, this building serves as the present West Fairlee School.

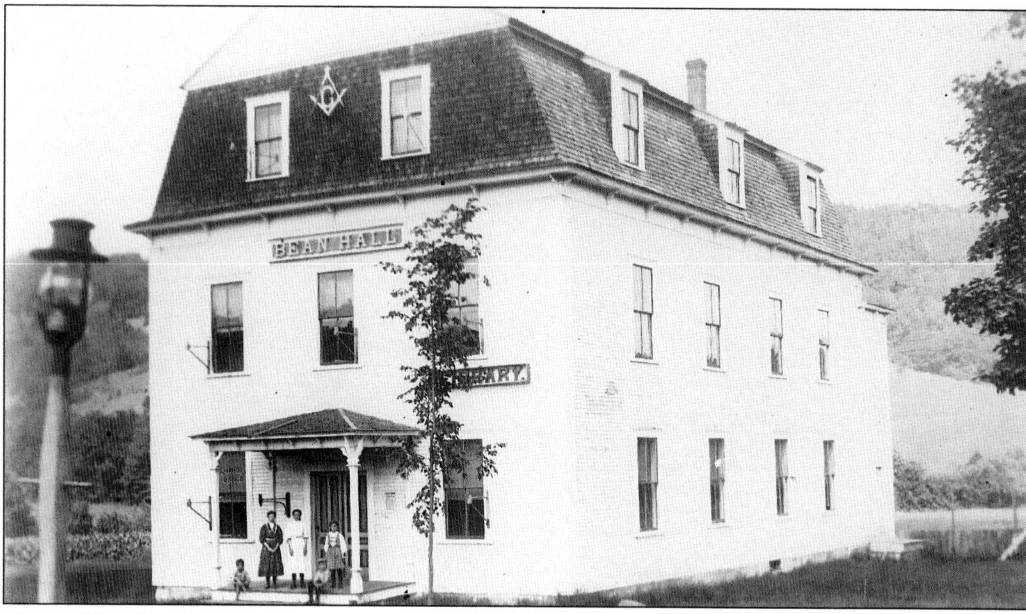

BEAN HALL, C. 1900. The town offices, the library, and the Masonic Hall are still located in this building.

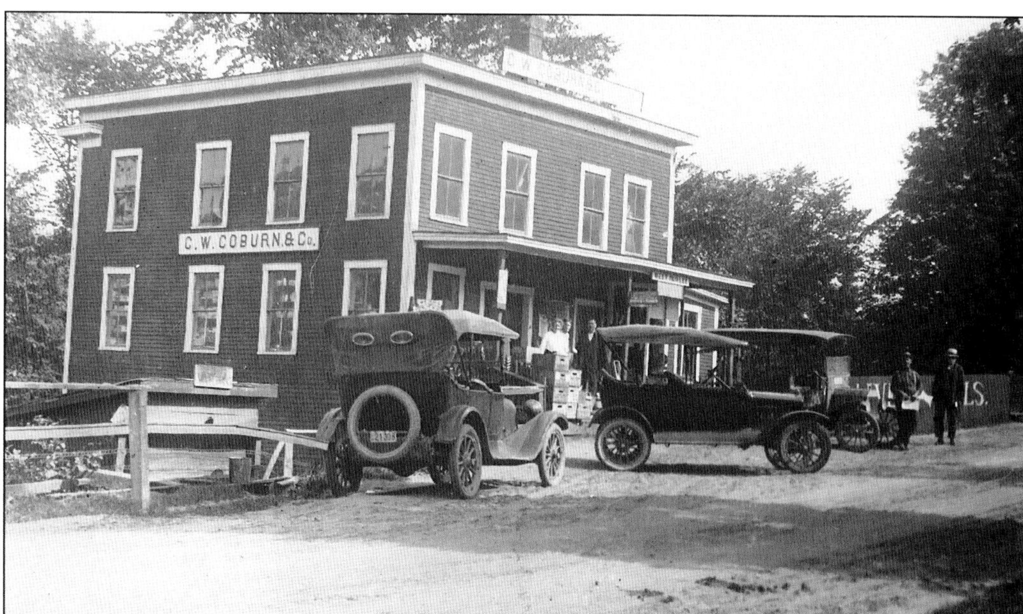

C. W. COBURN AND CO. GENERAL STORE, 1920s. This building was located on the east side of Main Street, near the bridge.

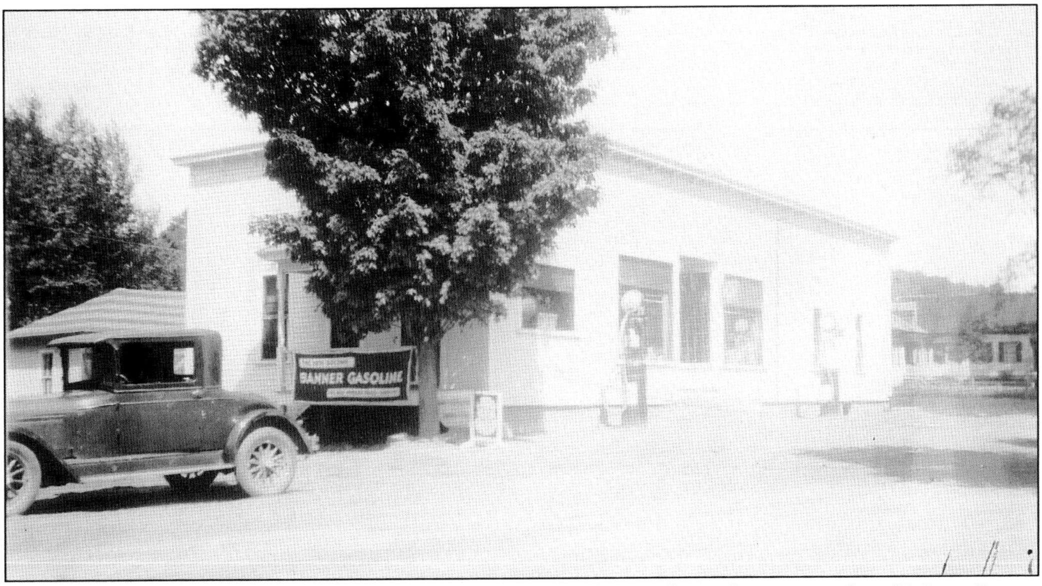

CLARENCE COBURN STORE, 1930s. This shop, located on the west side of Main Street near the bridge, later became Ladds Store.

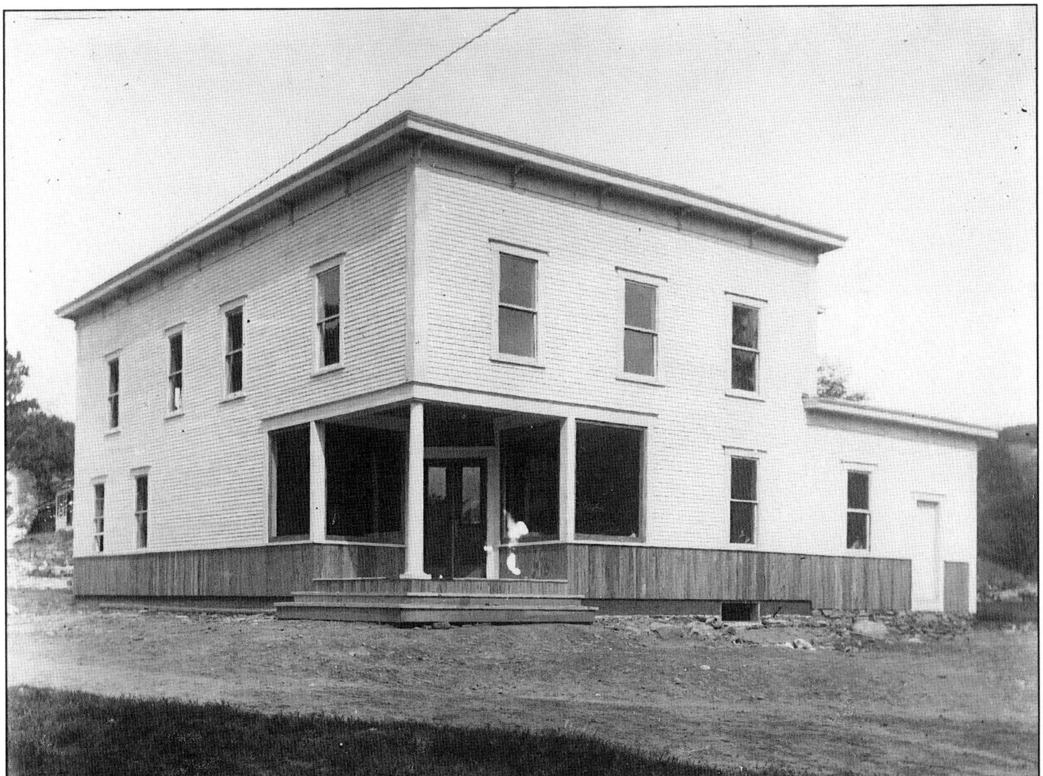

PAUL & HAYWARD STORE, 1930s. Located on the corner of Main Street and Mining Hill Road, this establishment continues to operate as a general store.

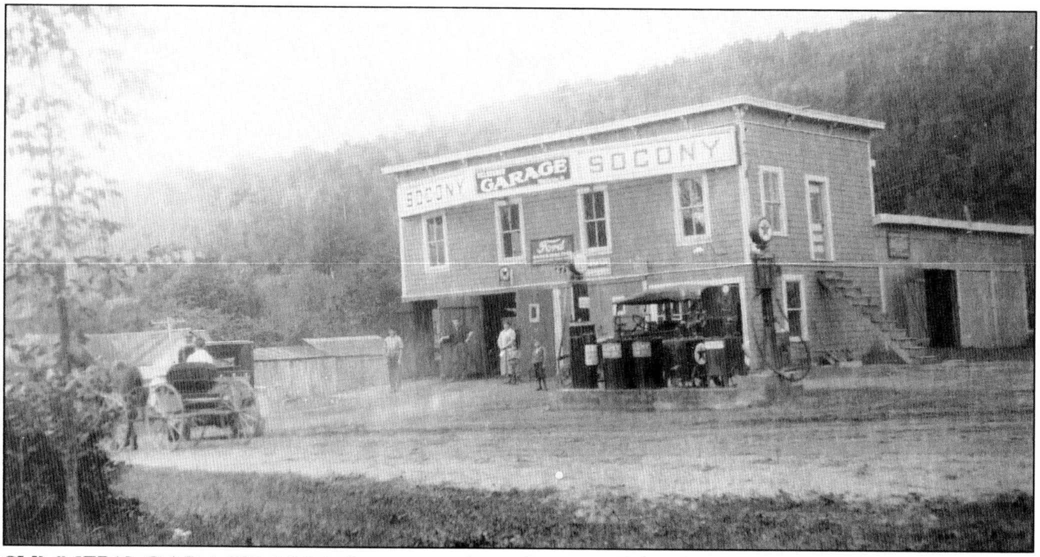

SUMNER'S GARAGE, 1926. Constructed on the site of the former Eagle Hotel, this building was later replaced by the present Eastman Garage.

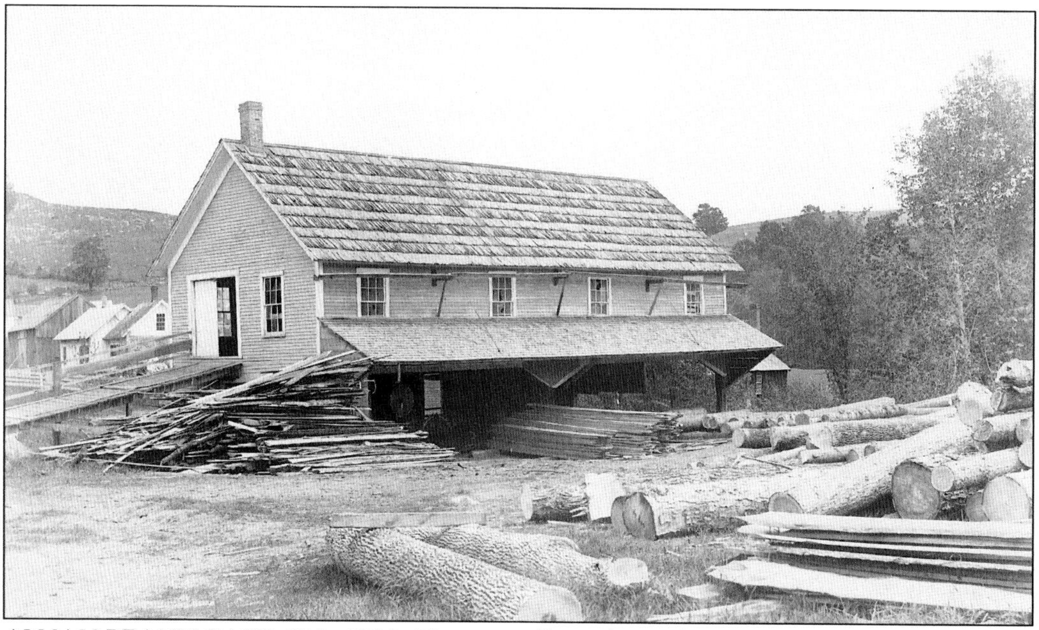

ALVAH BEAN'S SAWMILL, 1890. This sawmill was located on Mill Street on the west side of the Ompompanoosuc River.

Two

Orford

NEW HAMPSHIRE
Grafton County
First Settled: 1765
Incorporated: September 25, 1761
Population in 1995: 1,022
Area: 35 square miles
Principal Settlements: Orford, Orfordville

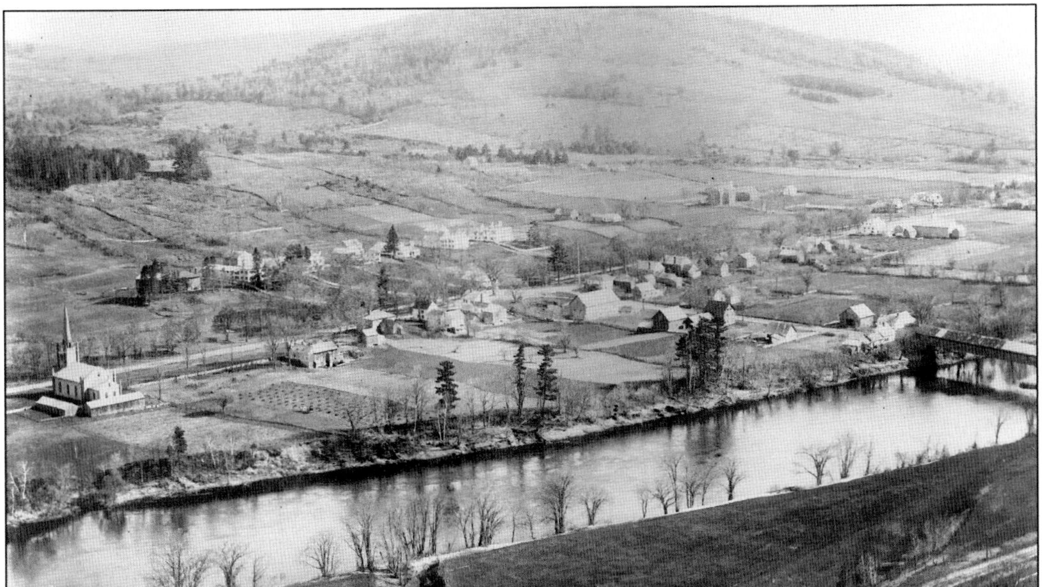

MAIN STREET, VILLAGE OF ORFORD. Photographed in the late 1800s from the Fairlee Palisades, the westernmost settlement within the town of Orford developed along the Connecticut River. Especially notable in this view are: the Congregational church, with its two horse sheds; the "Ridge Houses", a row of Federal and Greek Revival houses built during the late 1700s to early 1800s on a ridge overlooking Main Street; the Academy building in the middle distance; and the open lands beyond the settled area, resulting from extensive clearing of the forests. (New Hampshire Historical Society photograph.)

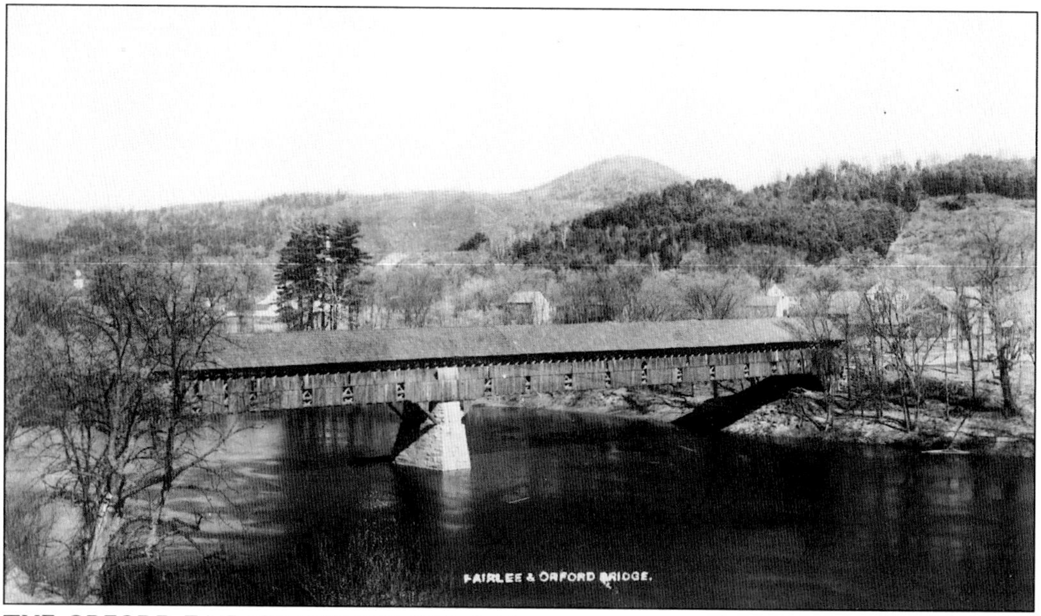

THE ORFORD-FAIRLEE BRIDGE. This bridge was constructed in 1857 on the site of two earlier uncovered bridges. Prior to the bridges, the Connecticut River was crossed by ferries, including one operated at this location by Orford resident Samuel Morey. The covered bridge was severely damaged by the March 1936 flood and demolished in 1937 to make way for the present steel structure. (Dartmouth College Library photograph.)

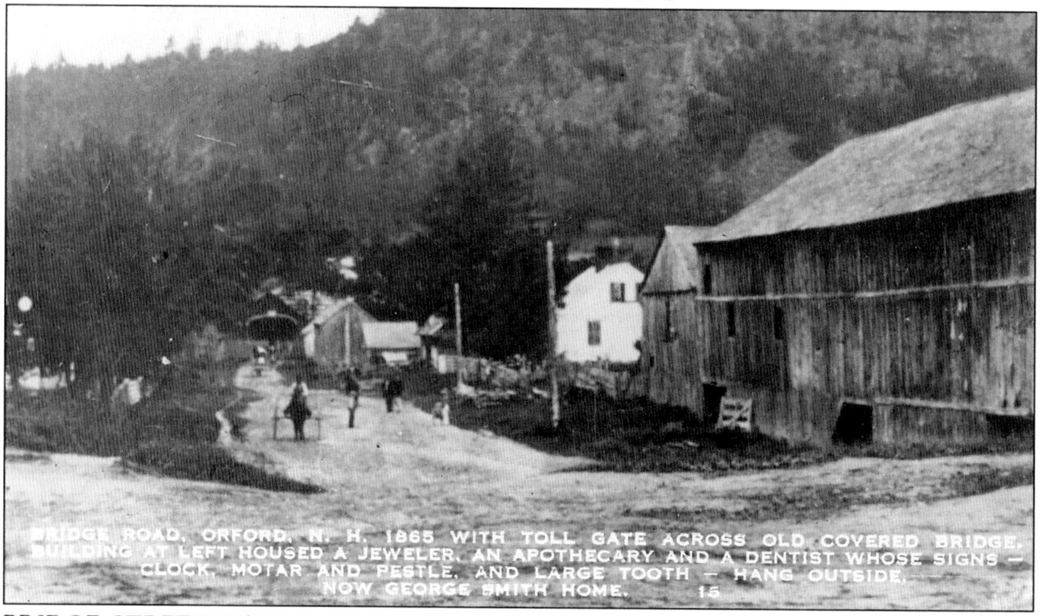

BRIDGE STREET. This is a view toward the Orford entrance of the covered bridge as it looked in 1865. Until 1894, a toll house collected fees from travelers, who were advised that horses were prohibited from being ridden or driven faster than a walk. This prohibition was to diminish sway in the long expanse of timbers. A building just visible on the left housed a jeweler, an apothecary, and a dental office; each signed with a clock, a mortar and pestle, and a large tooth, respectively.

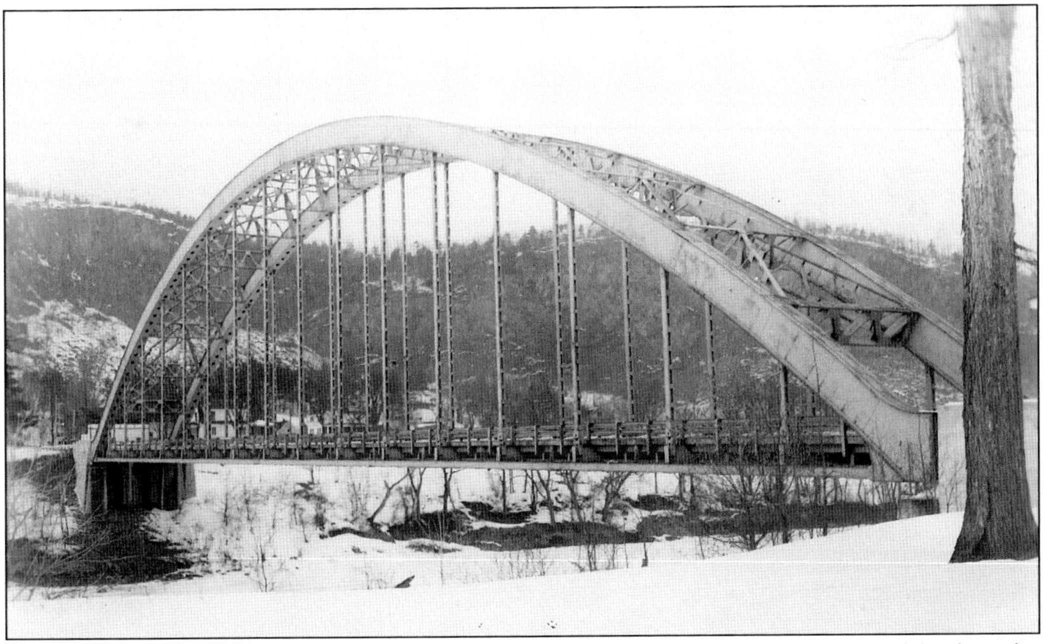

UNIQUE BRIDGE. Completed in 1938 to replace the flood-damaged covered bridge, the Samuel Morey Memorial Bridge is a highly unusual, tied-through steel arch design, now one of only four remaining steel-arch bridges in New Hampshire.

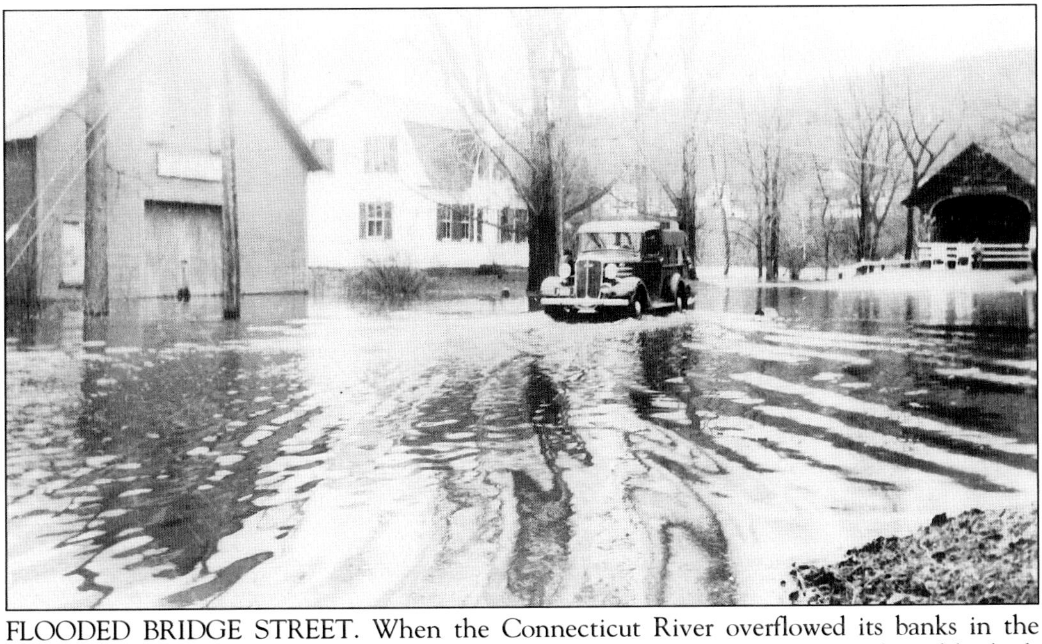

FLOODED BRIDGE STREET. When the Connecticut River overflowed its banks in the recordbreaking flood of March 1936, the Orford-Fairlee bridge was badly weakened by high water. Access to the bridge was blocked at both sides, as seen here.

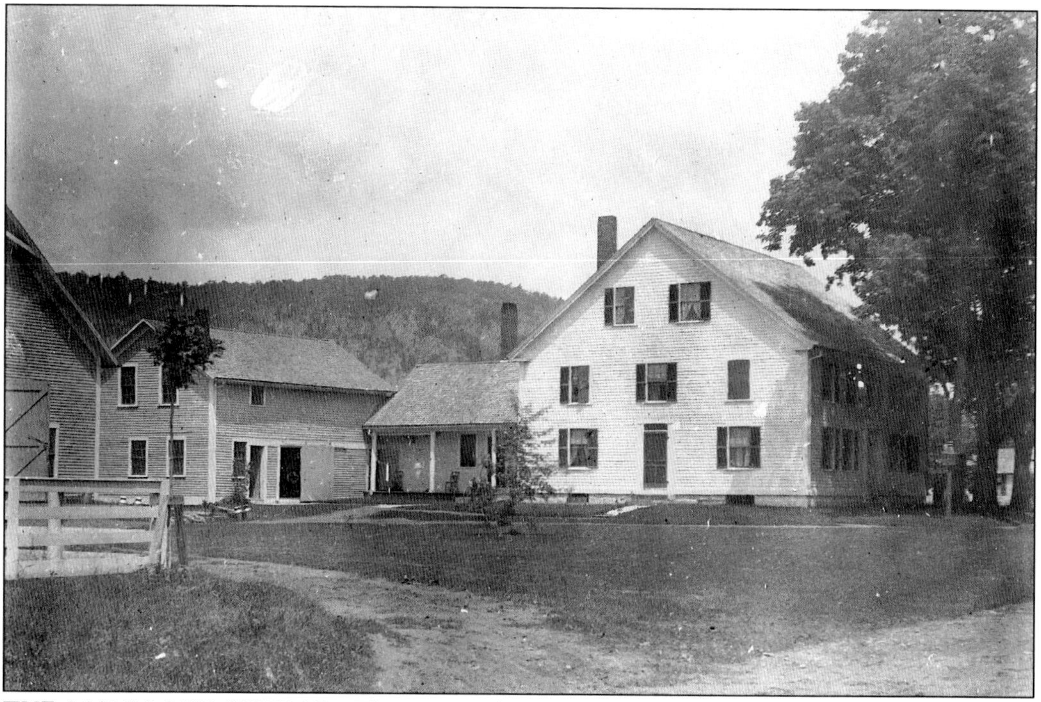

THE MANN HOMESTEAD. This 1908 photograph shows the original tiny, shed-roofed structure built by John Mann in 1788, which later served to connect the front house to the rear building. John Mann, Orford's first settler, packed his pregnant bride on his horse and walked north from Hebron, Connecticut, in 1765. He bought fifty acres of riverfront for $50 from the absentee proprietors of the town, which was chartered and incorporated by England's King George III in 1761.

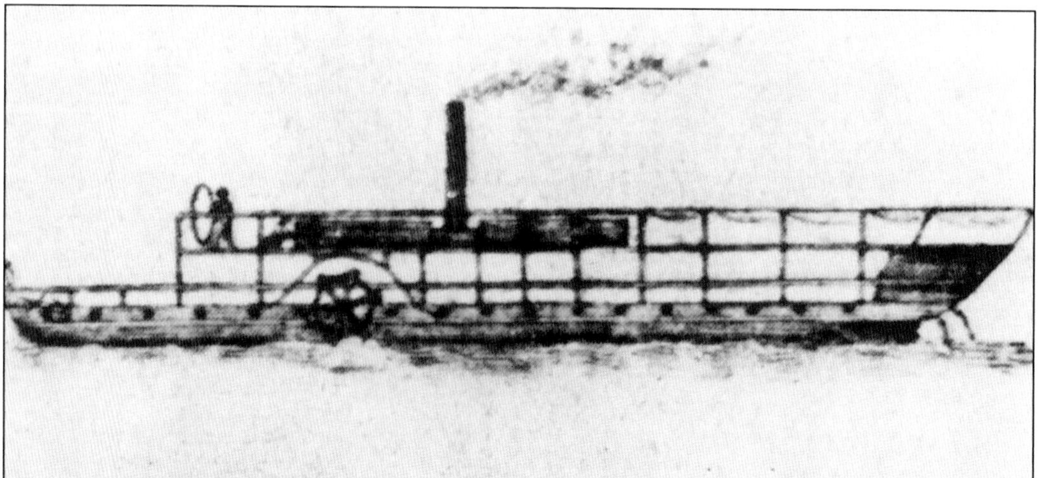

THE FIRST STEAMBOAT. Orford inventor, lumberman, and mill-owner Samuel Morey built an experimental boat, actually a log dugout, which he outfitted with his steam-powered engine. He successfully launched this craft on the Connecticut River and ushered in America's steam age. Illustrated here is an early sketch of Morey's invention, showing the revolving steam engine, which he patented in 1815. Morey never received due credit, however, because Robert Fulton first secured the financial backing to produce the steamboat commercially.

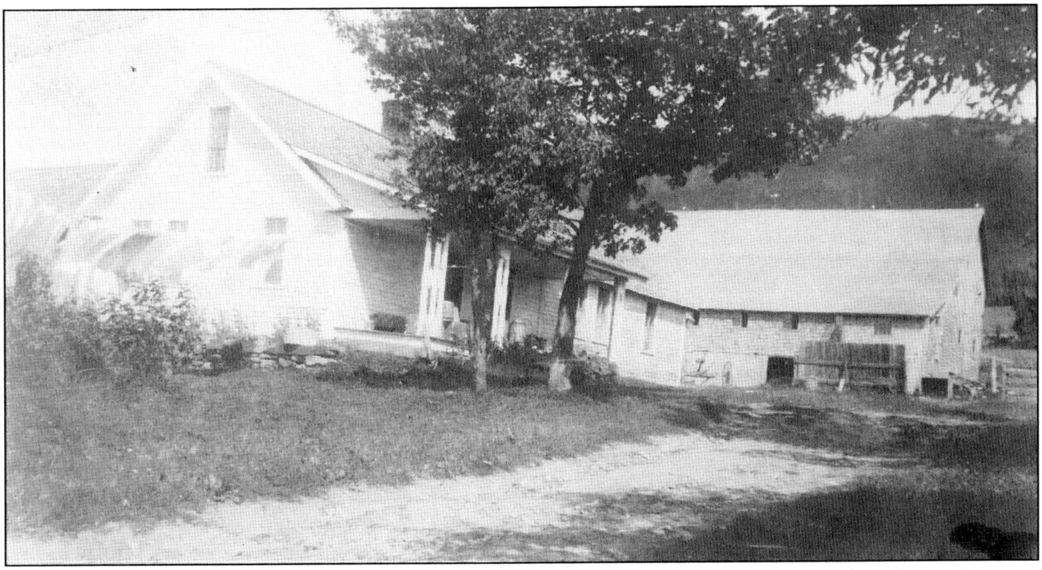

AN EARLY HOMESTEAD. Elijah Palmer built the Finney home in 1784 for Eleazar Finney and his wife and father. It was on the west side of Mount Cube in Orfordville. Seven generations of Finneys resided there. Direct descendants of this pioneer family live in Orford today.

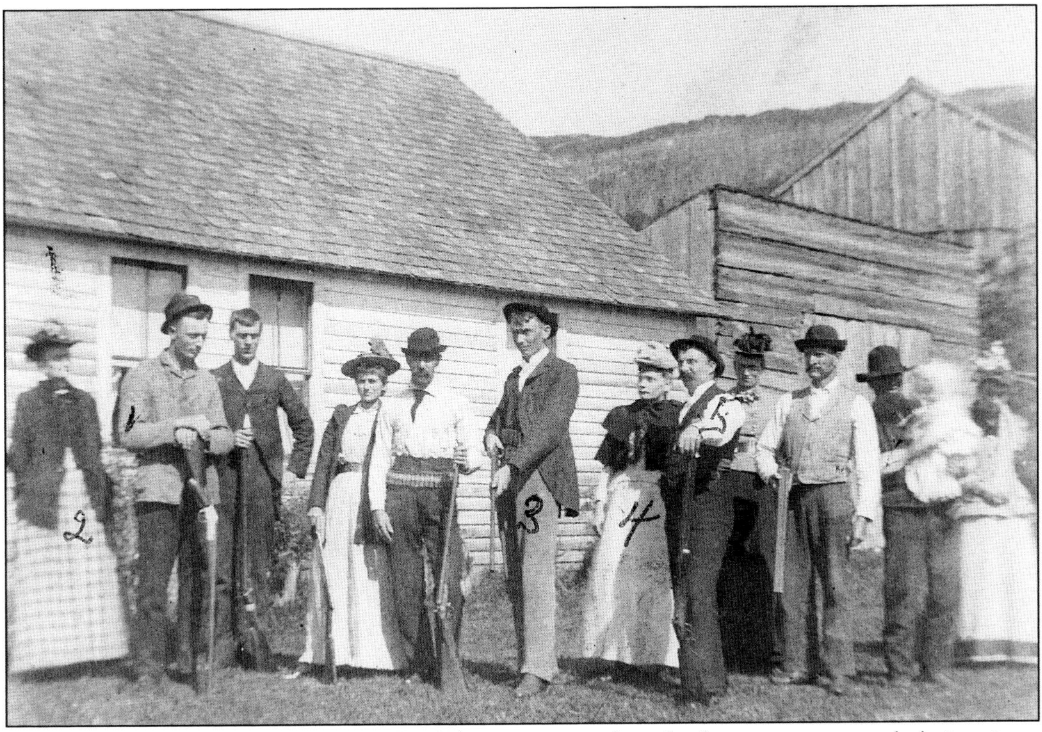

A FINNEY GATHERING, C. 1870. The men posed with their weapons and their wives. Among those pictured are: Mrs. Henry Finney (Mary Emerton); her sons, Frank and Charles; her daughter, Mattie; and Mattie's husband, Frank Seymour.

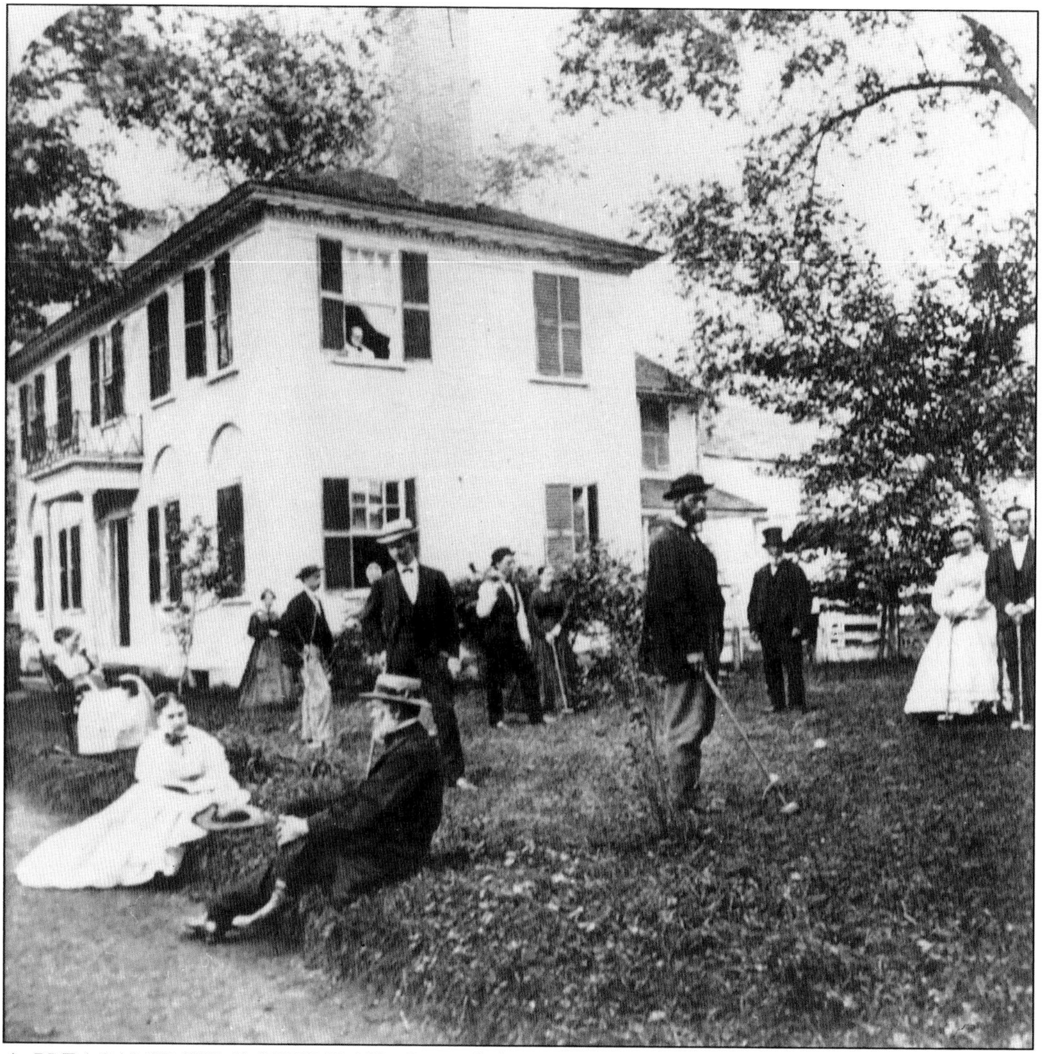

A PLEASANT SUMMER'S DAY. One of the "Seven Sisters" houses on the Orford Ridge, this house was built in 1817 by John Rogers, a lawyer and longtime selectman in Orford. The house features a "good morning staircase"—a double set of stairs accessed from a single staircase and which leads to second floor bedrooms. In 1868, when this photograph was taken, the house was owned by the Hartwell Cushman family. Mr. Cushman is seated in the foreground wearing a straw hat. His daughter, Pleasantine, and her fiance, Boston lawyer John T. Wilson, are at the extreme right with croquet mallets. John J. Cushman is wearing a top hat at the rear right. Family members and guests complete the composition.

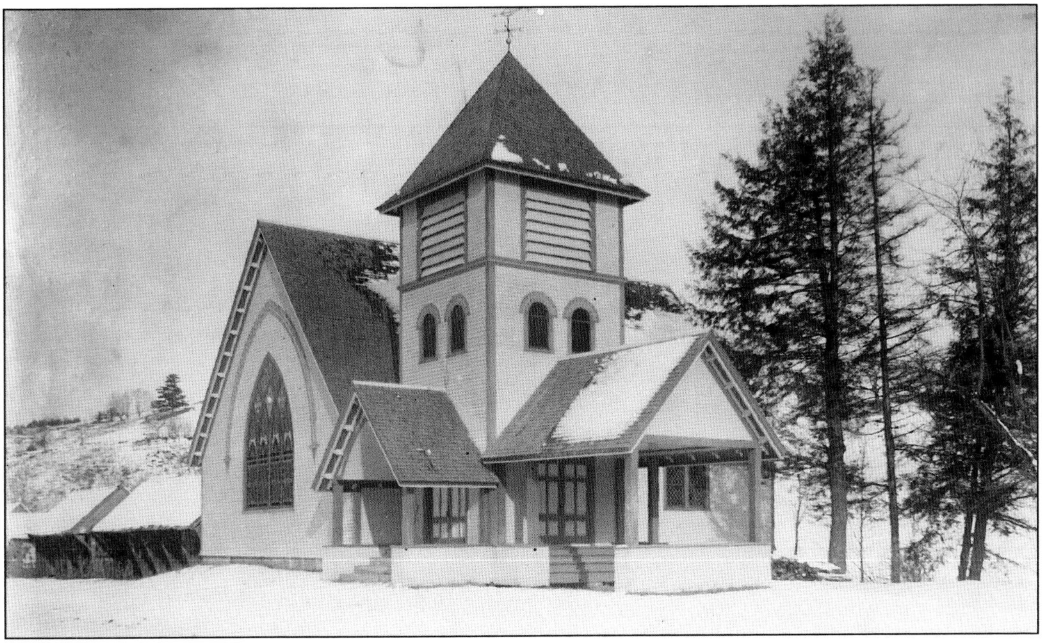

THE CHURCHES OF ORFORD. A winter's view of the First Congregational church of Orfordville. The first minister was Obadiah Noble, who established a Presbyterian church in the late 1700s. By 1795, a meeting house was built on Dame Hill. In 1833, the members built a brick building next to the Orfordville store, which served as a Congregational church. This structure was destroyed by fire in 1895 and rebuilt as the church in current use. This church contains the oldest pipe organ known to be in use in New Hampshire, a gift from the Royal Beal family who operated a chair and mattress factory in Orfordville.

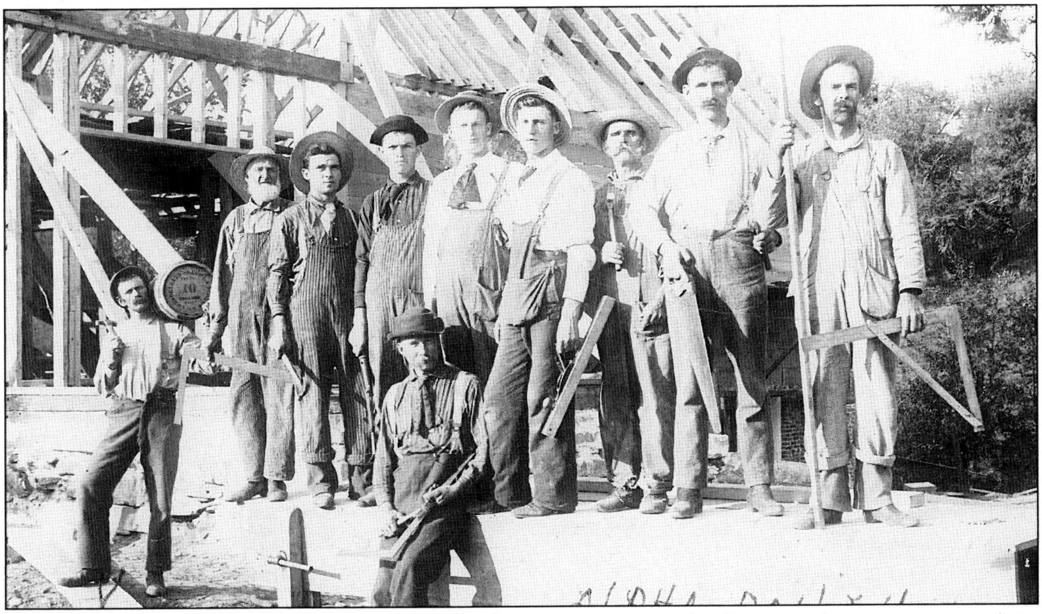

REBUILDING THE CHURCH. The workmen posing with their tools were engaged in rebuilding Orfordville's Congregational church following the 1895 fire. The only man identified is Alpha Bailey (extreme left) hefting the keg of ten-penny nails.

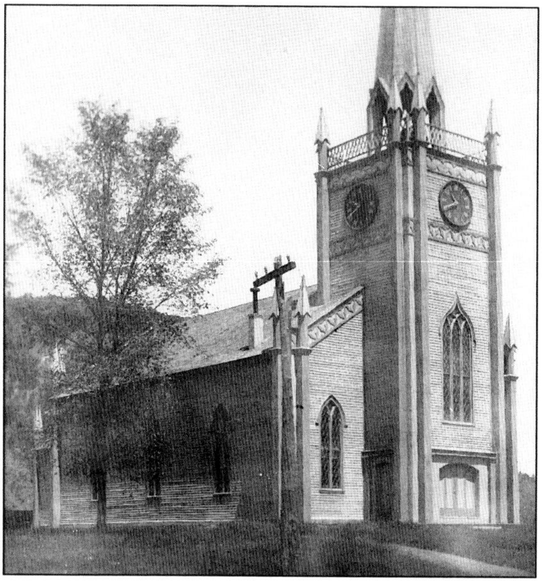
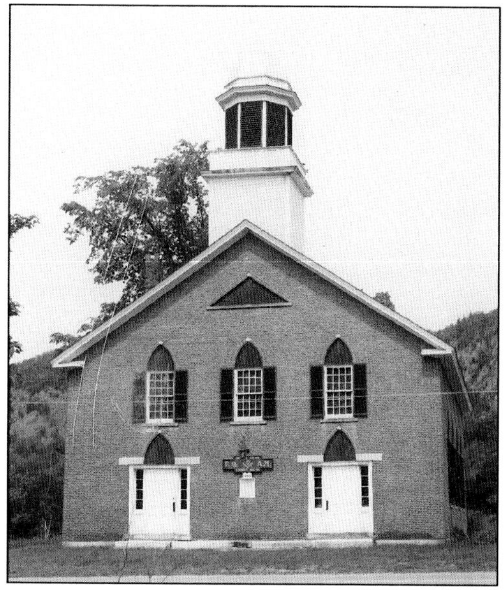

THE WEST MEETING HOUSE. Now the Congregational church of Orford, this church was first established in 1797, a year after the Dame Hill Meeting House was constructed. The building, with its soaring steeple, was designed by Lebanon native Moses Wood in Gothic Revival style and built in 1854/55. It cost $2,900 and was paid for, in part, by the sale of pews—one family reportedly bought ten. Prices ranged from $50 to $100 per pew.

THE UNIVERSALIST CHURCH. Erected in 1840, this Federal-Gothic Revival brick church was supported by worshippers from Orford and Fairlee and was active for some twenty-five years. The building was sold in 1878 and transformed into a "Union Hall" for public entertainments. In 1904 it took on its present role as the Masonic Hall.

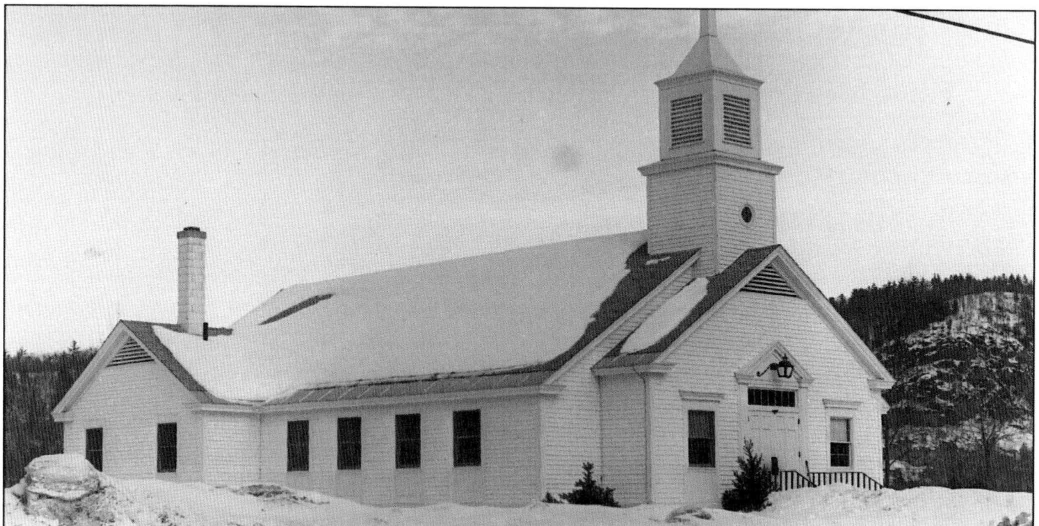

OUR LADY, QUEEN OF PEACE. This 200-seat Catholic church, designed as a typical New England house of worship, was completed in 1977. For fifteen years, the church was housed in the completed basement until sufficient funds could be accumulated. Located on Route 10, the church is distinctive for its seventeen-pane window behind the altar, which encompasses the west wall and overlooks the Connecticut River.

THE GENTLEWOMEN OF ORFORD. The ladies on this page represent those who worked side-by-side with their men, hoed the gardens and preserved the produce, nurtured and taught the children, and thereby tamed the wild places and fostered a civilization and a culture. Pictured here *c.* 1915 are: Florence Cushman (right), Gladys Huckins (below, left), and Lurlene Blodgett (below, right).

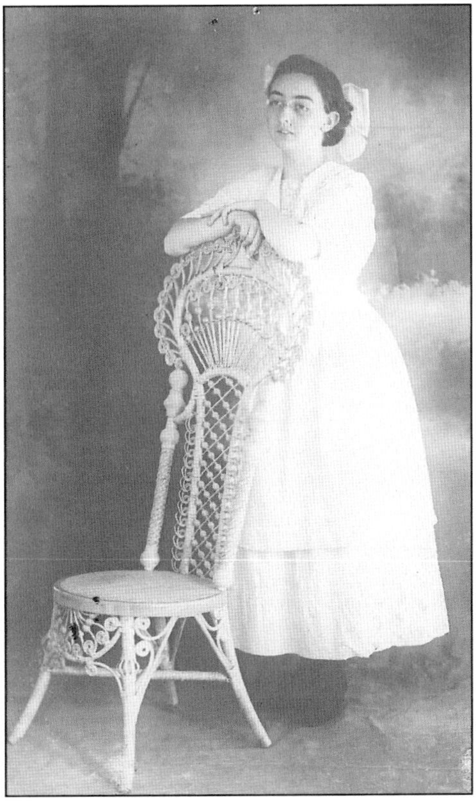

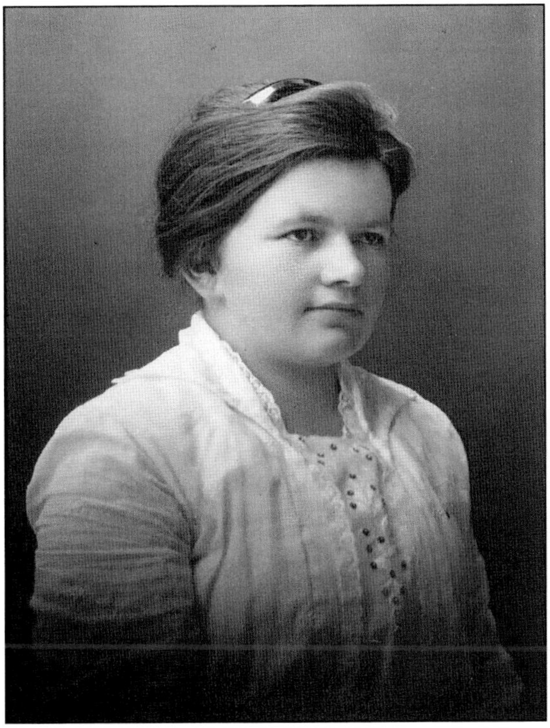

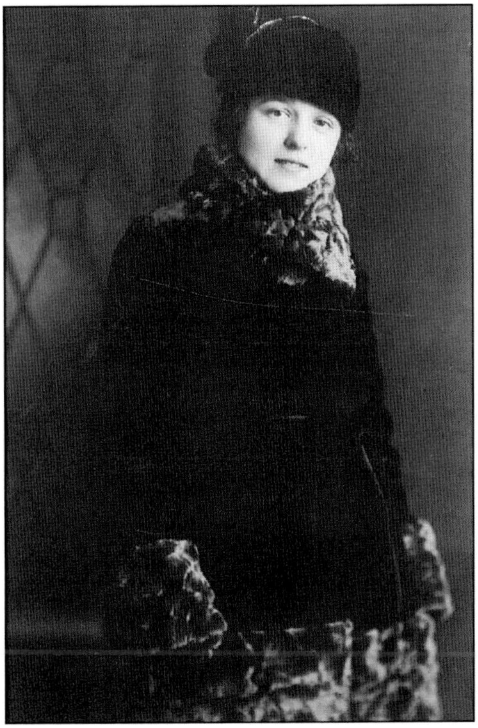

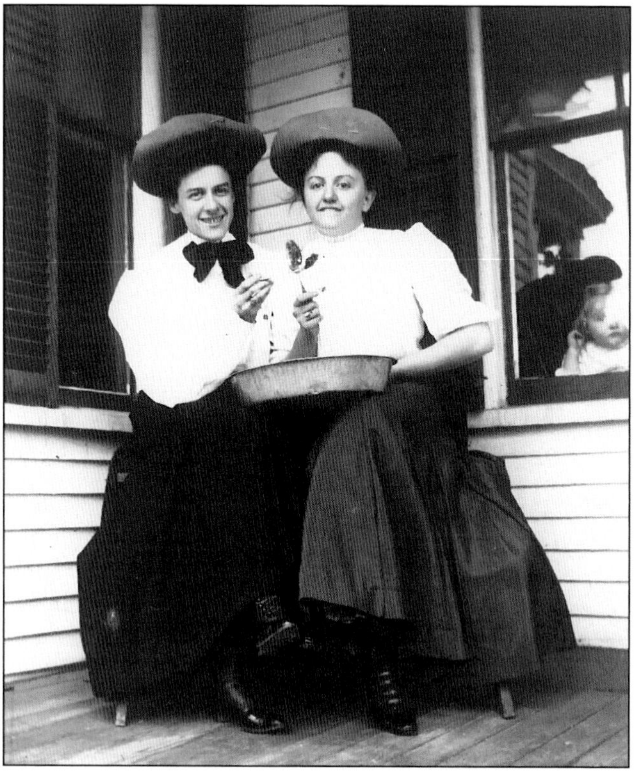

TWO CHUMS ENJOYING A SUMMER'S DAY, C. 1901. Irma Carr (right) and her friend prepare flowers for drying. Barely visible, a small child looks on from the window (extreme right). Irma's husband Henry worked with his father, Robert O. Carr, in the family's general merchandise business at the corner of Orford and Bridge Streets.

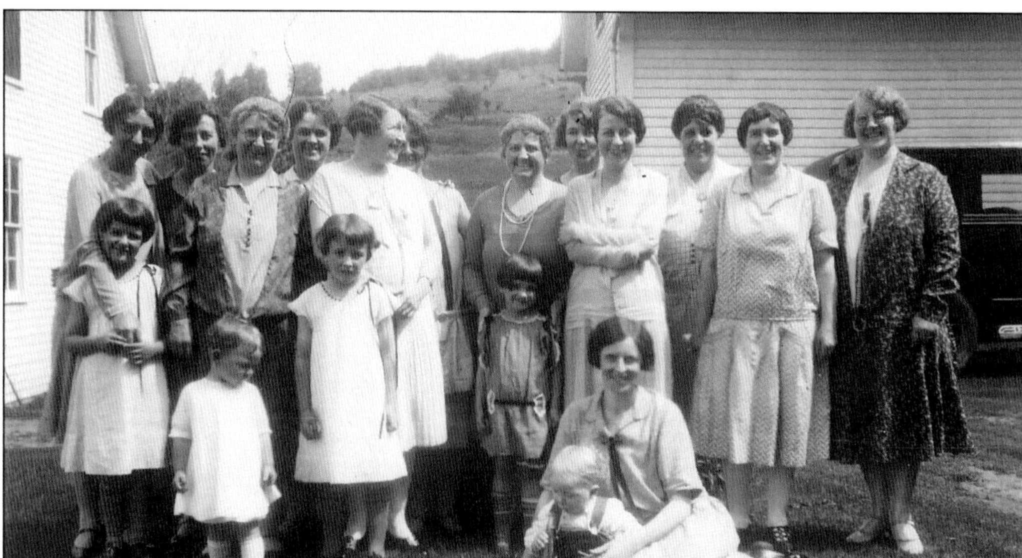

A "SOROSIS" GATHERING. In 1928, this ladies' club gathered at "The Veranda," a house on Route 10 south of town which later was used as an inn and is now an apartment house. Shown here are: Ella Wilson, Hattie French, Florence Cushman Bohn, Marion Swan, Eliza H. Wilcox, Bess Cushman, Alice Washburn Jennison, Maude Harris, Erma Carr, Katherine Saunders, Ruby Carr, Ella Wilson, Bess Horton, and Hazel Huckins with her baby son, G. Roger. Also included are the Washburn girls: Laura, Lucille, Jeanne, and Joyce.

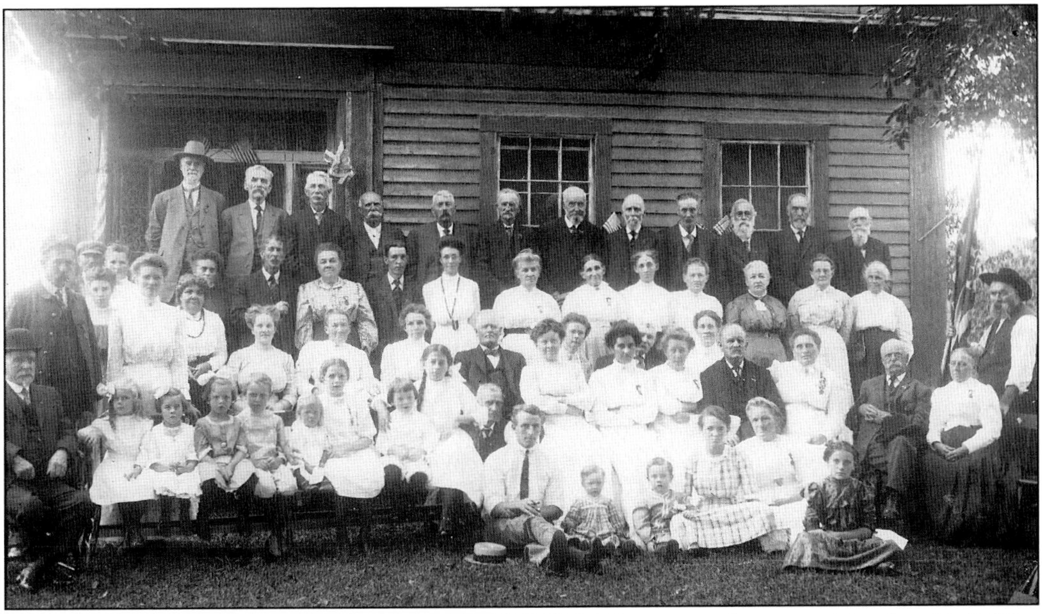

GRAND ARMY OF THE REPUBLIC REUNION. The men who served in the Civil War gathered at annual picnics to honor all those who had fought in America's wars. With their families, the men met here in August 1911 at the home of Walter Horton in Orfordville. Included are: Ruth Kibling, Charlie Craig, Gracie Chase, Freda Smith, Ralph Gaskill, Verna Rich, Celia Dike, Dorothy Smith, Walter Horton Sr., Walter Allan Horton, Jesse Horton, Floyd Horton, Bernice (Washburn) Horton, Mary Stone Horton, Bess Kenyon Horton, and Frank and Josephine Hall. Note the youngsters lined up decorously on the bench.

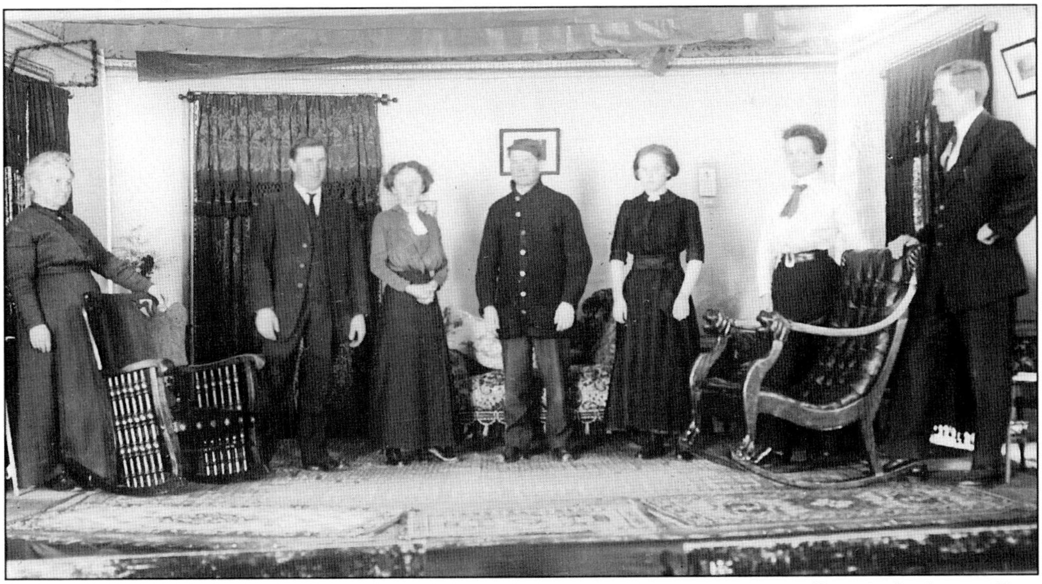

THE PLAY WAS THE THING. Plays were presented at the Masonic Hall in Orford as well as at the town hall in Orfordville. On stage here at the latter venue is the cast of *Cranberry Corner*, a drama produced in February 1914. Players are, from left to right: Mrs. Walter Horton, Harry Marshall, Florence Russell, Jesse R. Kenyon, Verna Greenley, Edyth M. Clough, and Samuel R. Morrison. Mrs. Morrison took the picture.

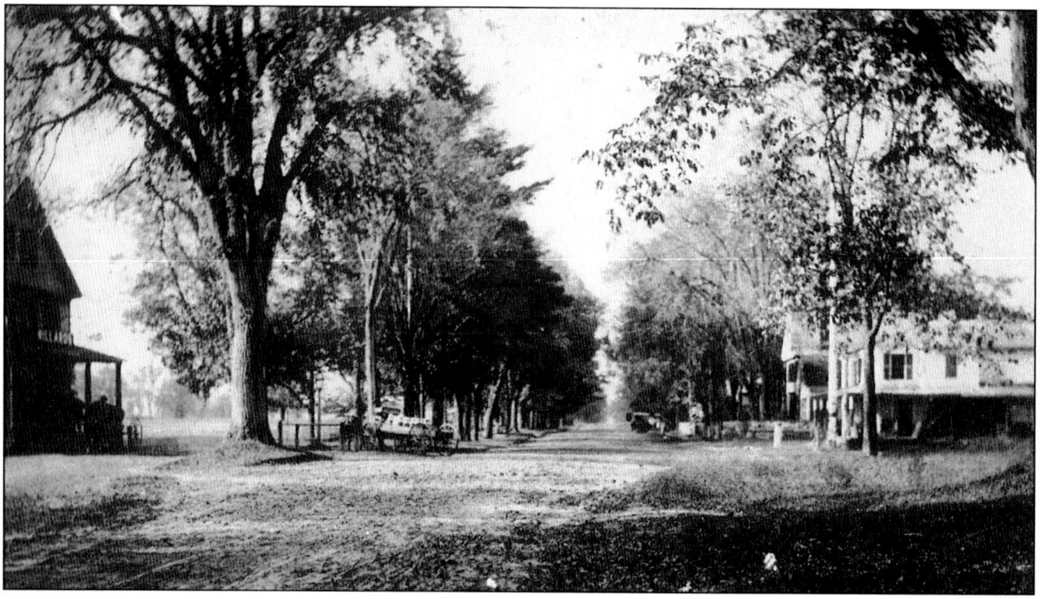

ORFORD STREET, LATE 1890s. This photograph looks down the tree-shaded main street of Orford (now Route 10), at the intersection of Bridge Street. Stedman Willard's store, which burned down in 1905, appears at the far left, and what was the Wheeler store is on the right.

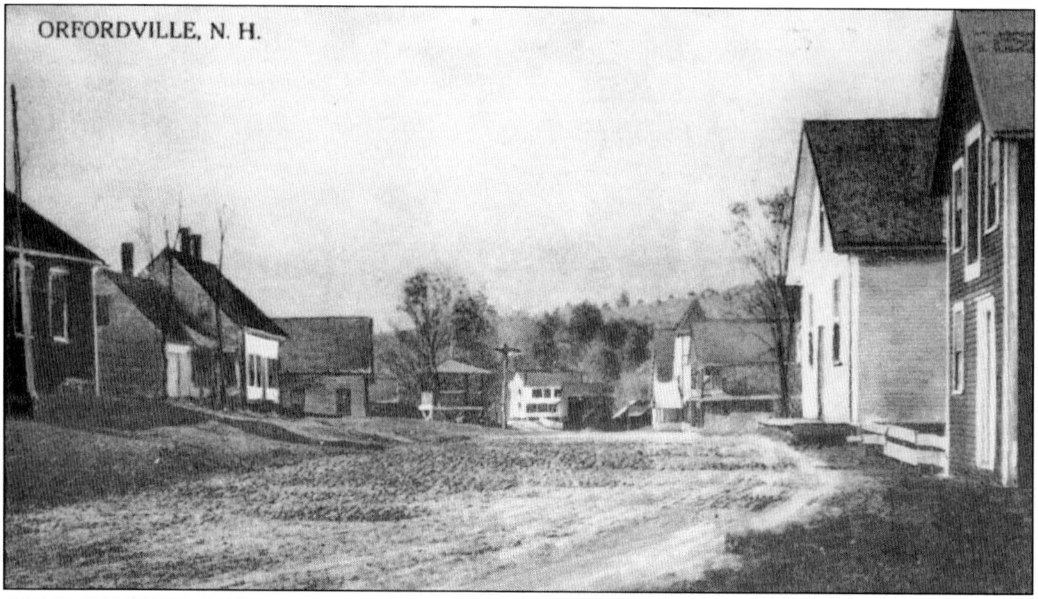

ORFORDVILLE, EARLY 1900s. The bandstand is visible (center left) in this view of the principal village street in Orfordville. Also included are the Beal house, which burned in 1937 (center); the town hall; and the casket factory (at right).

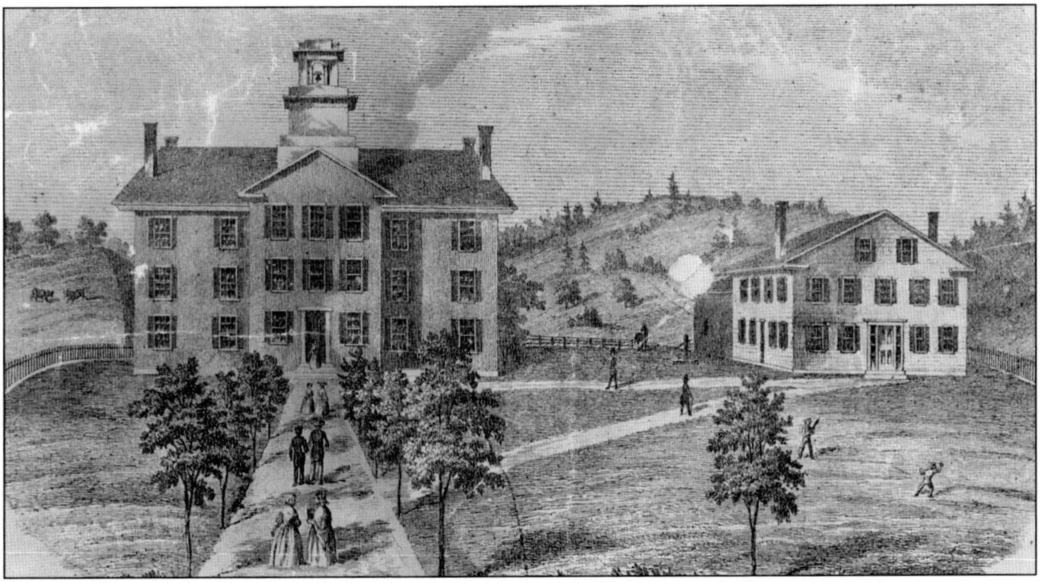

ORFORD ACADEMY AND BOARDING HOUSE, C. 1855. Built in 1851, the Academy is the oldest public building in Orford. The Academy was first established in 1797 as a private school near the present Masonic Hall. Two years later the school was turned over to the town and operated as a public secondary school. Following a fire it was removed to the present location on the south end of the Ridge. The boarding house functioned as a girls' dormitory while the third floor of the high school, "Patterson Hall," was the boys' dormitory.

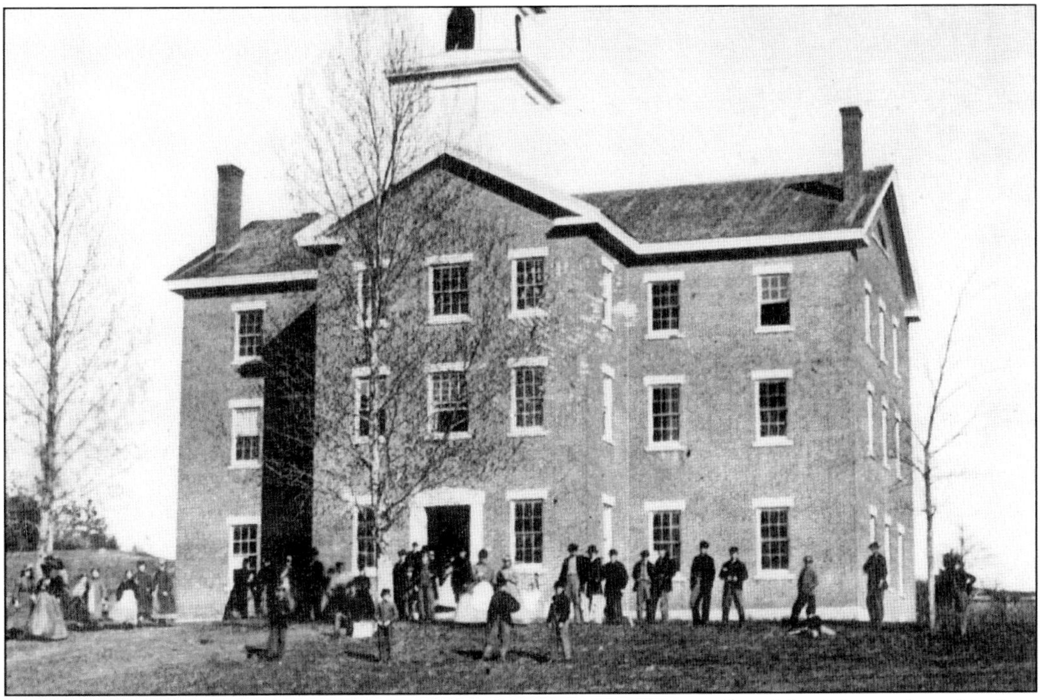

THE HIGH SCHOOL IN 1865. The Academy is the oldest school building of its kind in continuous use in New Hampshire. The school building looks much the same today and still serves both local students as well as those tuitioned in from neighboring towns.

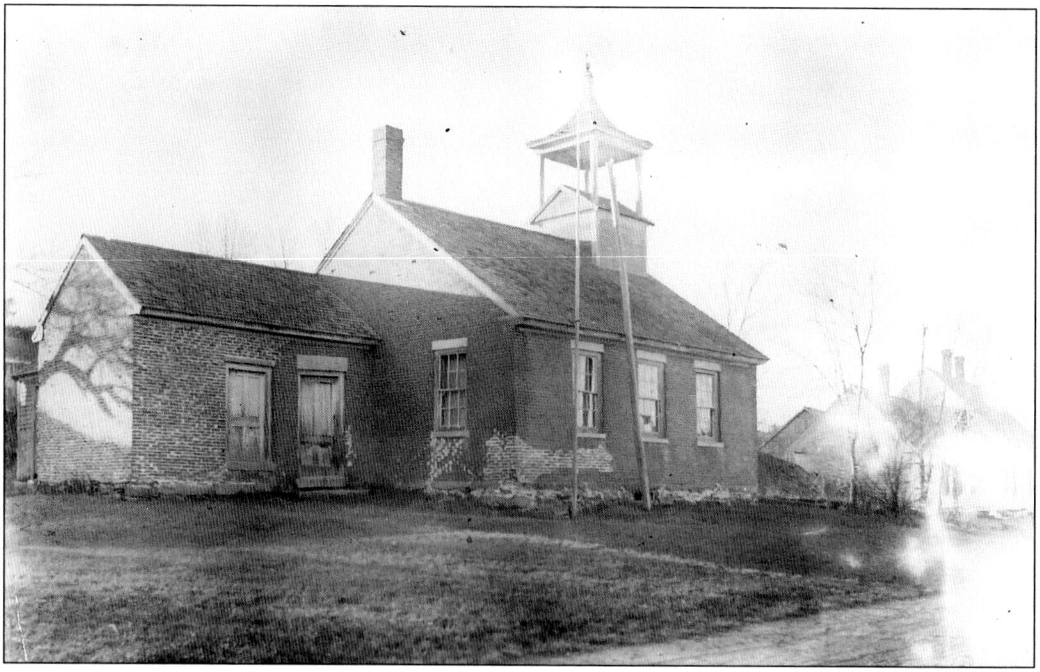

THE OLD BRICK SCHOOL. Built in the village of Orfordville in 1832, this brick grammar school was one of sixteen "district" (mostly one-room) schools built throughout the town and serving more than 400 students in that era. This building later served as the town office and library. It burned in 1933 and was rebuilt. Today it is in use as the Orford Free Library, one of Orford's two libraries. The Orford Social Library, once a millinery shop, is on Route 10 between the former parsonage and the general store.

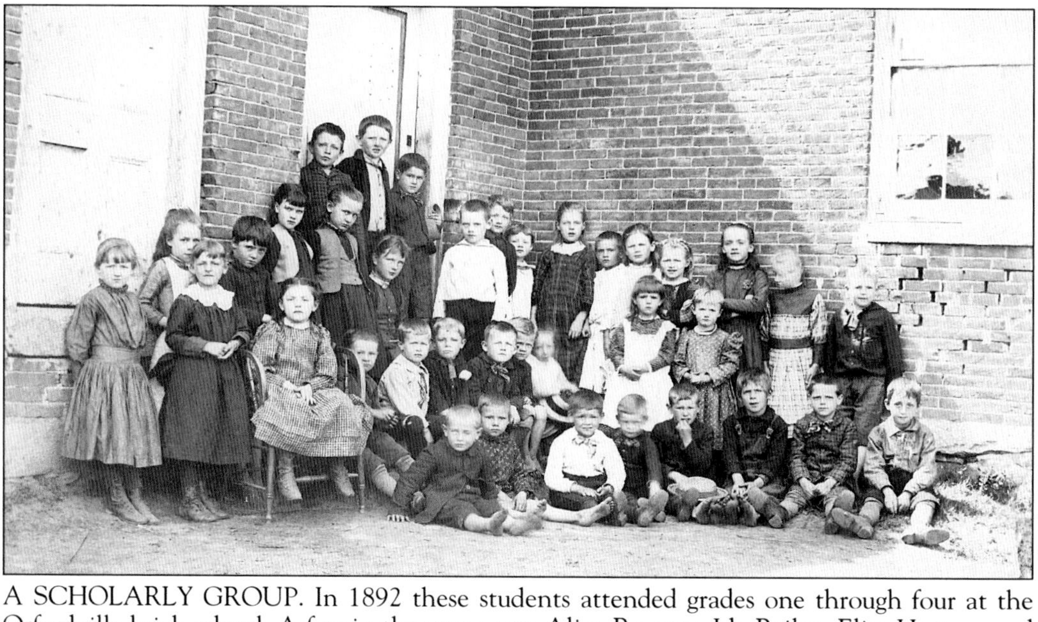

A SCHOLARLY GROUP. In 1892 these students attended grades one through four at the Orfordville brick school. A few in the group are: Alice Ramsey, Ida Bailey, Eliza Horton, and Alice Washburn. Some of the youngsters wore their high-button shoes for the camera while others opted for the comfort of bare feet.

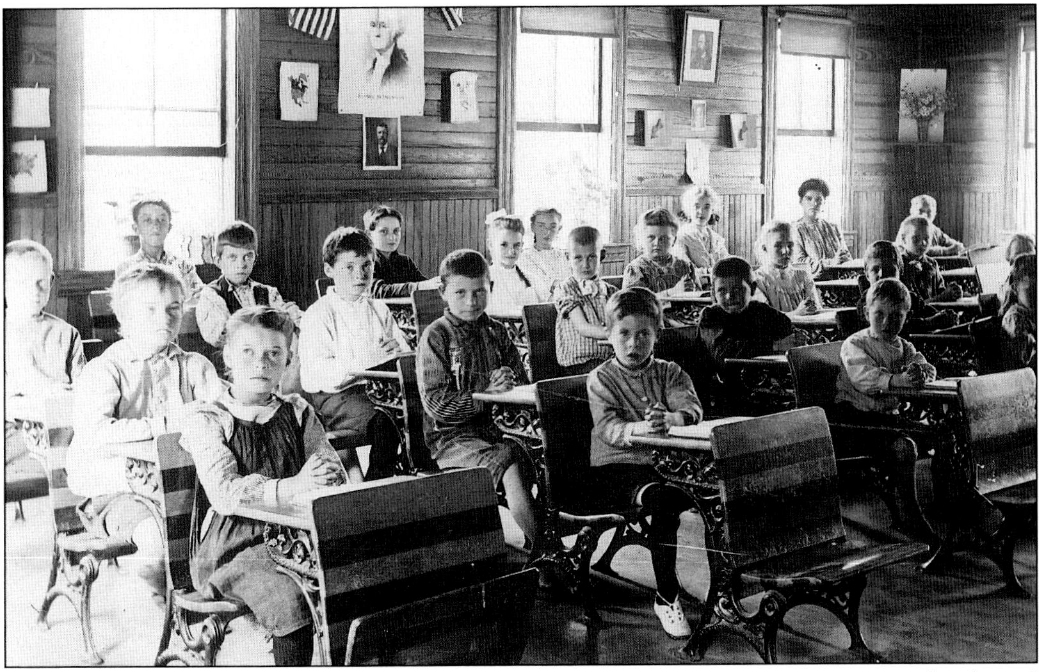

ORFORDVILLE SCHOOL HOUSE, BUILT 1898. This building was in use as a school until February 1990—it is now the Orford Town Offices. In 1906, the students included: Moses White, Bernice Horton, Florence Cushman, Gladys Huckins, and Verna Greenley.

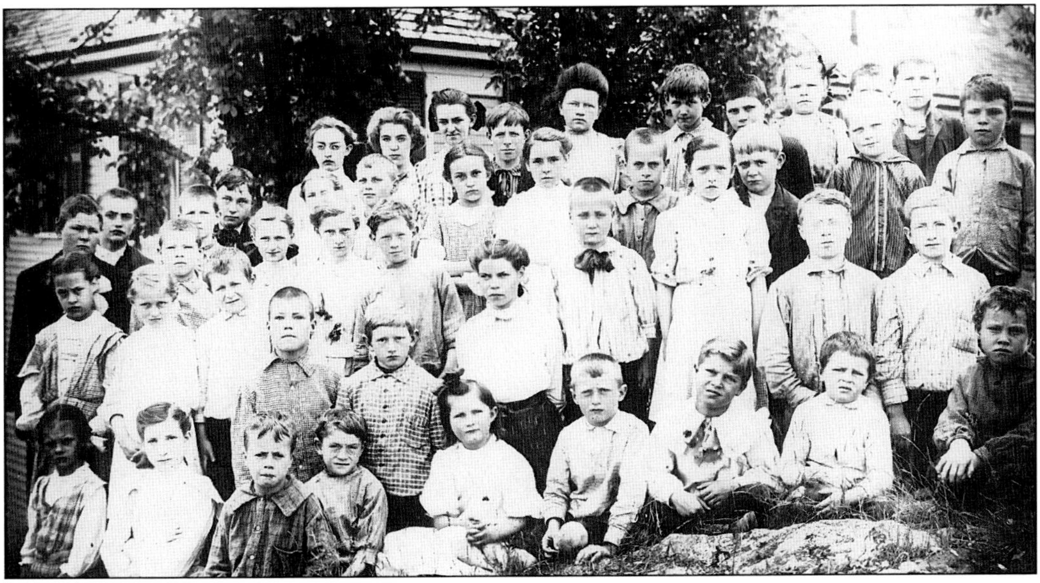

ORFORDVILLE STUDENT BODY, 1908. The entire student body included: Ruth Cross, Fred Mosely, Guy Finney, Ralph Wright, Doris Finney, Brad Baker, Leon Marsh, Ralph Bean, Lettie Rhodes, Lem Manchester, Marion Trussell, George Niles, Carl Hibbard, Lurlene Blodgett, Barnard Bennett, Clifton Huckins, Ernest Hibbard, Dorothy Love, Max Mousley, William Hall, Walter Marsh, Roy Sanborn, Florence Cushman, Kate McPherson, Bernice Horton, Warren Greenley, Gladys Huckins, John Whitcher, Fred Baker, Gertrude Hall, and Harry Baker.

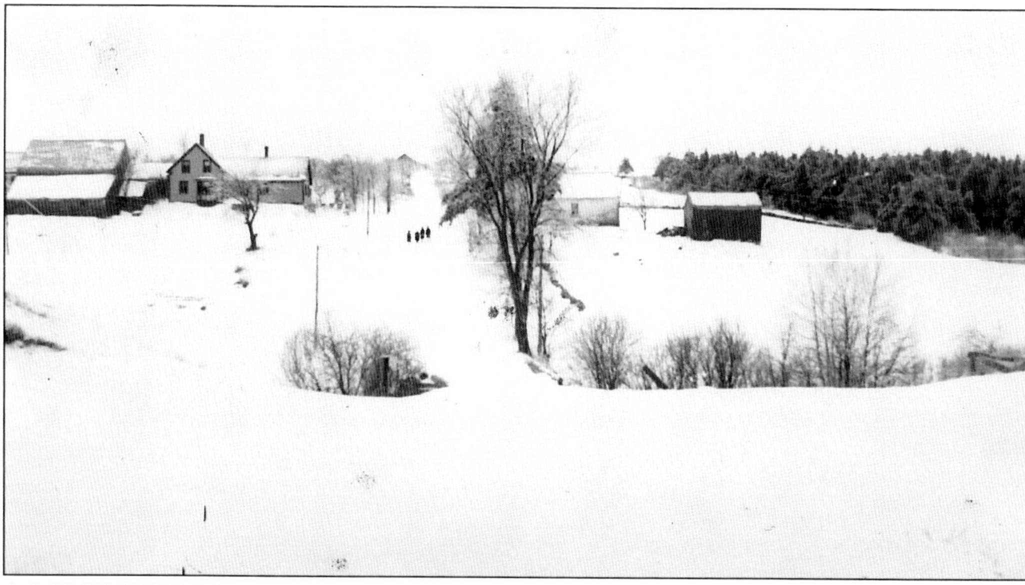

A LONELY WINTERSCAPE, C. 1895. Looking bleak and lonely, this is the Franklin farm, established in 1831 by Nathaniel Haselton and his son, John. Benjamin Franklin bought the property in 1852.

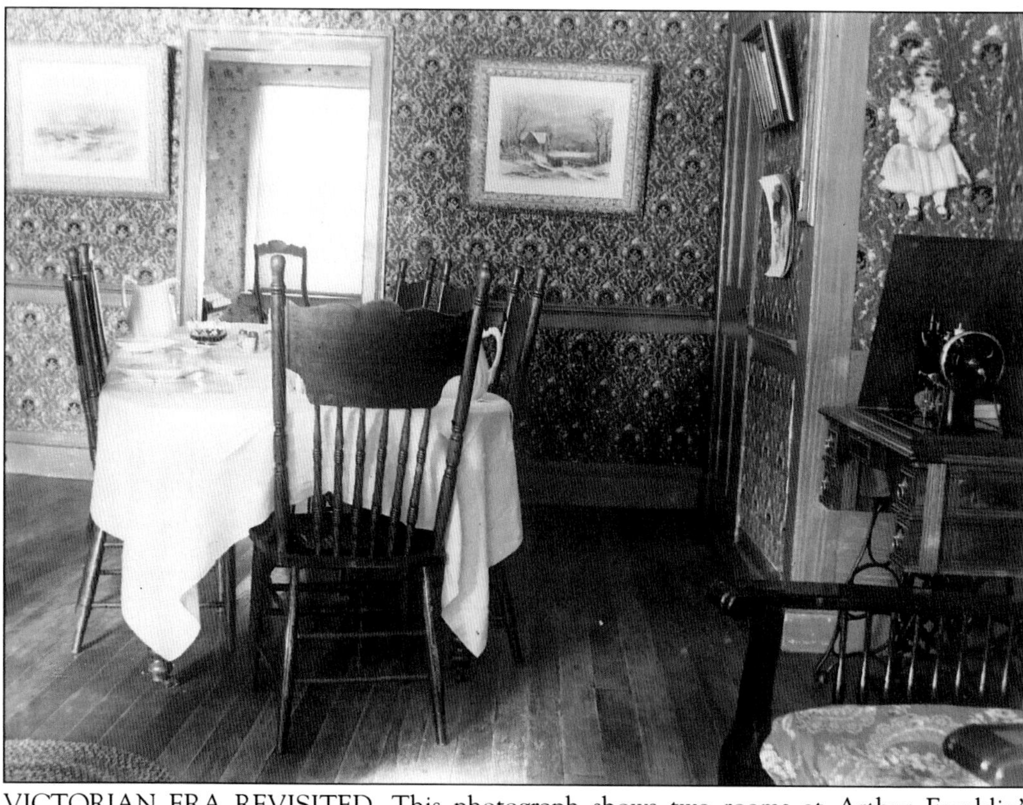

VICTORIAN ERA REVISITED. This photograph shows two rooms at Arthur Franklin's house (Benjamin was his father). These rooms appear to exhibit typical decor for that time and location.

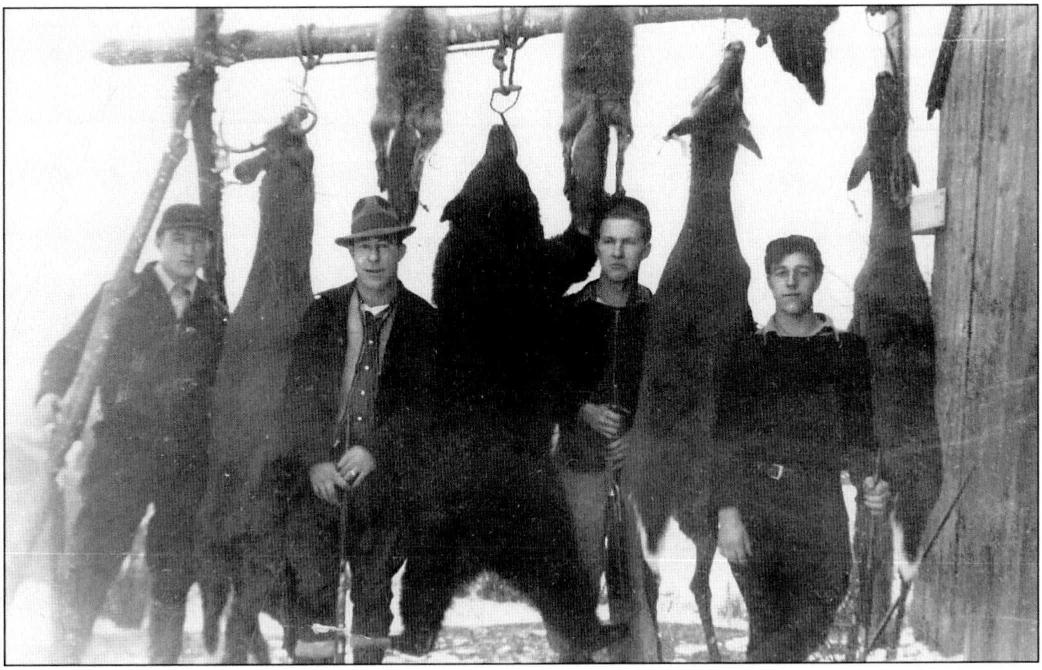

MAKING A LIVING. From the time of the first settlers, hunting wild game to put food on the table and for hides to sell, as well as fishing the ponds and streams of Orford, often made the difference between hunger and a well-fed family. In 1937, these hunters showed the results of their skill. From left to right: Maurice Chase and Walter, Delbert, and Ralph Mack (brothers), with the deer, fox, and bear they had taken in a day's hunting and trapping.

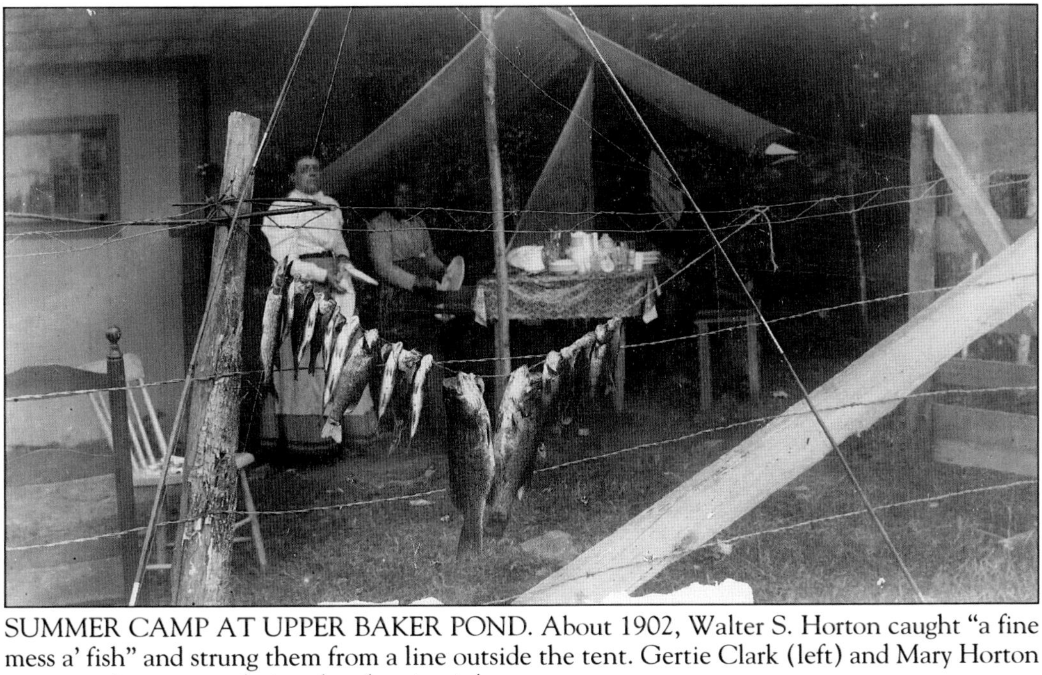

SUMMER CAMP AT UPPER BAKER POND. About 1902, Walter S. Horton caught "a fine mess a' fish" and strung them from a line outside the tent. Gertie Clark (left) and Mary Horton appear to be contemplating the cleaning job.

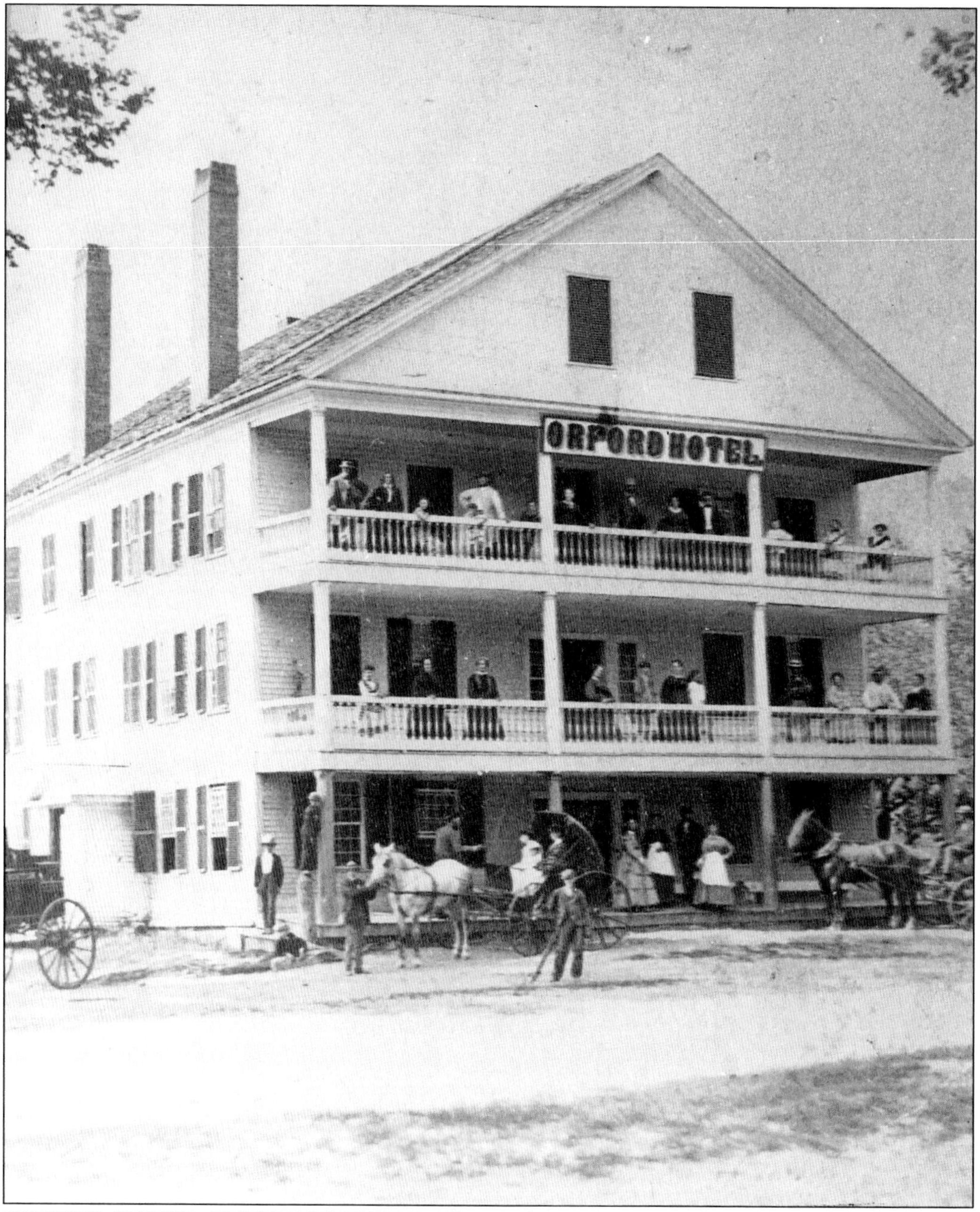

ORFORD HOTEL BEFORE THE FIRE. This striking view shows the Orford Hotel, a fine example of the flourishing tourist economy in Orford during the 1800s and early 1900s. Formerly the Solomon Mann Tavern (Solomon one of John Mann's fifteen children), it was built in 1802, and burned to the ground in December 1875 while owned by John Haselton. The site, at the northwest corner of Bridge and Orford Streets, later became the Elm Corner Store, owned by Mr. and Mrs. Guy Hebb. It is now the offices of Orford Enterprises, a real estate and development business. There were several other hotels and inns in Orford, as well as tourist cabins that operated seasonally for several decades.

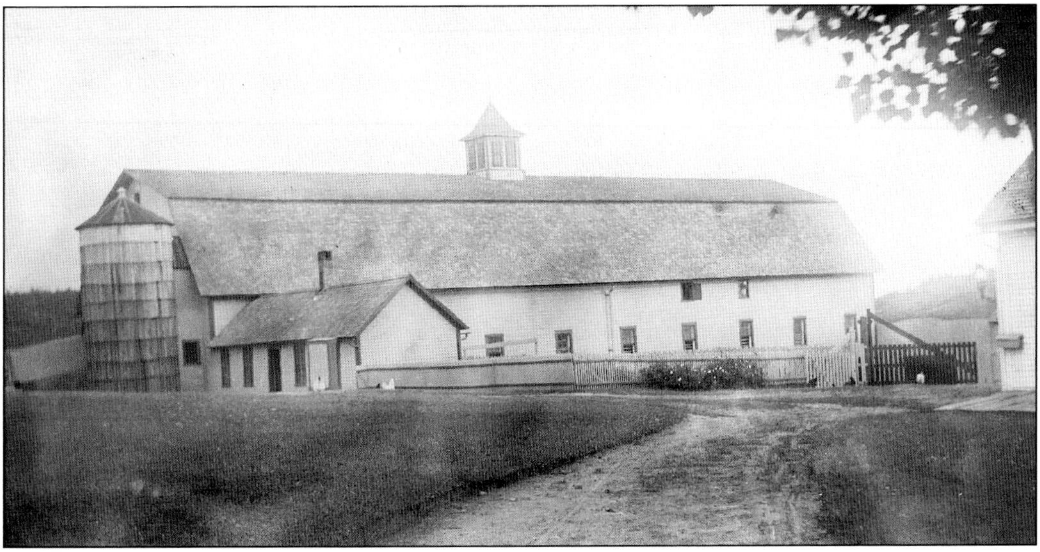

FARMING AS AN INDUSTRY. This is a view of the famous long barn at the Marston Stock Farm in Orford. Mills for sawing lumber, making starch from potatoes, carding wool, cutting shingles, separating clover seed from dried blossoms, and making mattresses and springs all helped Orford enjoy a diversified economy for its first 170 years. Still, it was farming that kept the community's economy alive and steady through the bad economic times as well as the prosperous periods.

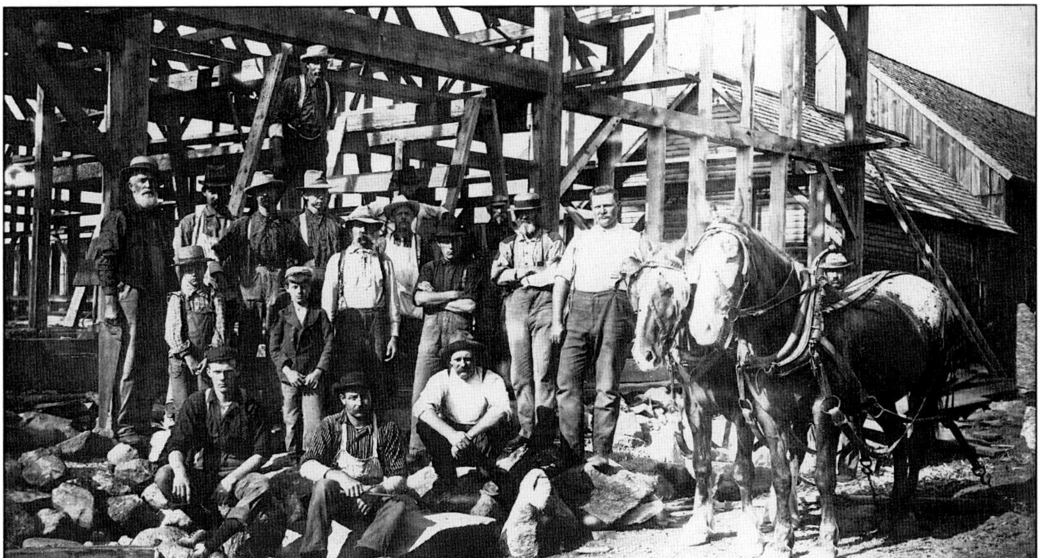

BUILDING THE BARN. The carpenters and joiners who built the long barn at the Marston Stock Farm posed for a photograph. The barn, finished in 1902, was a full 120 feet long. By 1915, Harry Morrison used the barn to house the largest herd of Herefords in all of New England. The Marston farm also had a large herd of sheep grazing its hills and fields. Pictured here, from left to right: (first row) Gene Cross, Ed Newhall, and Dwight Cross; (second row) Fay Russell, the two grandsons of Harry Morrison, a Mr. Bellford, Carroll Blon, Morrison, and Ed Veasey; (third row) Frank Tallman, Raymond D. Page, Harvey White, Charles Cushman, Walter Kimball, Jim Tallman, Ben Weed, and Stillman Wade.

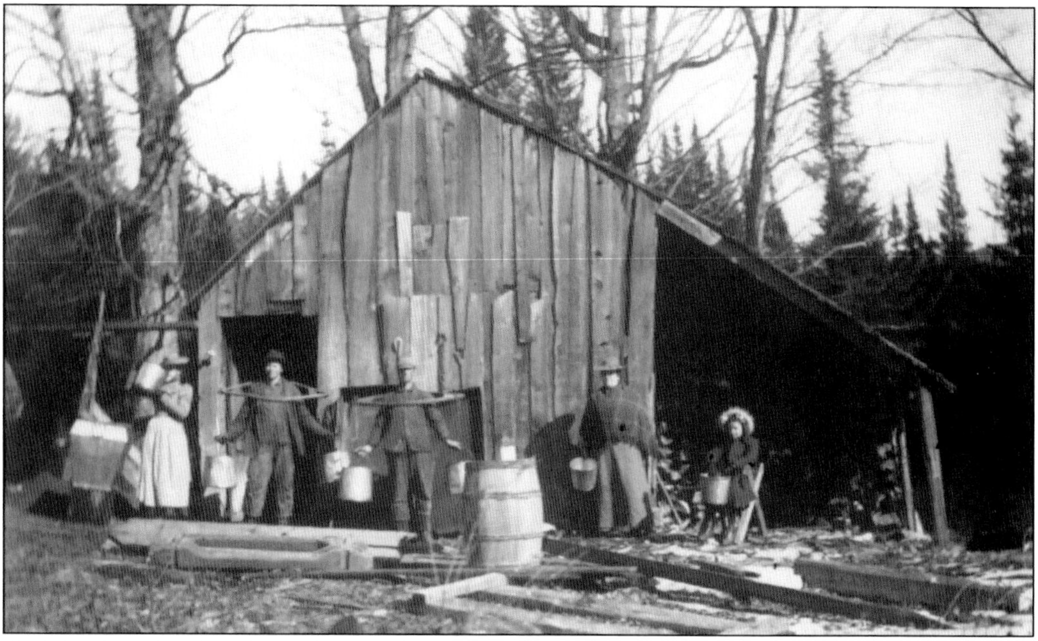

CONTINUING PURSUITS. From the earliest days of this local settlement, converting the sap from sugar maples into the sweet, coveted syrup (a process learned from Native Americans) and the logging industry have been the commercial staples for Orford. Maple producers continue to supply the nation with their gourmet produce while logging remains the largest industry. Shown here is an early sugar shack, with the men of the family bearing the yokes used to transport the sap buckets from the woods.

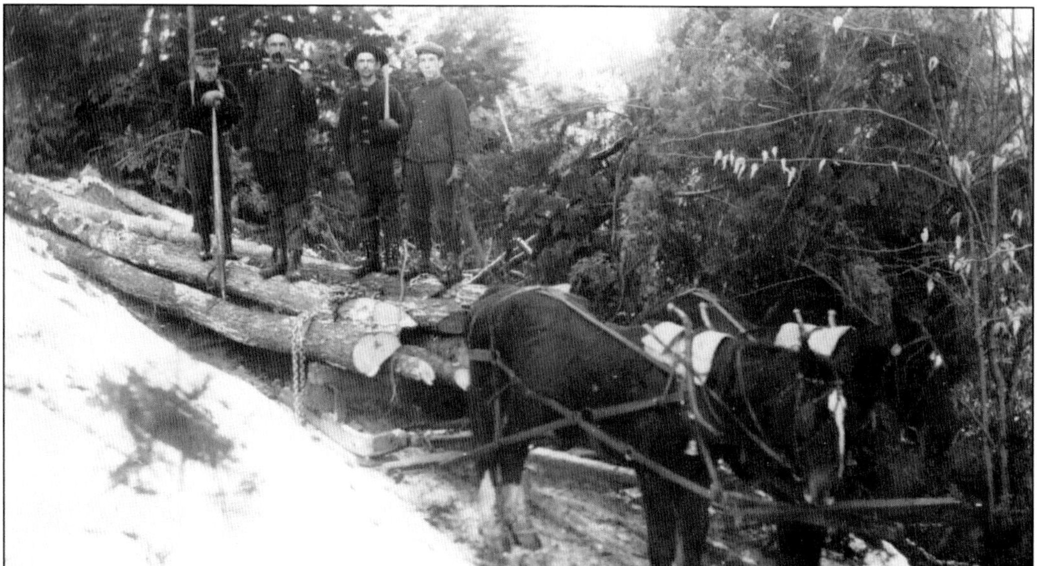

HAULING LOGS, C. 1910. While the team waited patiently, the men secured great logs to be dragged out of the forest. Shown here are: Lee Mousley, Harvey White, Alfrado (Raol) Quint, and Caspet Wible. Often, the logs cut in winter were floated down the Connecticut River to the sawmills in the spring when the ice went out.

Three

Bradford

VERMONT
Orange County
First settled: 1765
Chartered: 1770
Population in 1990: 2,522
Area: 29.8 square miles

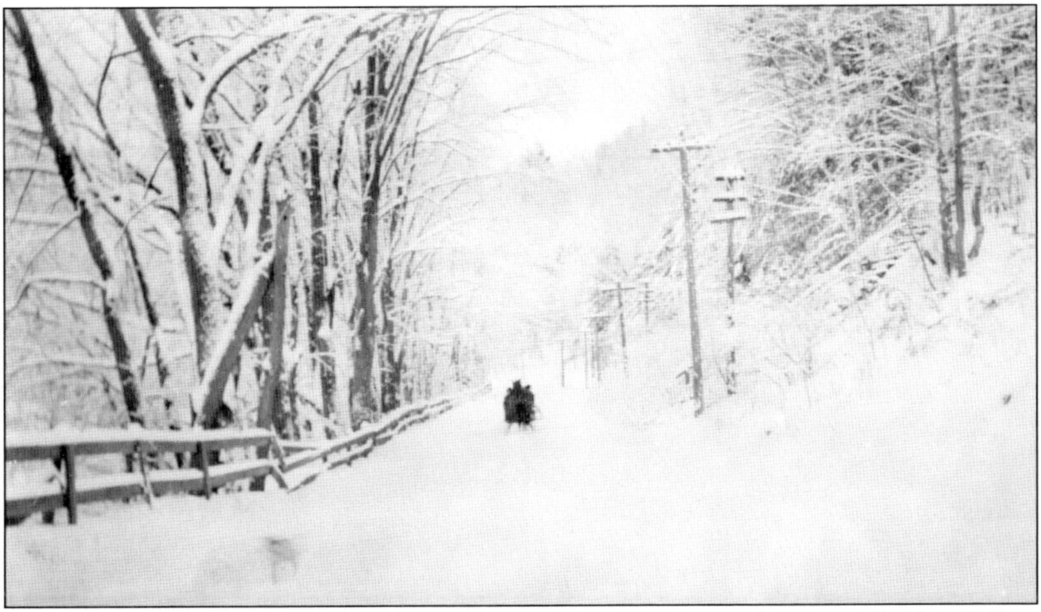

WELCOME TO BRADFORD, VERMONT! This was the scene riding through Bliss Hollow on Route 5 on a snowy day, *c*. 1900.

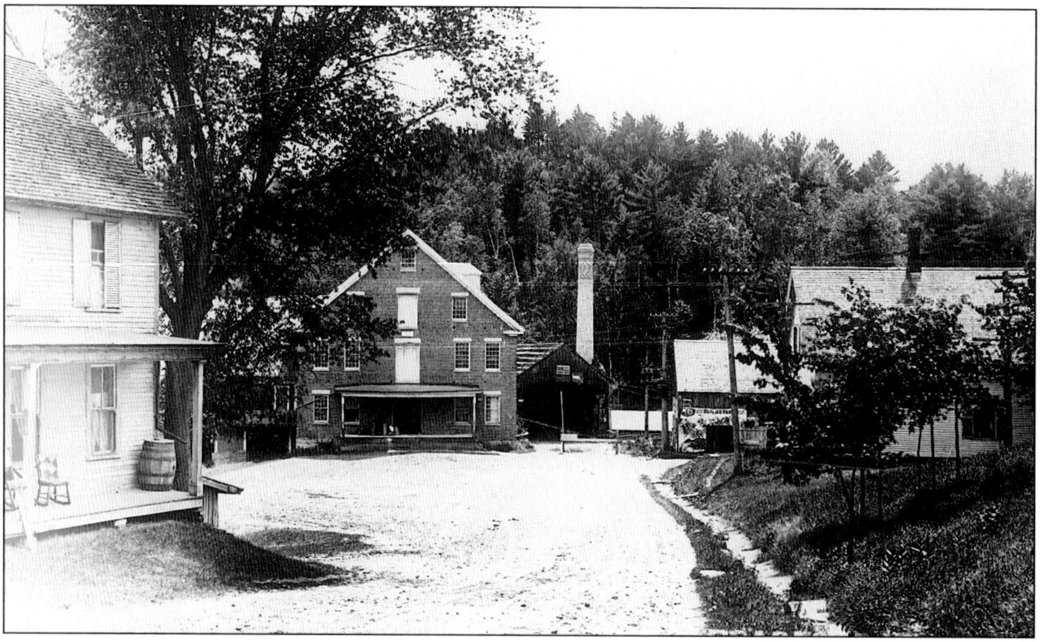

ASA LOW'S GRIST MILL, C. 1906. This mill was located alongside the old covered bridge over the Waits River. The stack is from the old Bradford Electric Company, now owned by Central Vermont Public Service. The old homes are no longer there.

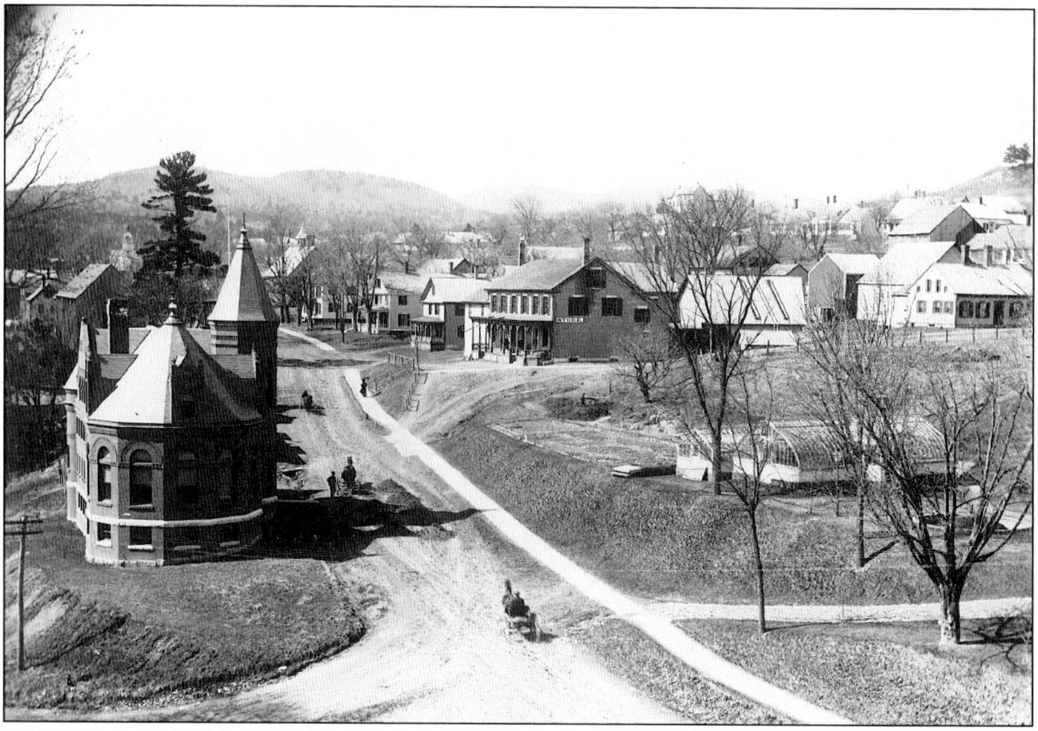

LOOKING DOWN SOUTH MAIN STREET, C. 1896. The new Bradford Library was completed in 1895. The greenhouses on the Low property and the brick building which is now home to the American Legion can be seen.

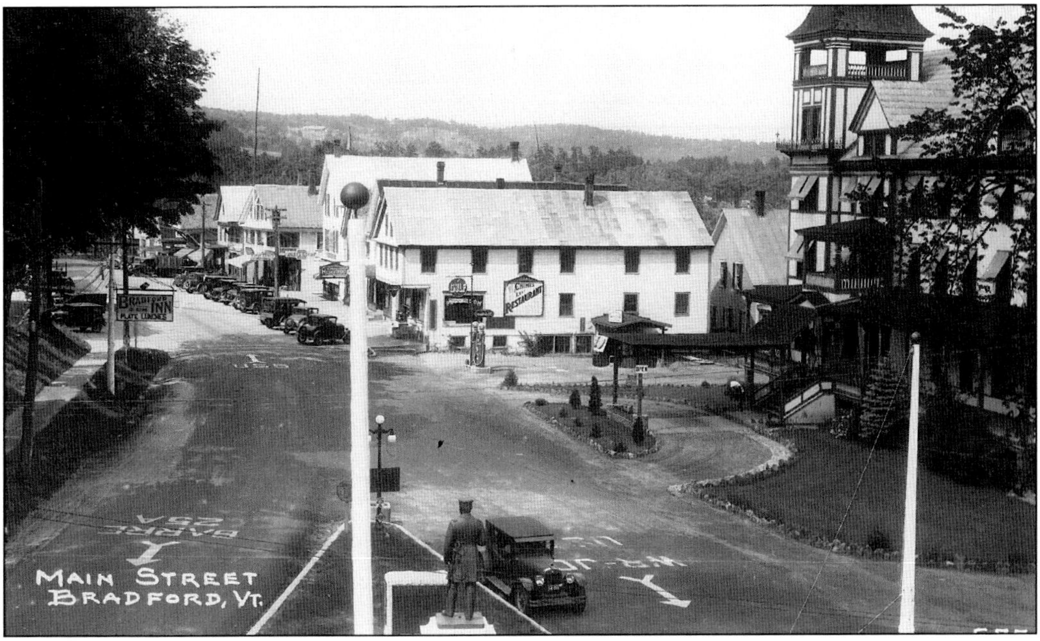

LOOKING NORTH FROM THE LIBRARY BUILDING TO BRADFORD'S MAIN STREET, C. 1930. Note the fancy three-globed light welcoming travelers to Bradford.

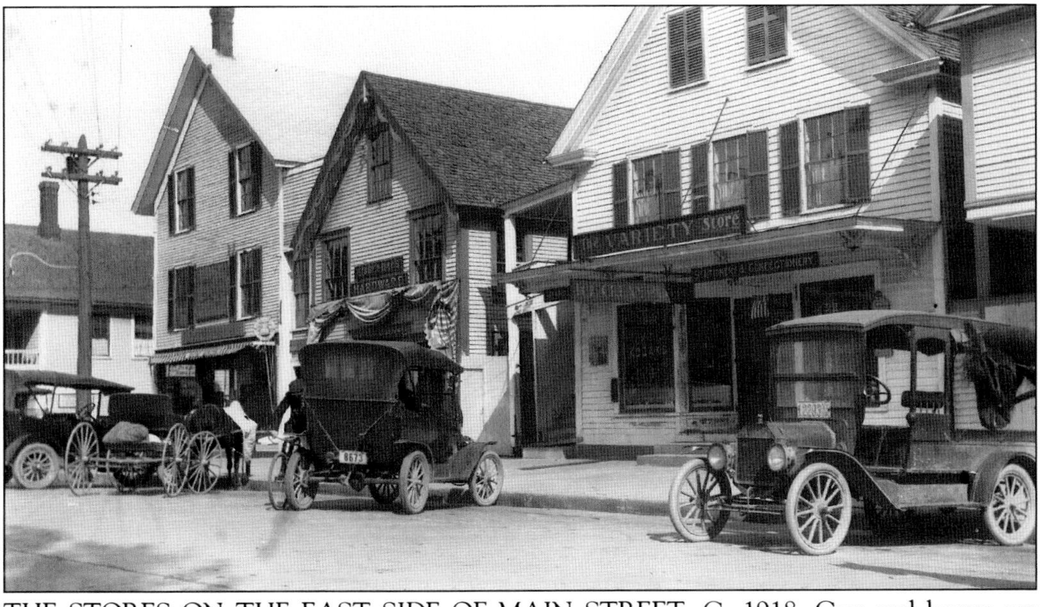

THE STORES ON THE EAST SIDE OF MAIN STREET, C. 1918. Cars and horses are meeting together.

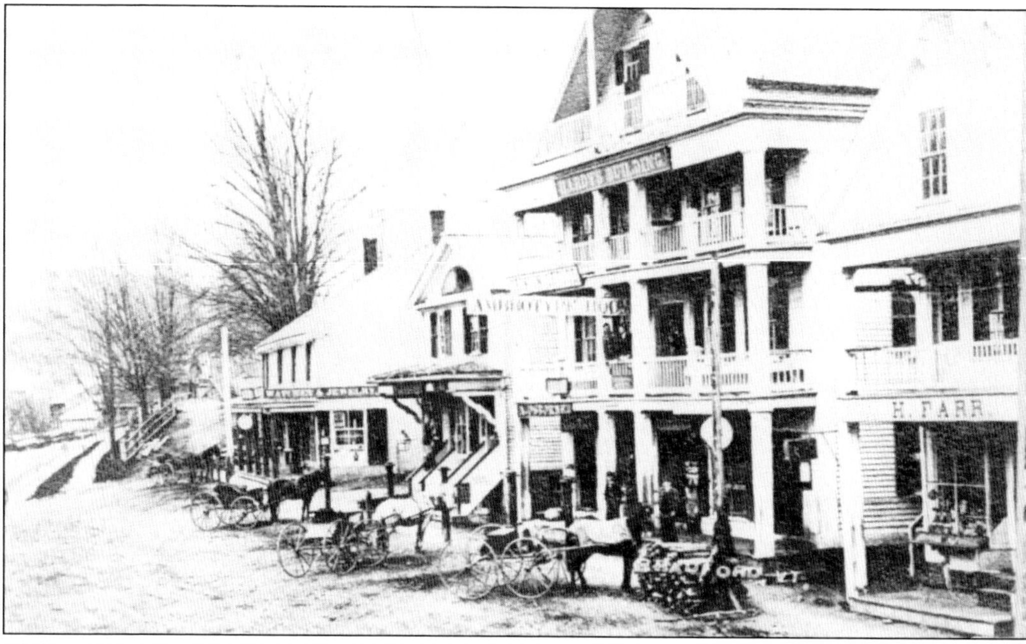

THE STORES ON THE WEST SIDE OF MAIN STREET NEAR BANK STREET. These buildings were all lost in the fire of 1883.

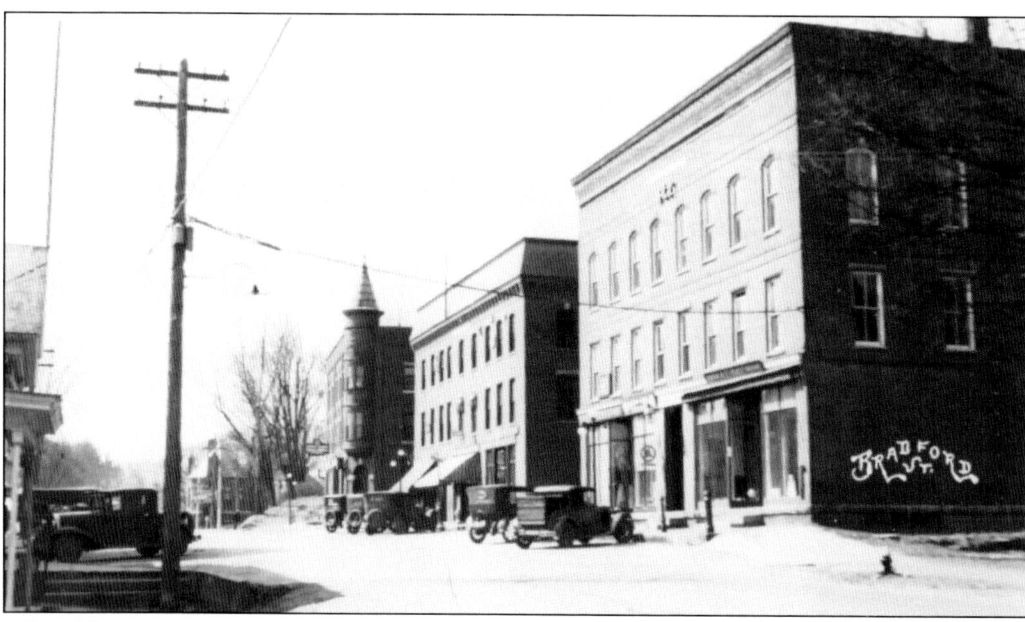

NEW BRICK BUILDINGS. This new group of buildings replaced the burned-out block. The bank building was built in 1891, the Union Block in 1883, and the Stevens Block in 1884.

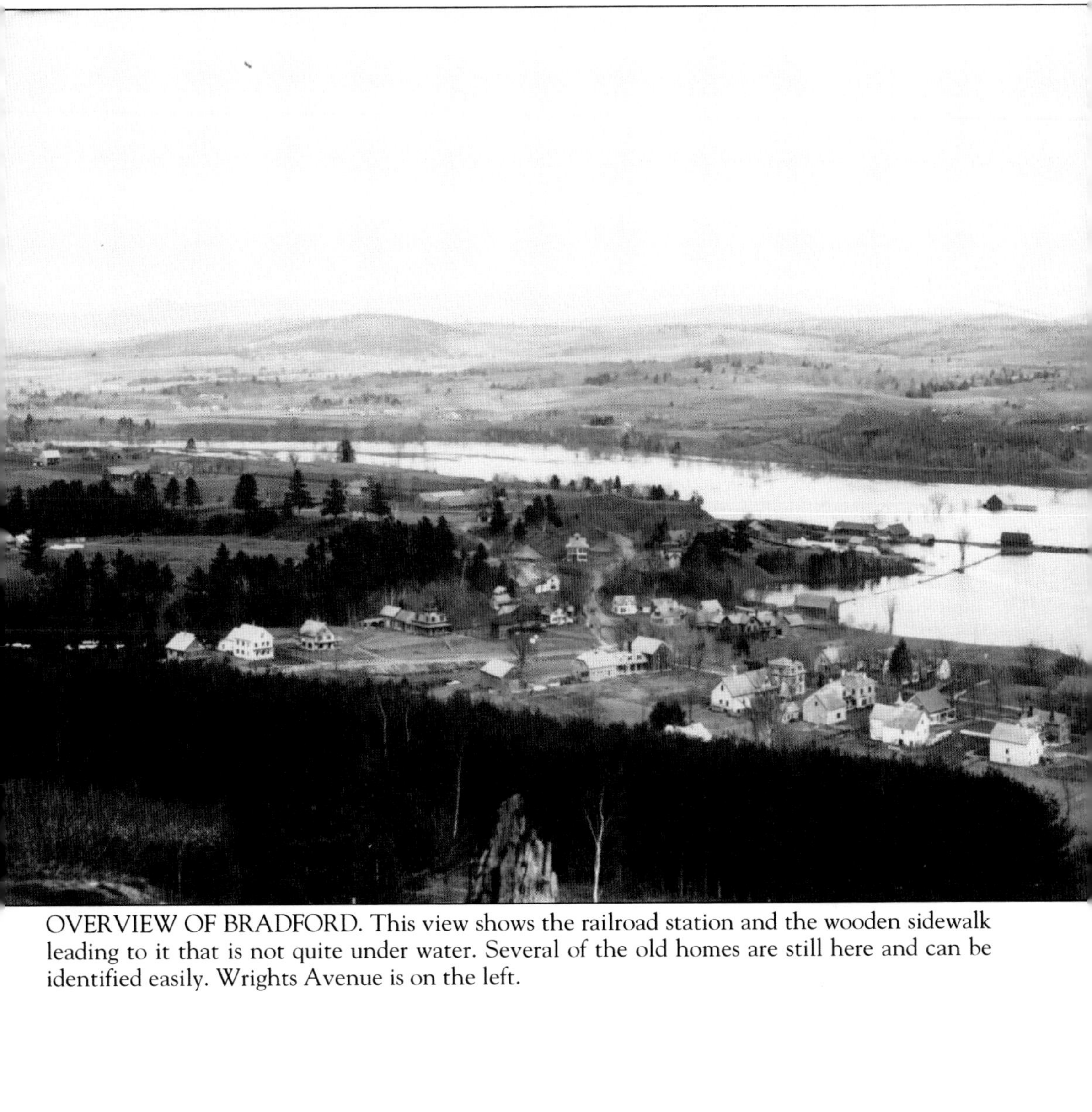

OVERVIEW OF BRADFORD. This view shows the railroad station and the wooden sidewalk leading to it that is not quite under water. Several of the old homes are still here and can be identified easily. Wrights Avenue is on the left.

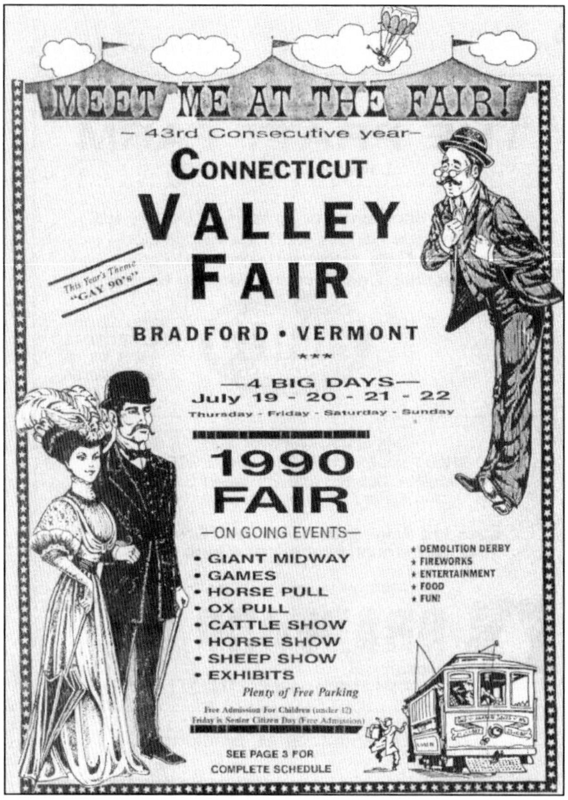

ADVERTISING THE FAIR. The Bradford Fair was an annual event from 1852 until 1913. It was located at the north end of the village in a two-level area on Fairground Road. The lower level, now the site of the State Armory and Elementary School, contained the half-mile track, racing stables, and area for judging livestock. The upper level provided space for the midway, exhibits, and eating places under canvas. Today's Connecticut Valley Fair started in 1948 on Memorial Field and is still an annual event with many of the same activities.

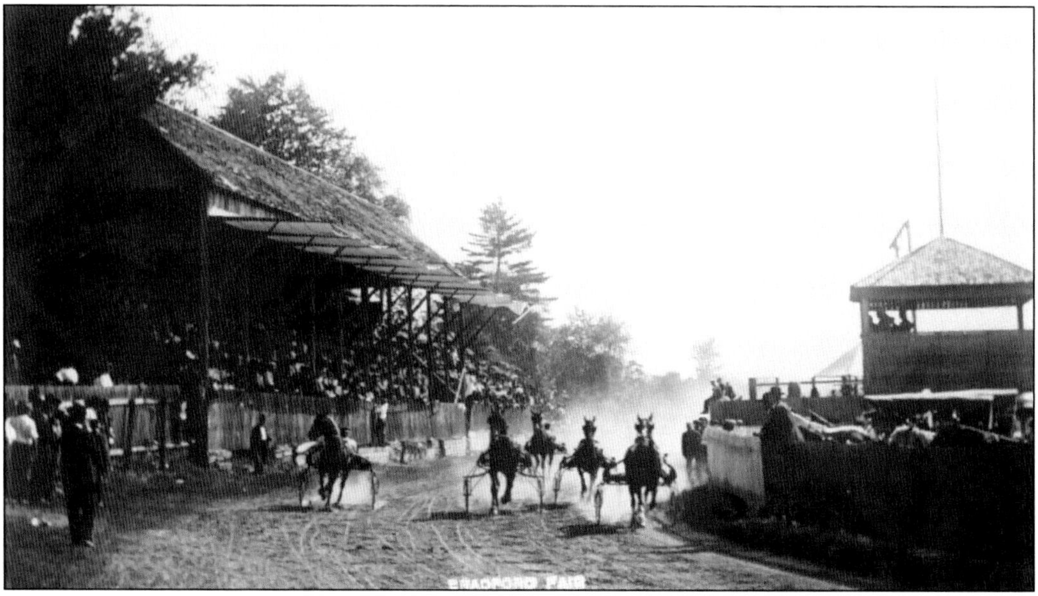

RACING DAY AT THE FAIR. Horse breeding, especially raising Morgan horses, was important to Bradford.

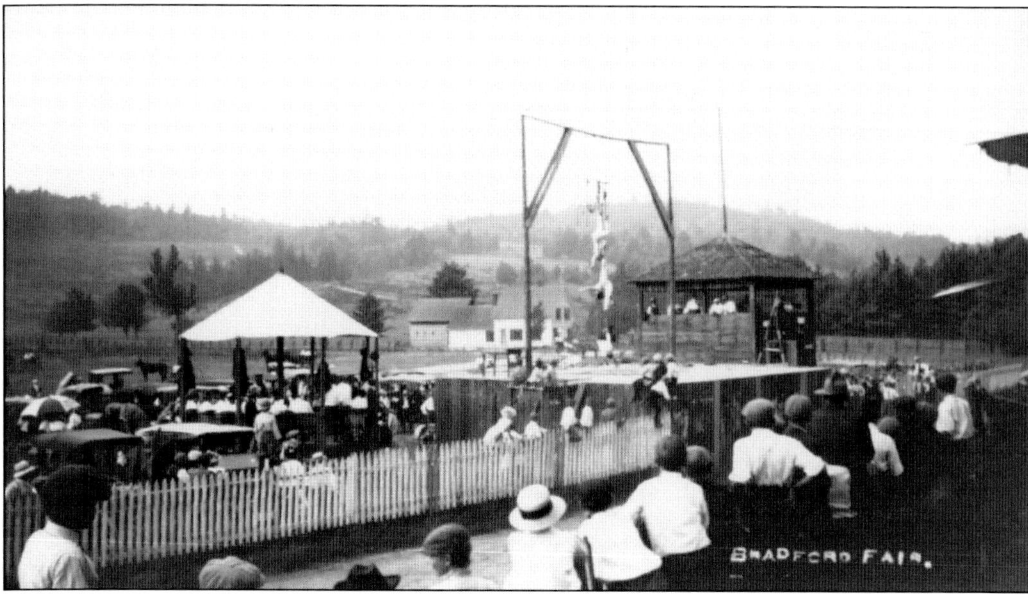

ACROBATS! The featured attraction on this day was the troupe of acrobats on a flying trapeze.

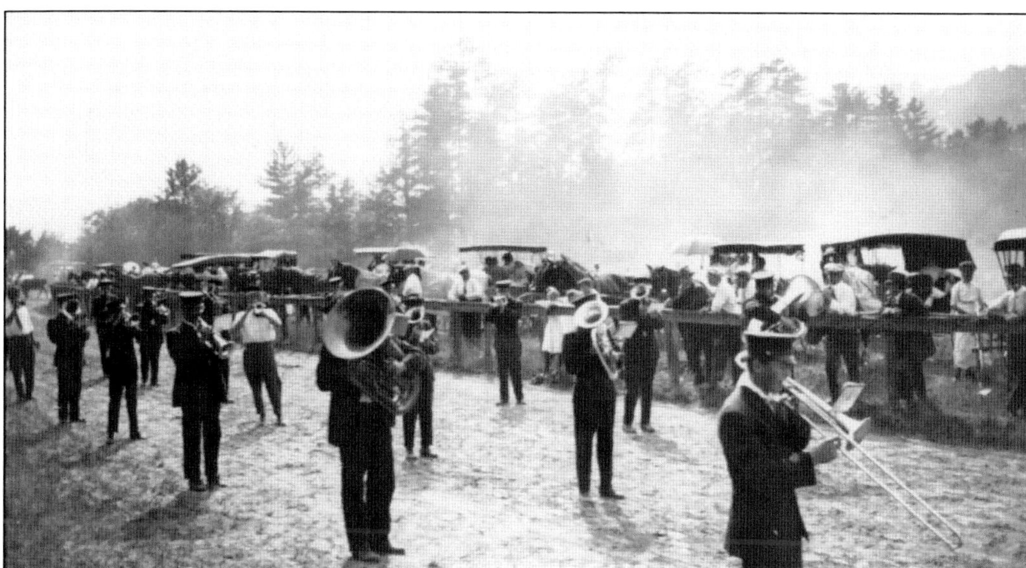
BRADFORD'S BRASS BAND ON PARADE AT THE FAIR.

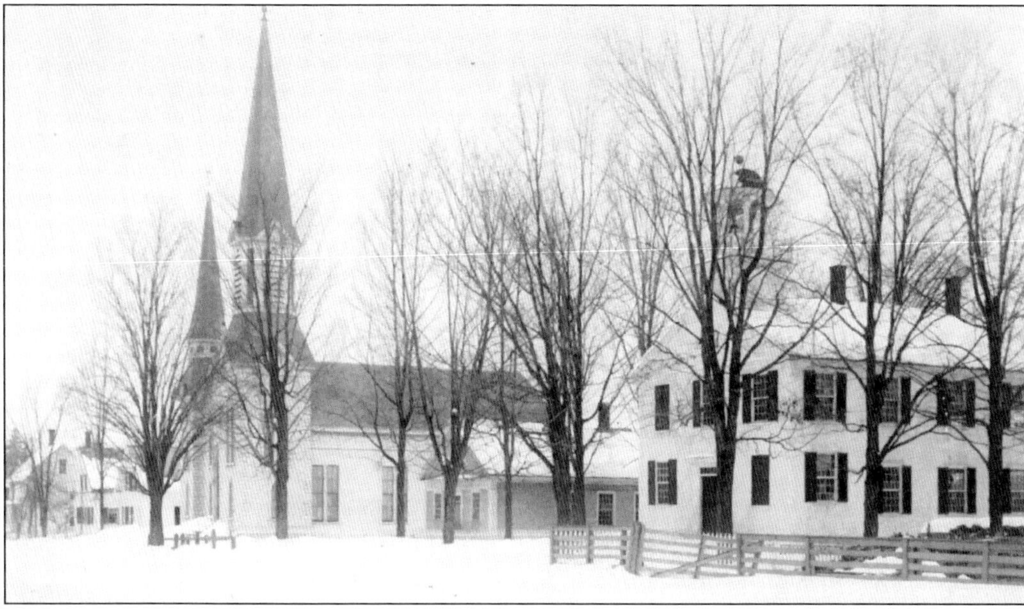

EDUCATION. Taken in 1888, this image shows the beautiful old Academy building chartered in 1820 (right), with District School No. 12 built prior to 1820 (center), and Grace United Methodist church (left). The new Bradford Academy was built behind these schools. The old Academy was sold at auction for $32, with District School No. 12 going for $25. Both were moved from the site.

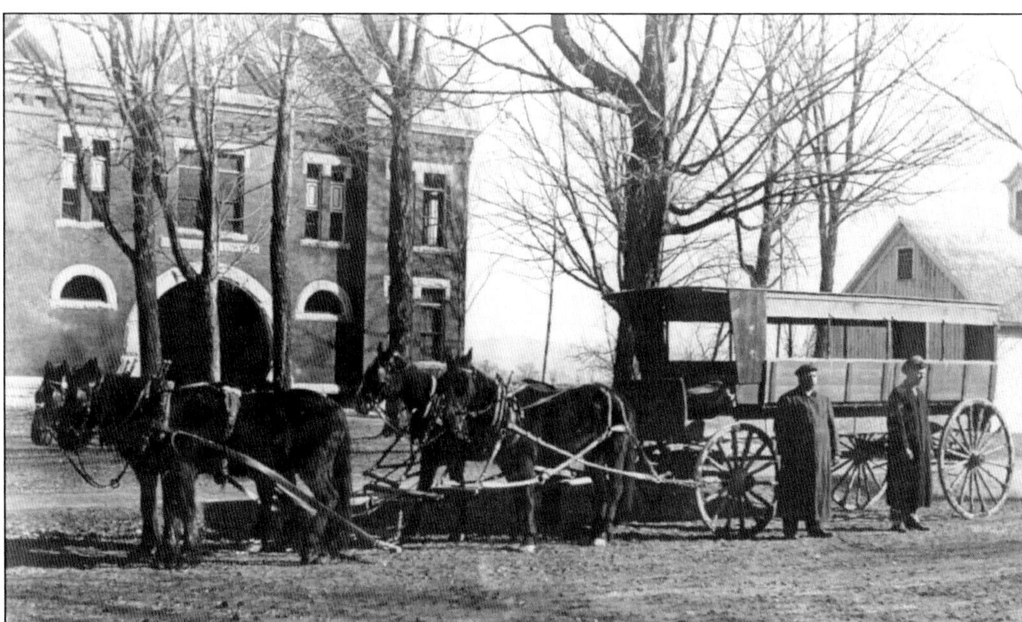

THE BRADFORD ACADEMY TEAM BROUGHT THE STUDENTS TO SCHOOL IN THE EARLY 1900s. When going up hills, the boys had to get off and walk. The Academy building, erected in 1893/94, was a gift of John L. Woods.

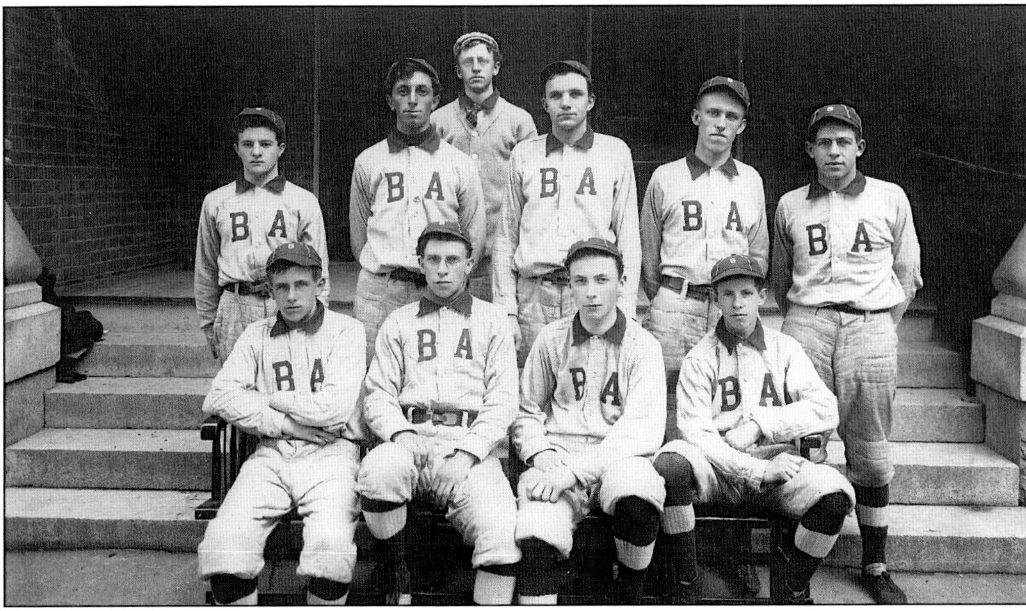

WINNING BASEBALL TEAM OF 1910. From left to right: (standing) Harry Colby, Clarence Caudrey, Frank Brigham, Clarence Pierce, Charles Haskins, Winn Taplin; (seated) Amos Sawyer, Conrad Shumway, Harold Haskins, John Gurley. Shumway pitched many no-hit, no-run games.

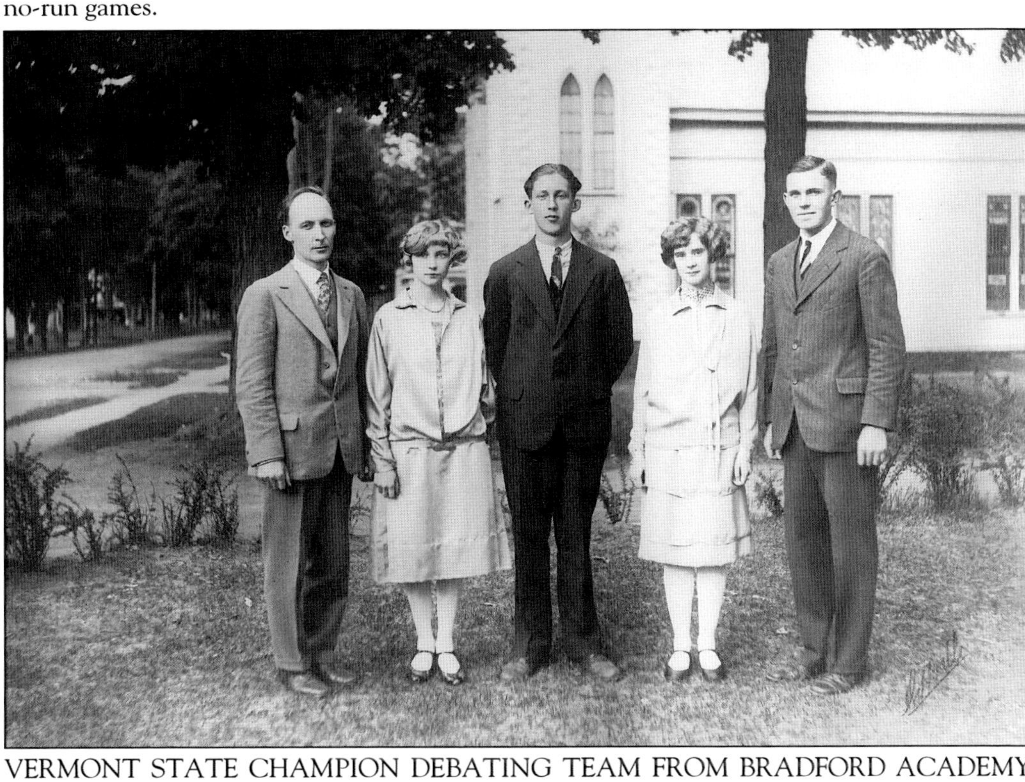

VERMONT STATE CHAMPION DEBATING TEAM FROM BRADFORD ACADEMY. From left to right: Harold Haskins (principal), Marion Pierce, Harold Slayton, Agatha Murphy, and Ronald Martin. Tree-shaded Main Street looked cool and inviting.

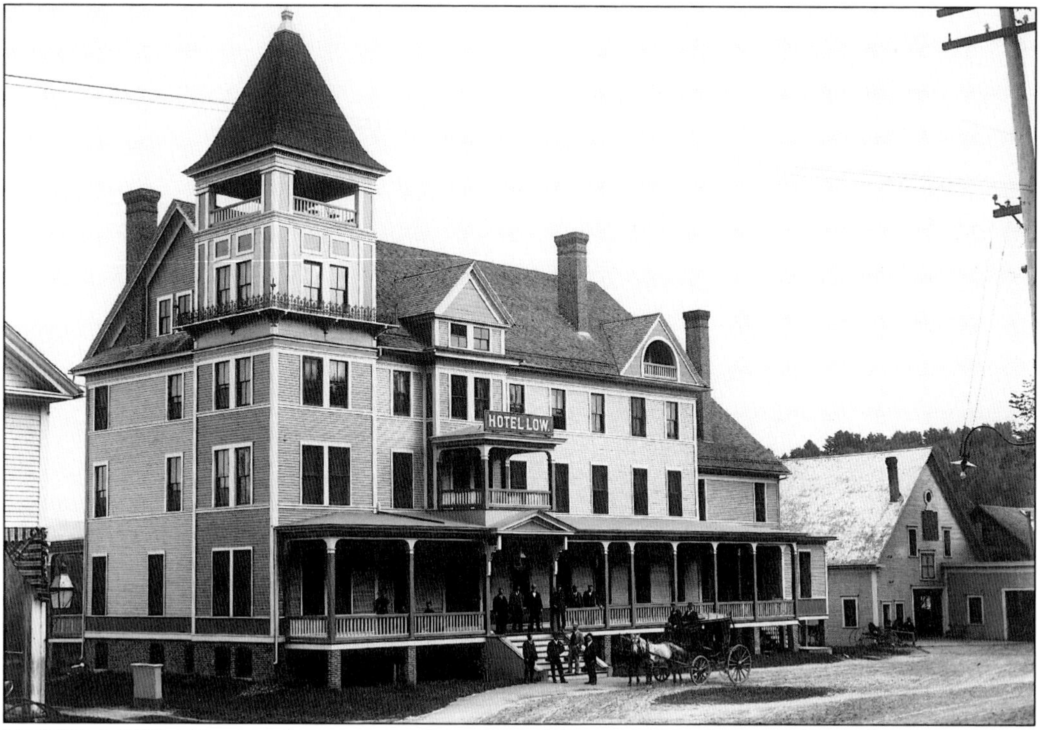

HOTEL LOW. This hotel was opened to the public in 1890, designed by architect Lambert Packard, and built by William Bray at approximate cost of $10,500. It was named in honor of Asa Low, one of Bradford's leading businessmen from 1825 to 1875. The hotel is shown here soon after it was erected. The coach, drawn by a pair of horses, is about to leave for the depot to meet a train. Known in later years as the Bradford Inn, the building was razed in 1960 to make room for a bank building.

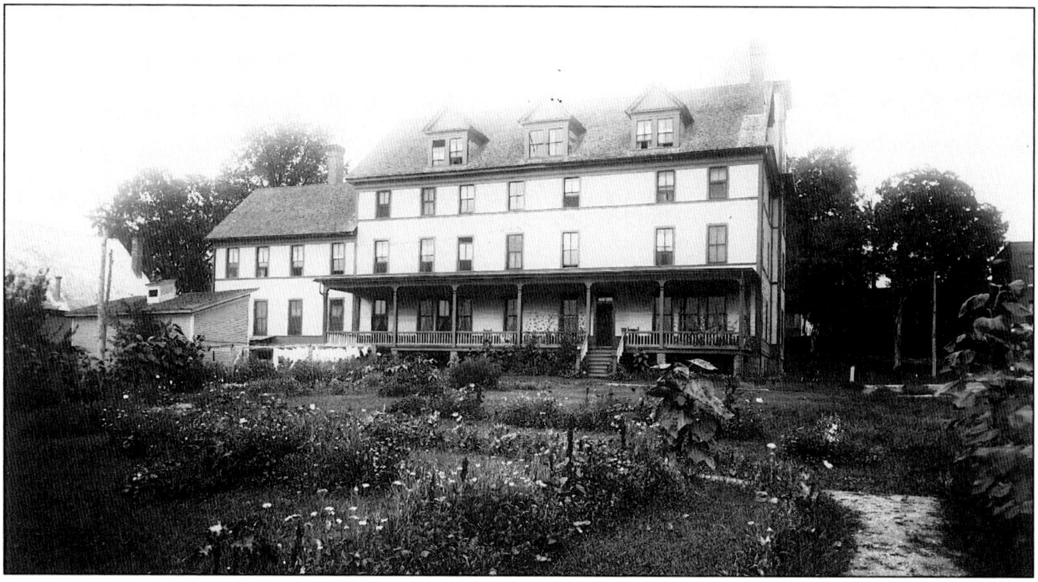

BEHIND THE HOTEL, 1920s. For many years, this flower garden and lawn were at the rear of Hotel Low. Golfers used to tee off from this lawn. This is now a parking area.

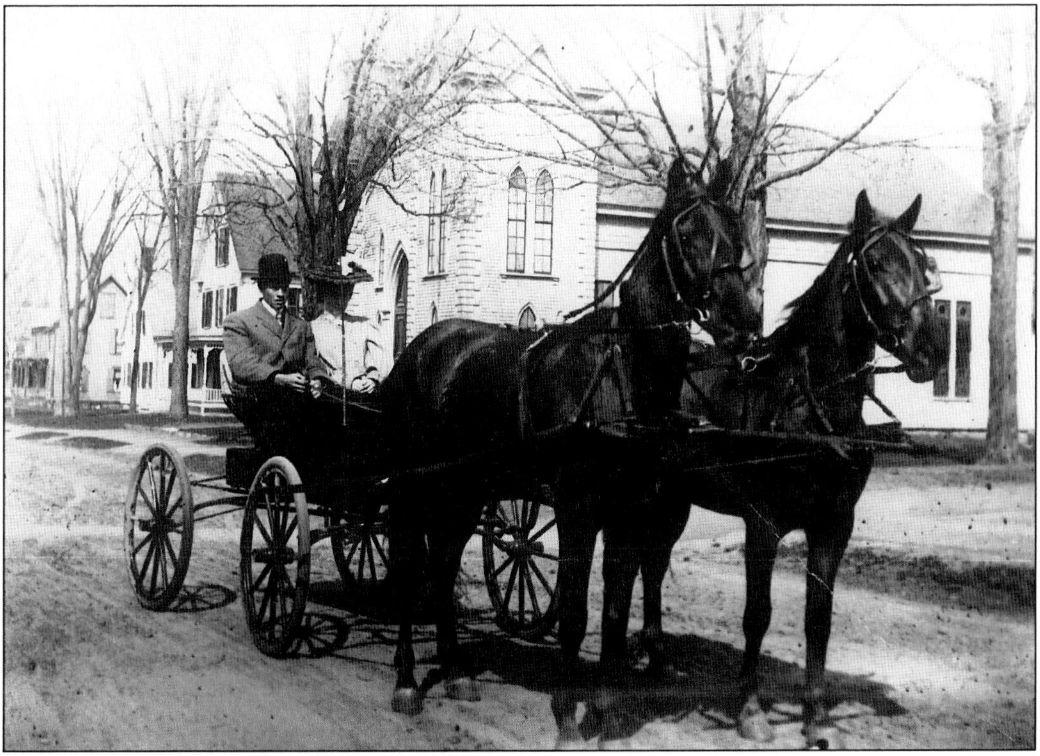

MR. AND MRS. EZRA EASTMAN SR. OUT FOR A DRIVE IN THEIR BUGGY, C. 1907.

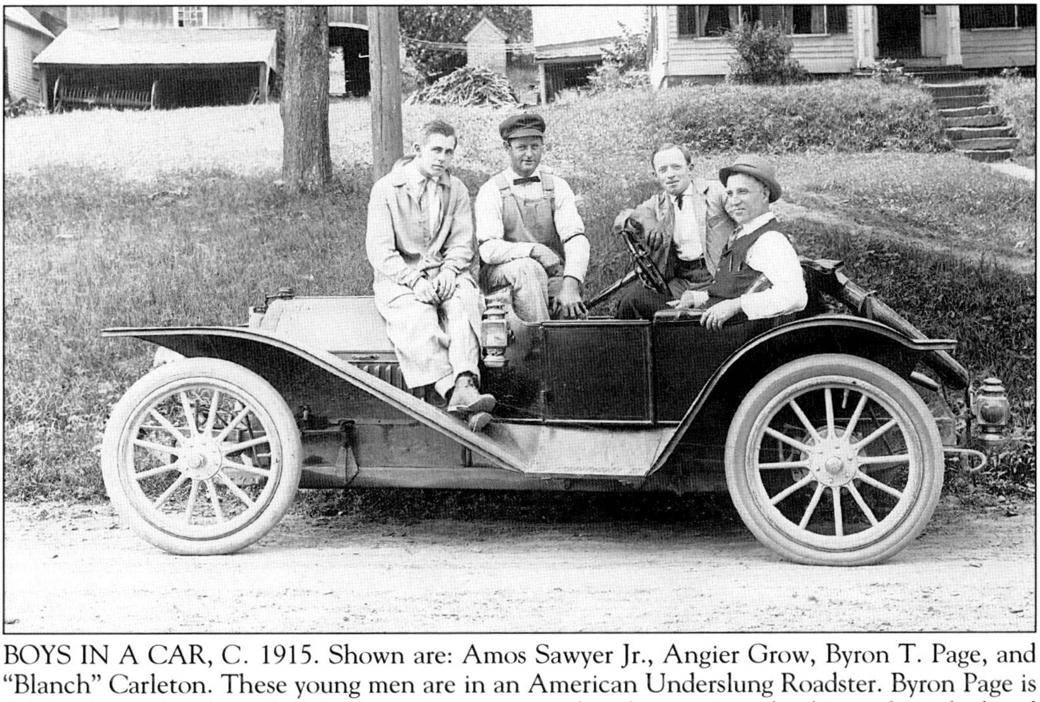

BOYS IN A CAR, C. 1915. Shown are: Amos Sawyer Jr., Angier Grow, Byron T. Page, and "Blanch" Carleton. These young men are in an American Underslung Roadster. Byron Page is driving (note the gloves!). It is interesting to notice that the steering wheel is on the right-hand side of the car.

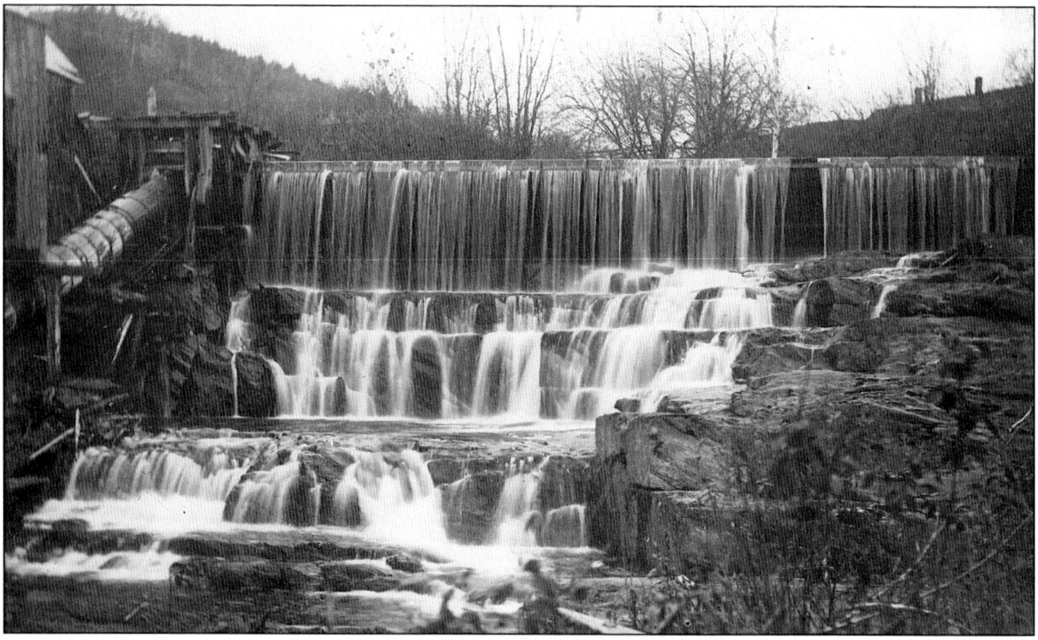

THE WAITS RIVER DETERMINED WHERE BRADFORD WAS SETTLED. A set of three waterfalls provided the energy needed for commercial ventures to prosper and grow. Over the years, new dams and sluiceways have been changed or added, but the water still flows and we still use the energy it produces.

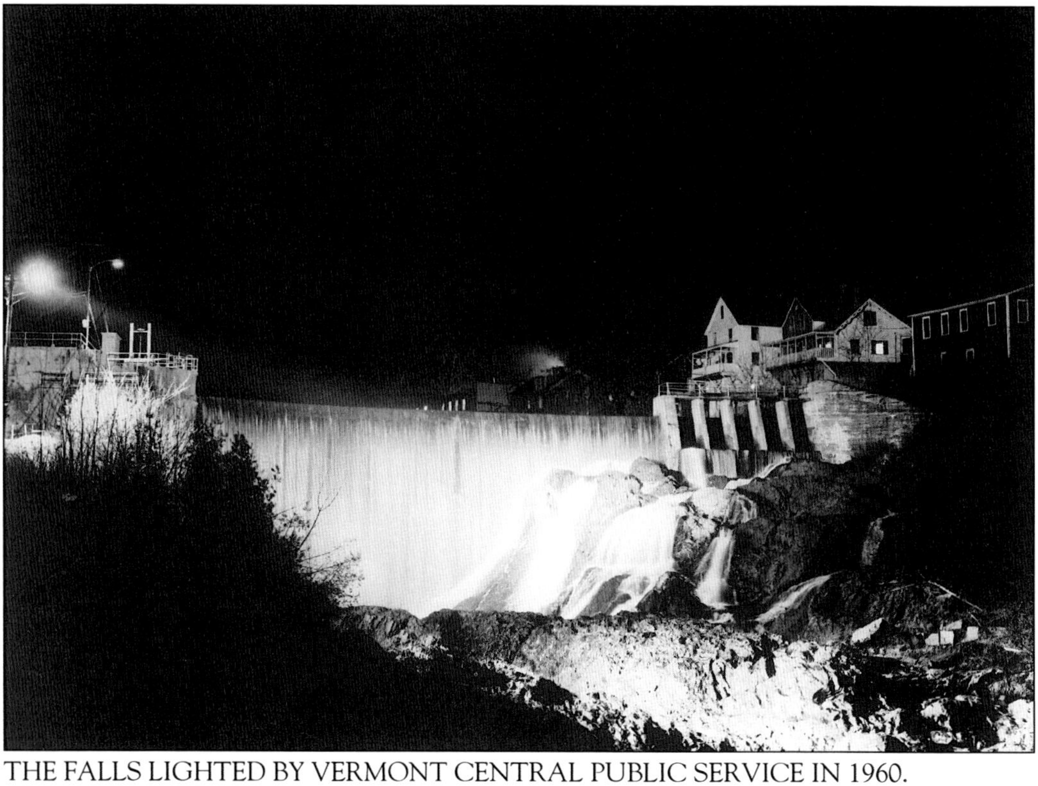

THE FALLS LIGHTED BY VERMONT CENTRAL PUBLIC SERVICE IN 1960.

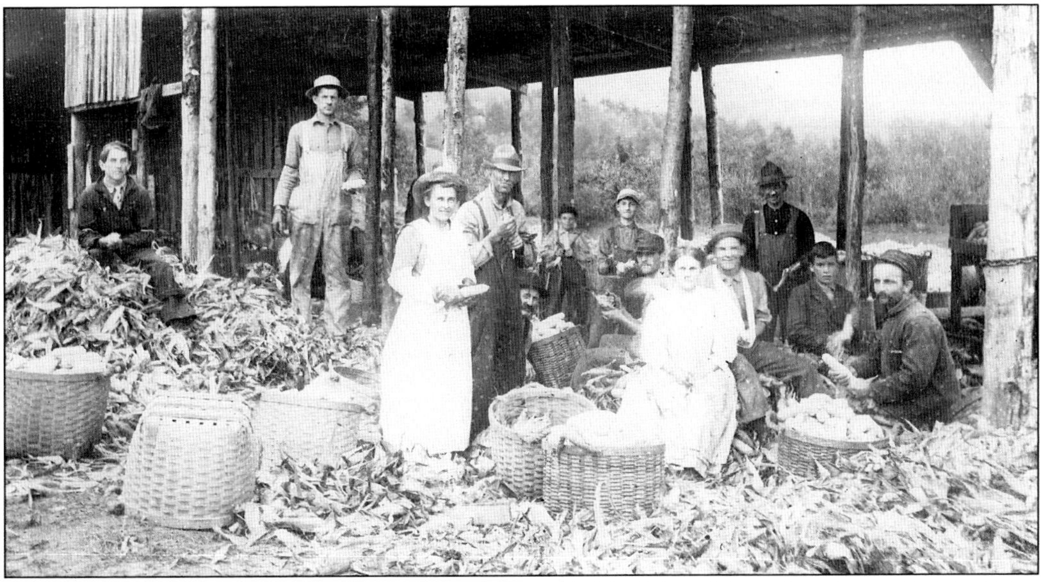

CORN HUSKING FOR BAXTER BROS. CORN CANNING FACTORY IN 1914. An output of 25,000 to 40,000 cans a day was not unusual during the late-summer canning season.

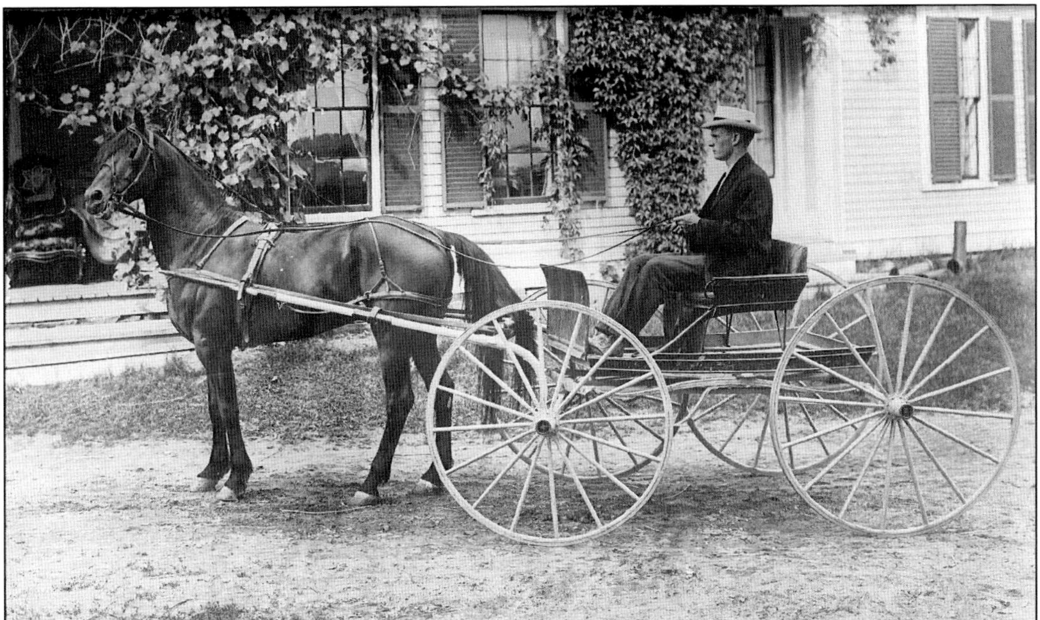

ETHAN ALLEN 2ND, C. 1908. This famous horse was driven by J. Edward Peters in front of the Peters Homestead. Ethan Allen 2nd has always been considered to be an ideal Morgan, and his descendants are found today from coast to coast in the U.S. and Canada. Peters families have lived in Bradford since 1770.

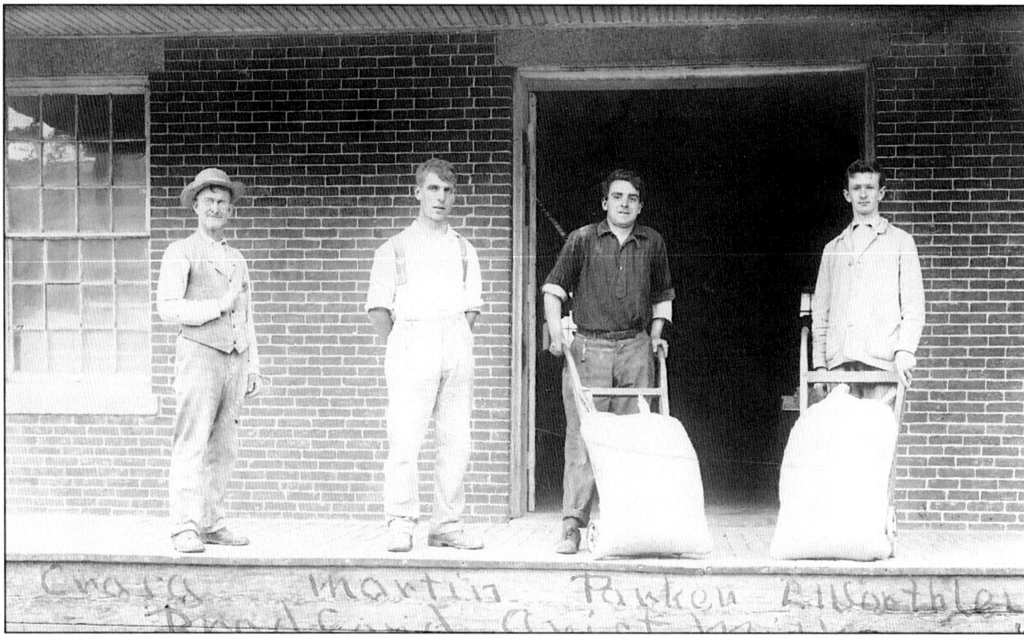

GRIST MILL WORKERS. From left to right: Craig, Martin, Parker, and Worthley. Built in 1847 by Asa Low, the mill still stands today at the falls—the gateway to Bradford.

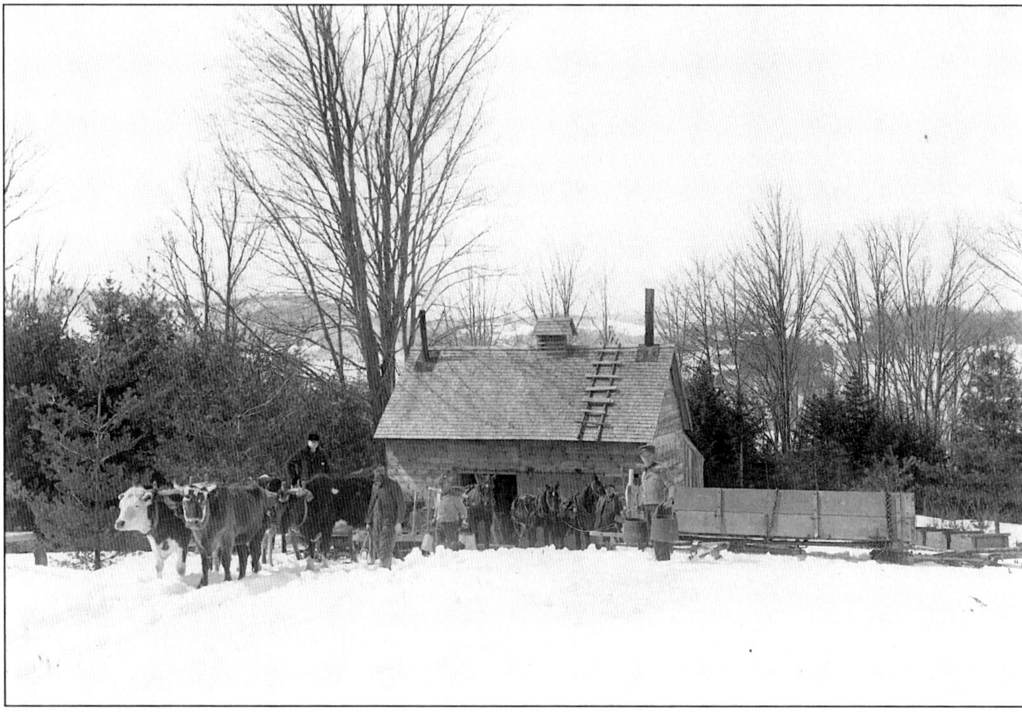

SUGARING IN BRADFORD, EARLY 1900s. This is Doe Brothers Sugar House on Sam Gove's lot in the Goshen area. N. R. Doe is behind the oxen. Also pictured are: George McGuire, Louis Woods, and Kenneth Wright. Fred Adams took the picture.

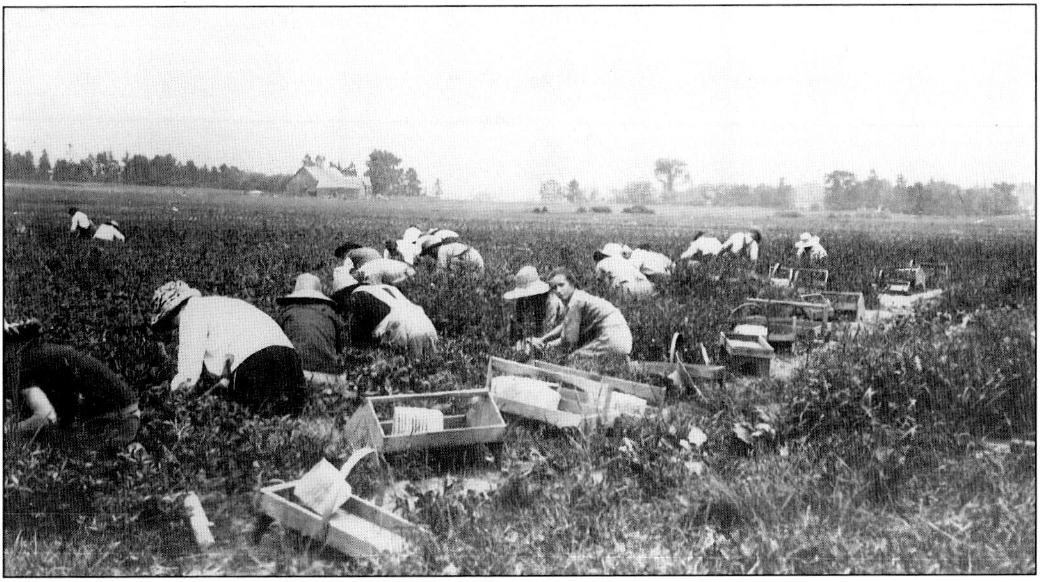

BRADFORD STRAWBERRIES WERE NOTED FOR THEIR QUALITY. During the short season, strawberry growing was a main industry in the area. Major production of this crop ran from 1878 to its decline in the 1920s, but strawberries are still grown and enjoyed from our local fields.

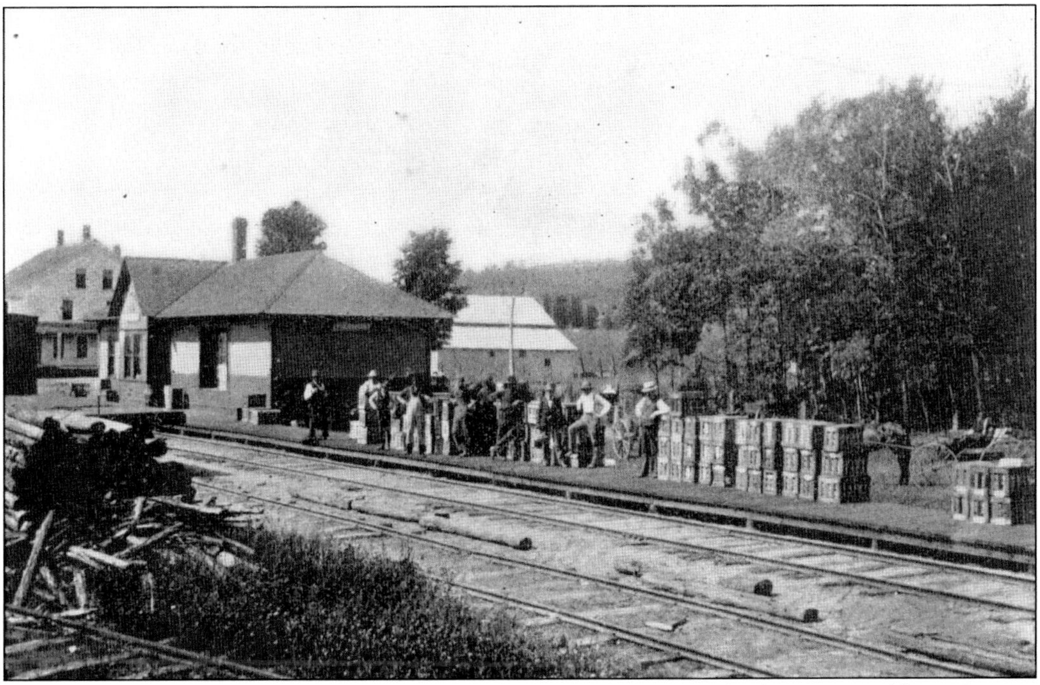

BERRY TRANSPORT. Trains made special stops to transport the berries quickly to Boston and the grand hotels of the White Mountains.

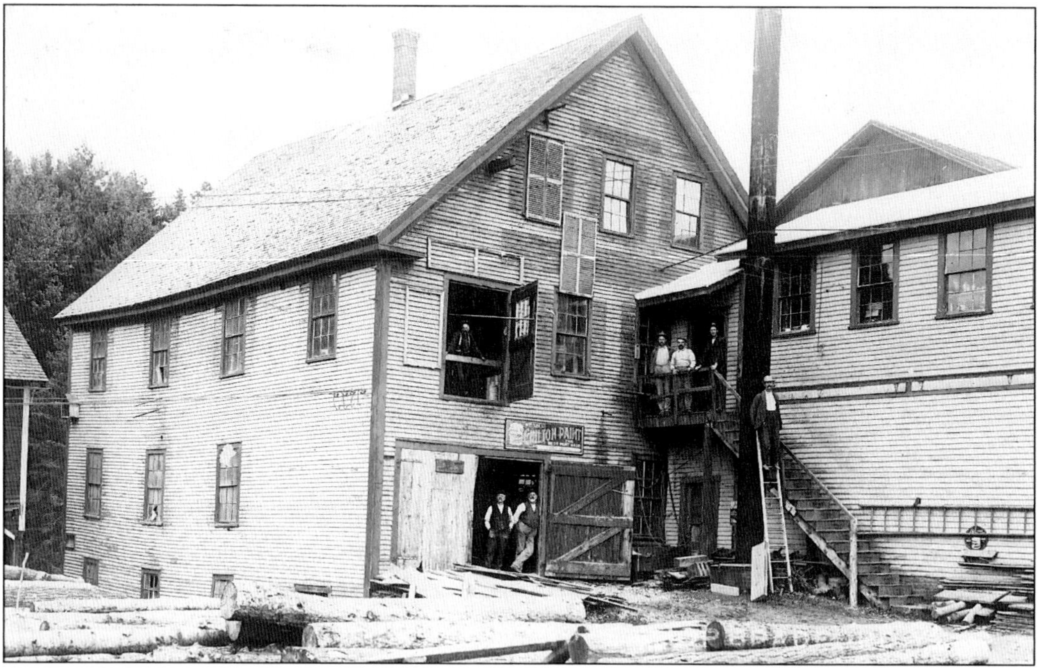

THE SASH AND BLIND SHOP. Long in operation on Mill Street, this enterprise burned in 1912. John C. Strong, then owner of the shop, stands on the right in the lower doorway. This was one of the many mills to obtain power from the falls on the Waits River.

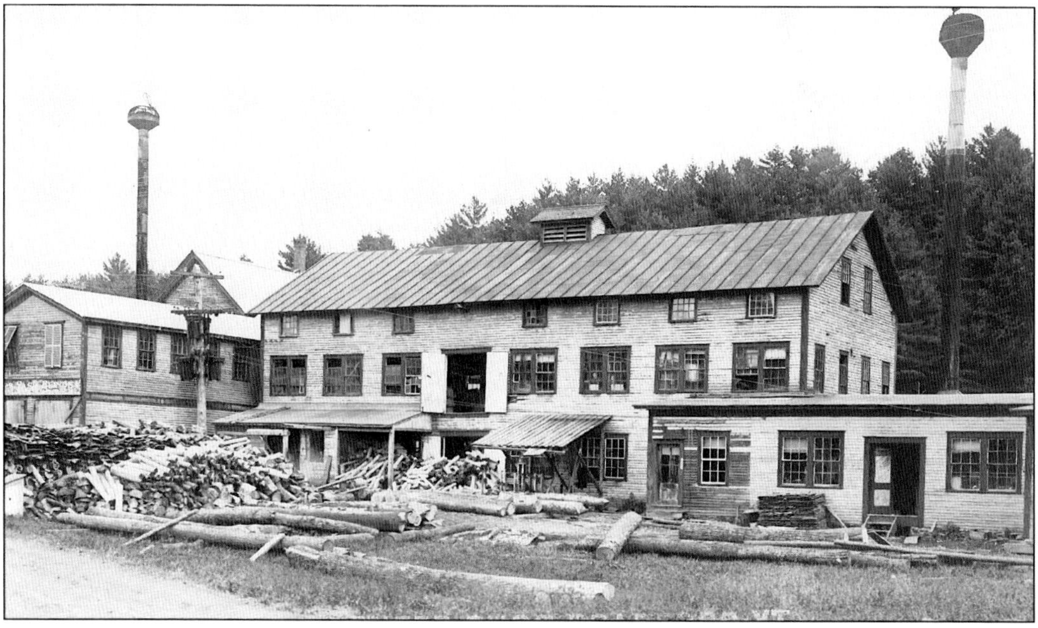

THE VENEER MILL. This company at the third falls started about 1909 and is still operating today.

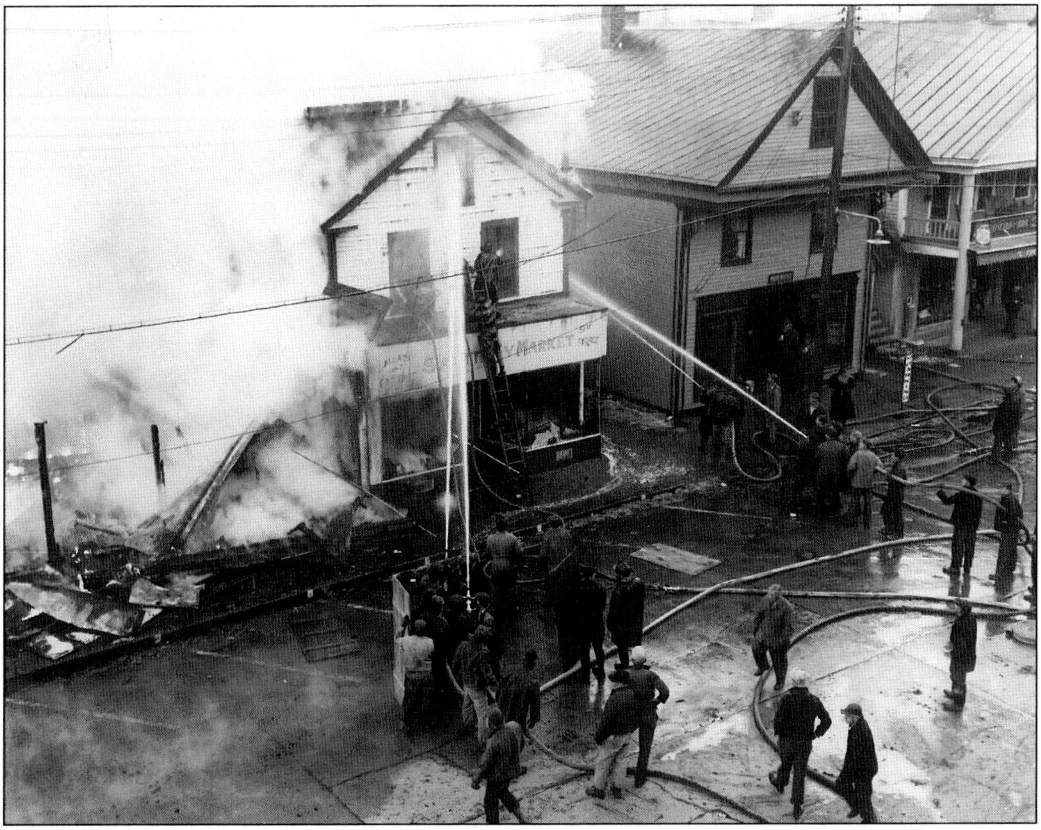

FIRE! FIRE! Bradford has had more than one devastating fire that has changed the character of the downtown area. This is the fire of 1947.

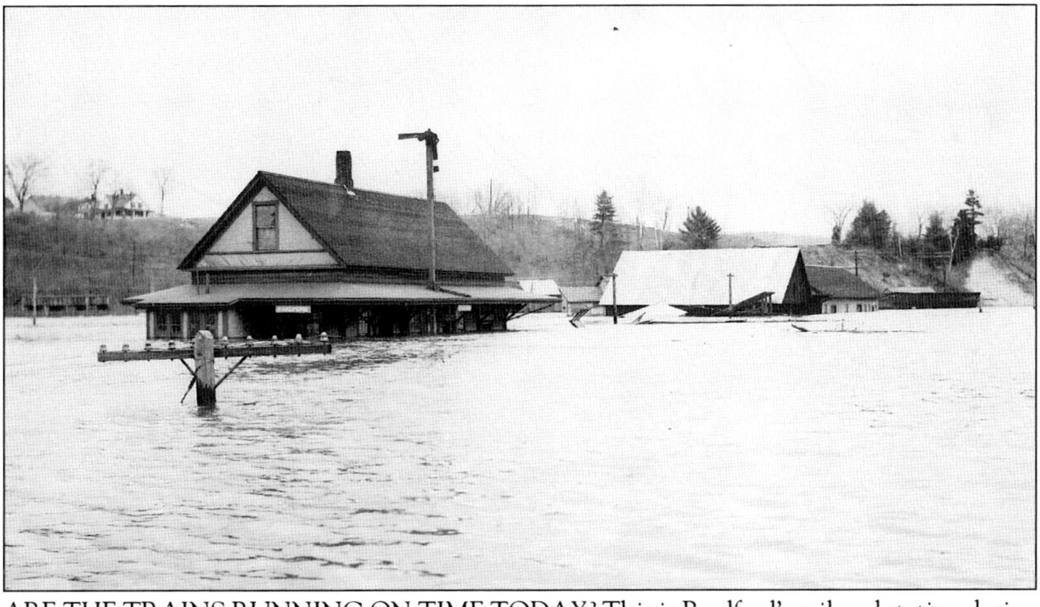

ARE THE TRAINS RUNNING ON TIME TODAY? This is Bradford's railroad station during the 1936 flood. Flooding was another hazard faced by our early settlers.

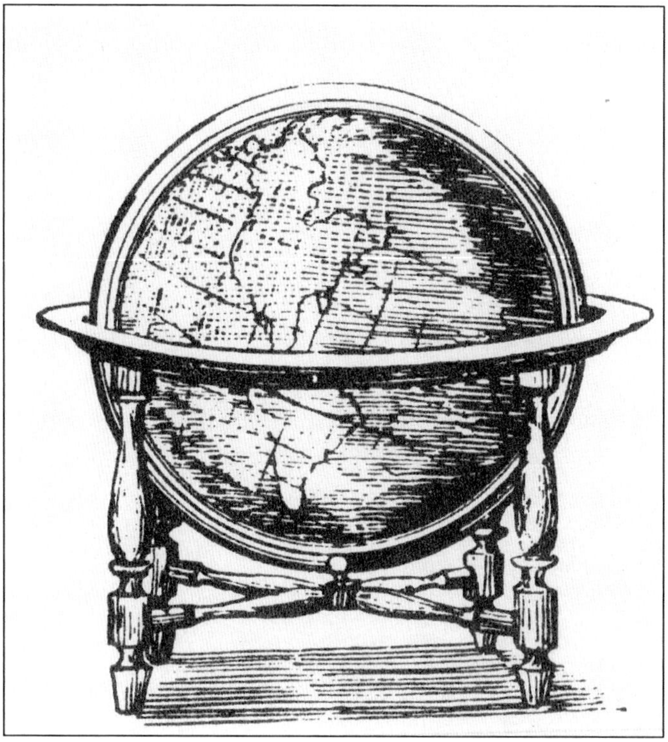

THE FIRST WORLD GLOBE. James Wilson of Bradford made the first globe produced in this country. He had little schooling and worked hard to educate himself in the knowledge of geography, astronomy, and science. He learned copper engraving from a man in New Haven, Connecticut. Reportedly, he had to walk there and back for the apprenticeship! His business started in 1810 when he sold his first globe. His sons later moved the business to Albany, New York, but Mr. Wilson remained in Bradford.

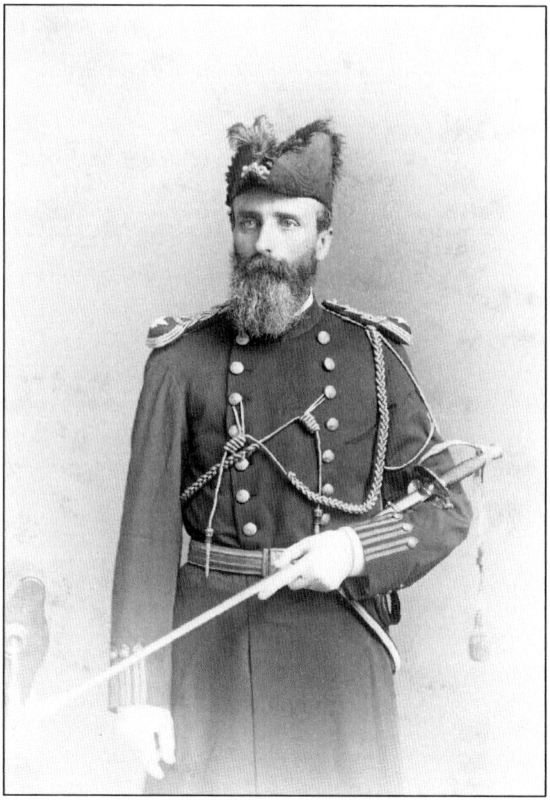

A CIVIL WAR COLONEL. Roswell Farnham moved to Bradford as a young man. He served as principal of Bradford Academy from 1854 to 1856, and he was a teacher, educator, lawyer, and statesman. He was governor of Vermont from 1880 to 1882. He served during the Civil War and was promoted to the rank of colonel.

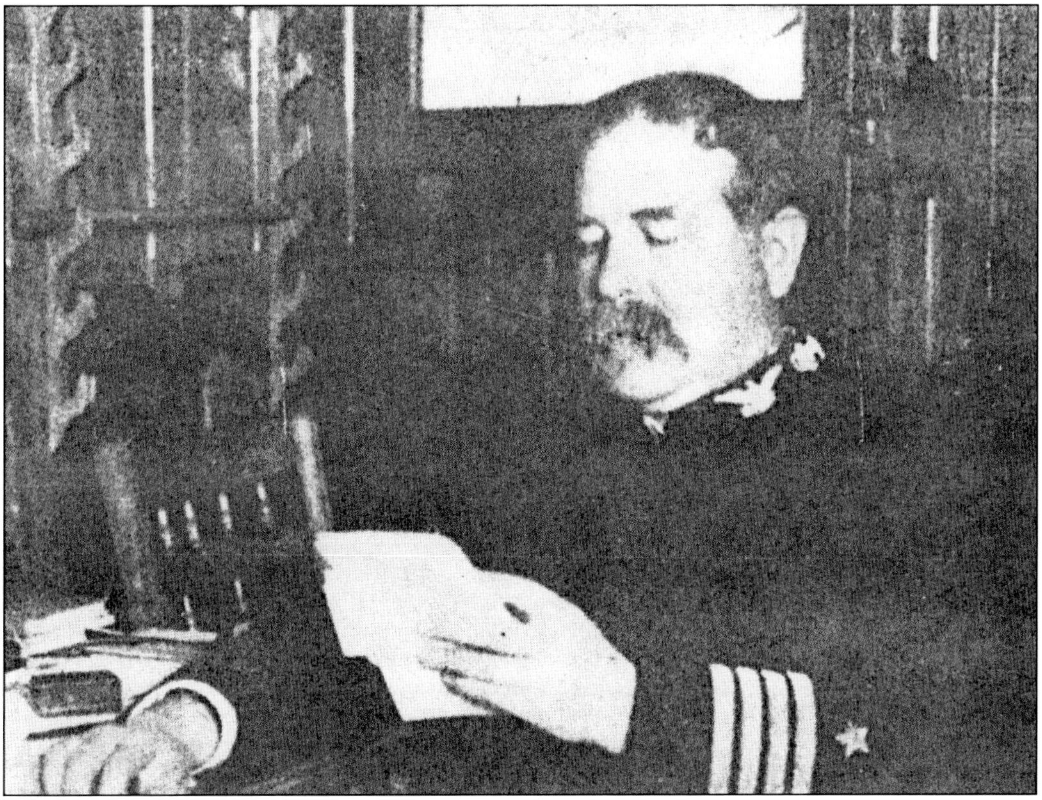

ADMIRAL CHARLES E. CLARK. A native of Bradford, Admiral Clark attended Bradford Academy and graduated from the U.S. Naval Academy in Annapolis. He was the captain of the *Oregon*, one of the U.S.'s first steam-driven battleships, when she made her famous trip from San Francisco to Santiago Harbor during the Spanish American War of 1898. The journey was nearly 15,000 miles and was completed in record time for that era.

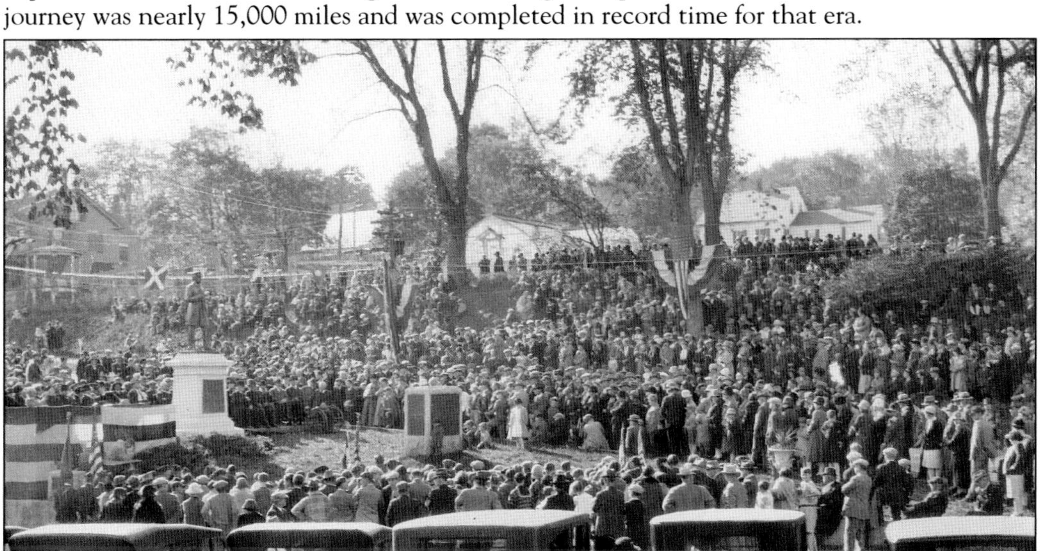

STATUE OF ADMIRAL CLARK, UNVEILED IN 1926. This statue stands in the library memorial park, and Clark looks out over the town. Thousands attended the dedication.

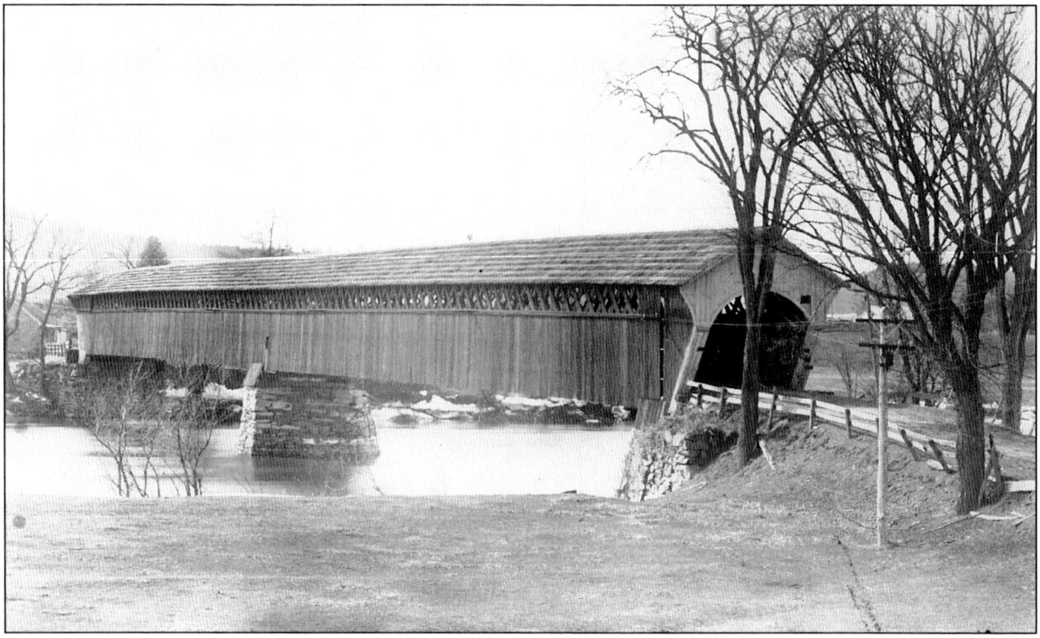

THE PIERMONT BRIDGE, CONNECTING BRADFORD TO NEW HAMPSHIRE. This structure was swept away in the flood of November 1927.

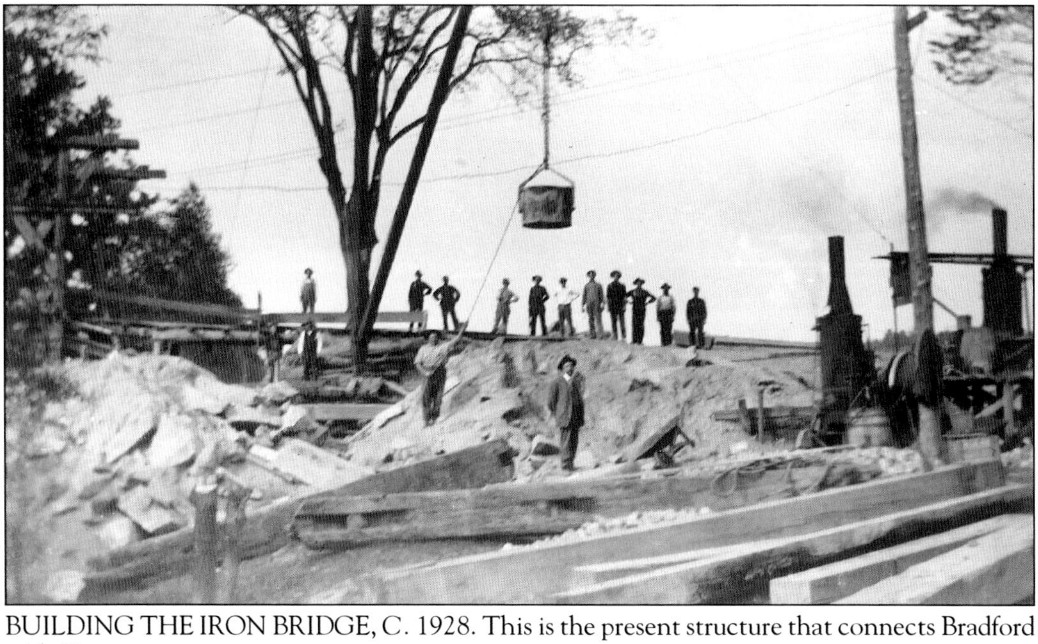

BUILDING THE IRON BRIDGE, C. 1928. This is the present structure that connects Bradford with Piermont.

Four

Piermont

NEW HAMPSHIRE
Grafton County
First settled: 1768
Chartered: 1764
Population in 1994: 641
Area: 40 square miles
Principal settlement: Piermont Village

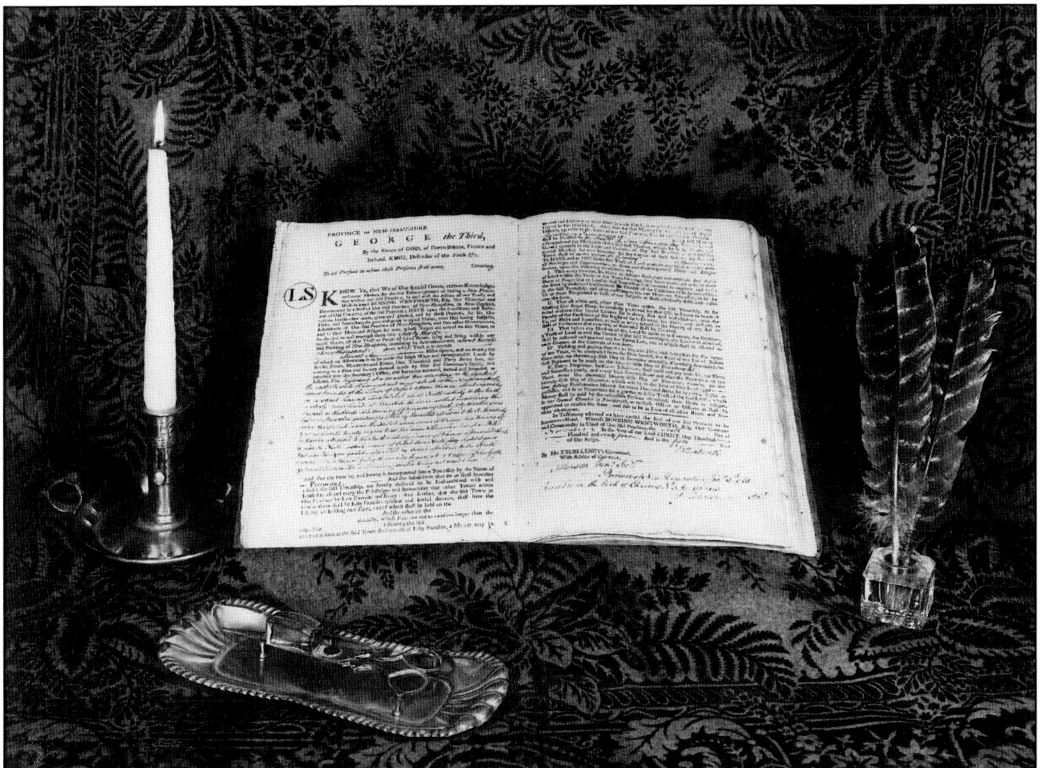

PIERMONT'S BEGINNINGS. The charter for the Piermont Township in the Province of New Hampshire was witnessed by Governor Benning Wentworth, Esq. on November 6, 1764, for George III, King of Great Britain, France, and Ireland.

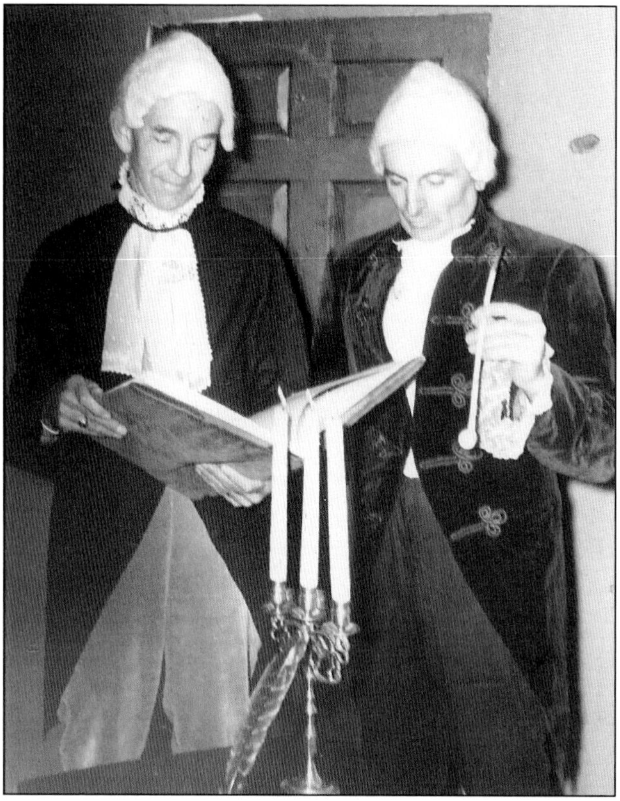

REENACTMENT OF A GREAT EVENT. During the Piermont Bicentennial Program in 1964, Stephen Underhill (right) and Philip Robinson examined the original charter.

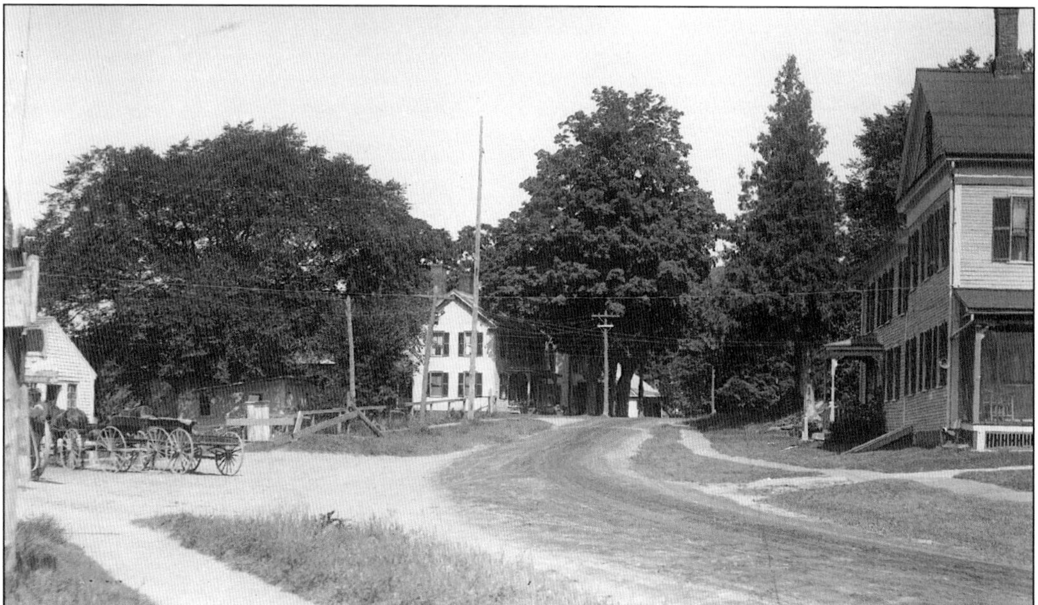

MAIN STREET IN PIERMONT. The present Piermont Inn, built about 1790, is shown in the right foreground. Since 1790, when it was operated as a tavern by Dr. Ross Coon, it has alternately been a home and an inn.

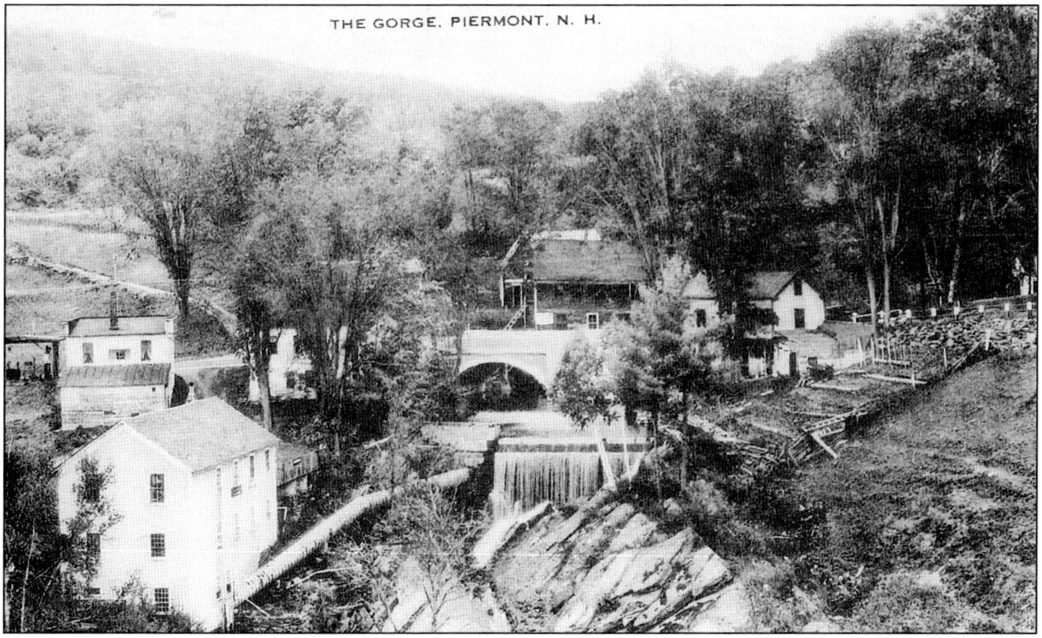

THE GORGE IN PIERMONT. Eastman Brook originates at Lake Tarleton and flows through the town in a westerly direction. It provided water power for thirteen mills, including Morrison's sawmill (foreground). Clayburn's butter box factory appears in the center behind the bridge.

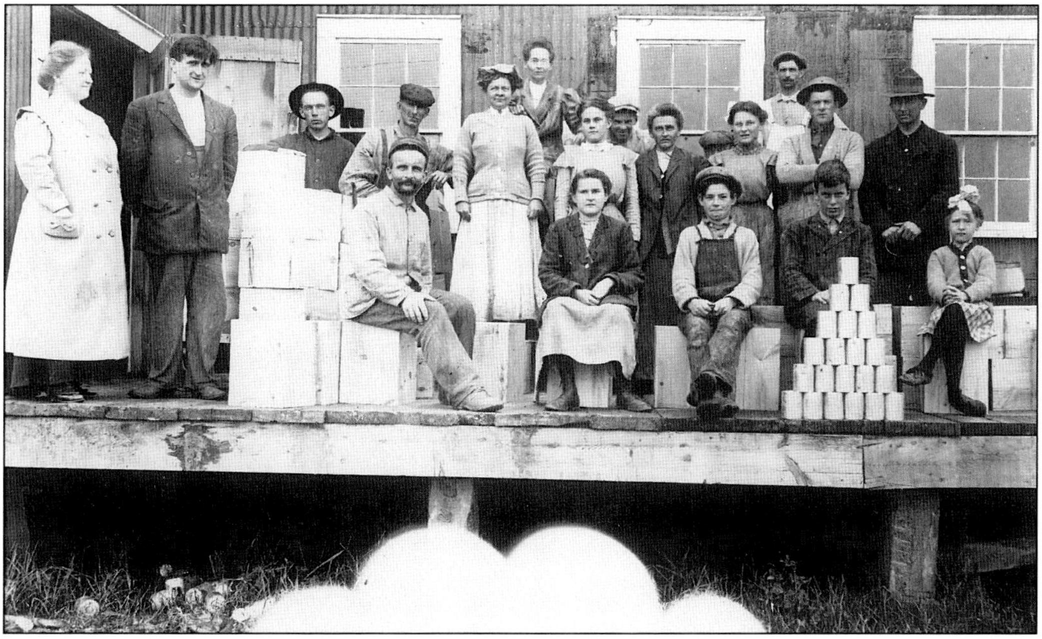

FAIRVIEW FARM CANNING COMPANY, C. 1911. This company canned local produce for a number of years at the site of the present Underhill Farm. Ernest Underhill, owner of the company, is shown seated at left in the front row. The company was sold to a Vermont canner who closed in 1930.

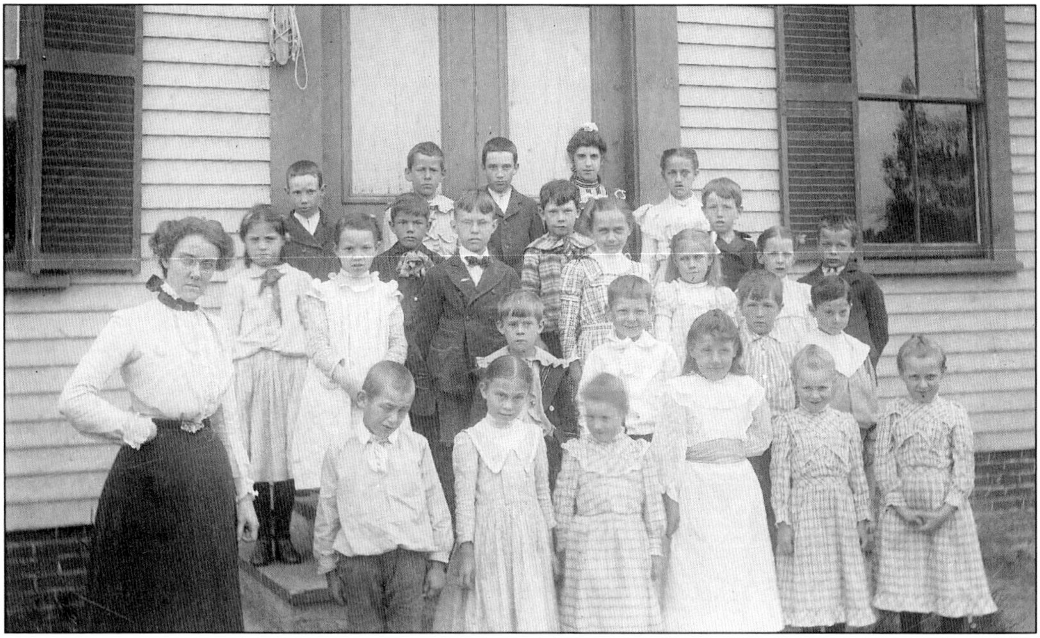

MISS CLARA B. TUTTLE WITH HER STUDENTS, 1902. From left to right: (front row) Earl Tarbox, Menta Ames, Edna Robie, Stella Cushing, Jessie Robie, Myrtie Robie; (second row) Walter Dennis, Harry Cushing, Guy Stanley, Harold Melendy; (third row) Elizabeth Smith, Annie Clayburn, John Ames, Leon Tucker, Ralph Simpson, Hazel Andross, Lona Ames, Arthur Evans, Florence Metcalf, Lester Corliss; (back row) George Clayburn, Albert Clayburn, Fannie Jacobs, and Lizzie Howland.

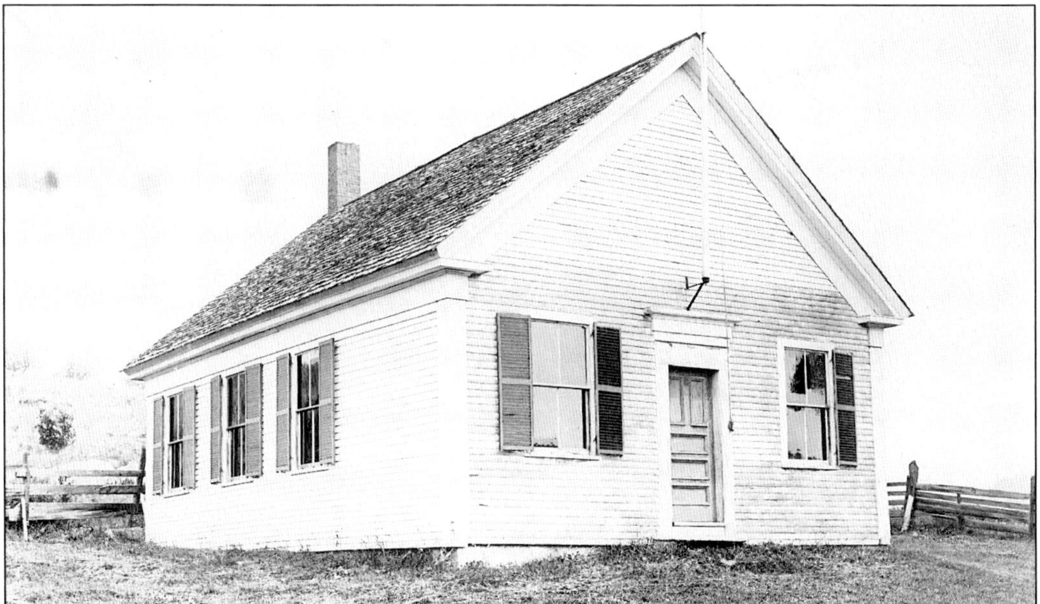

ONE-ROOM SCHOOLHOUSE. This photograph of a Piermont schoolhouse represents a turn-of-the-century design typical of the sixteen rural schools in Piermont. In 1819, 434 students were enrolled in Piermont schools.

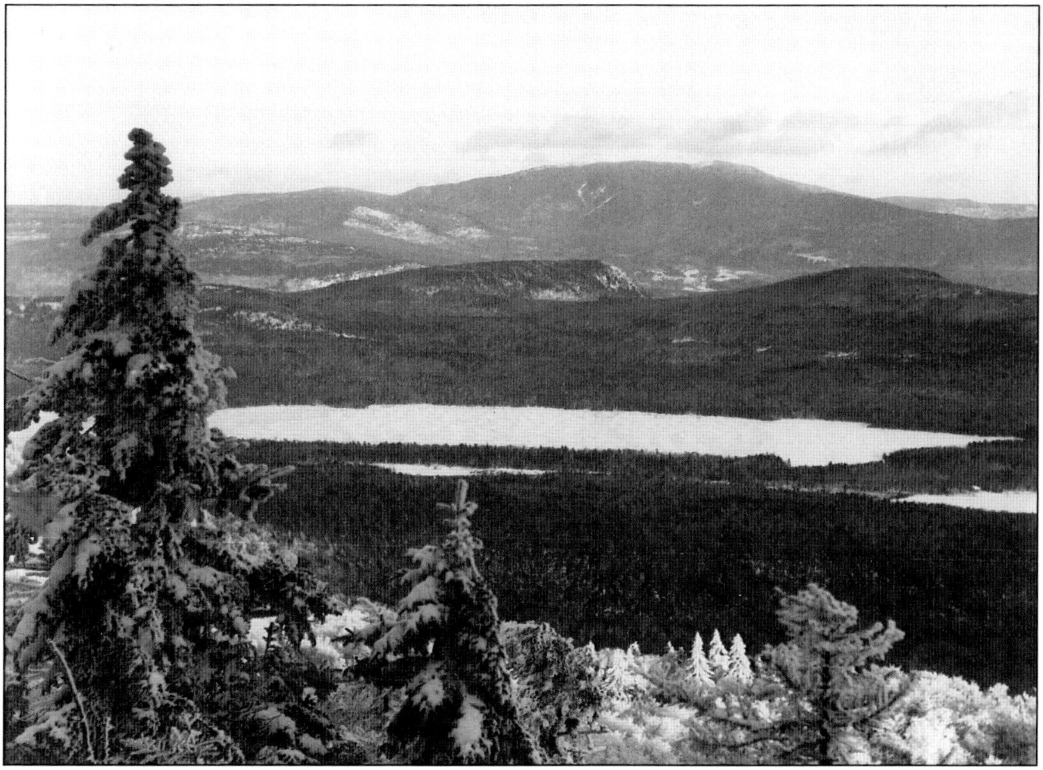

LAKE TARLETON. Viewed from the top of Piermont Mountain, Mount Moosilauke provides a backdrop for Lake Tarleton. For most of the first half of the twentieth century, this was a popular vacation spot catering to a clientele from all over the northeast.

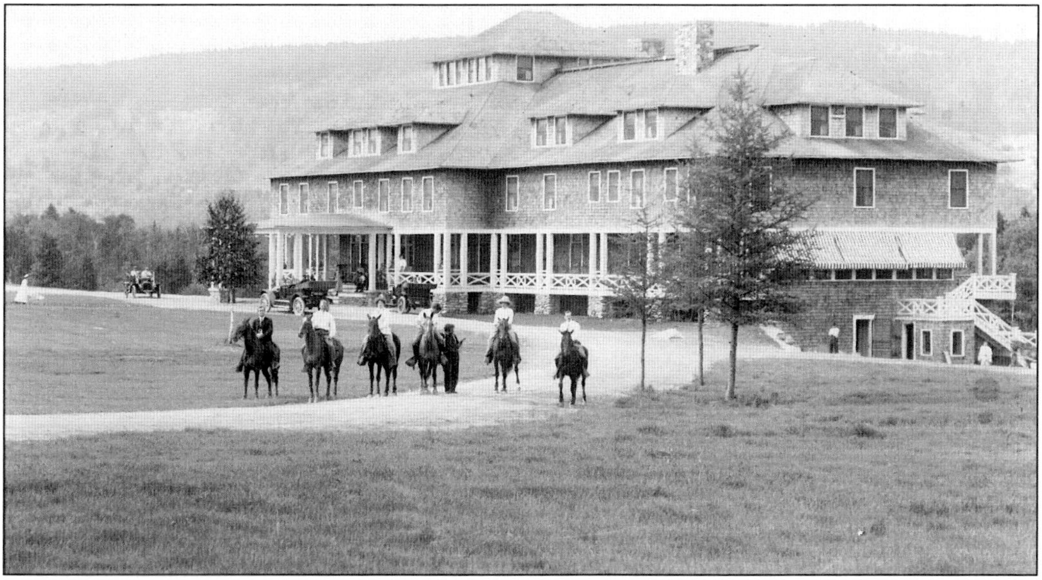

LAKE TARLETON CLUB HOTEL, 1912. The Club and its many recreational facilities were located on the site of the 1774 Tarleton Tavern. It was established in 1911 by E. Bertram Pike and encompassed 2,500 acres.

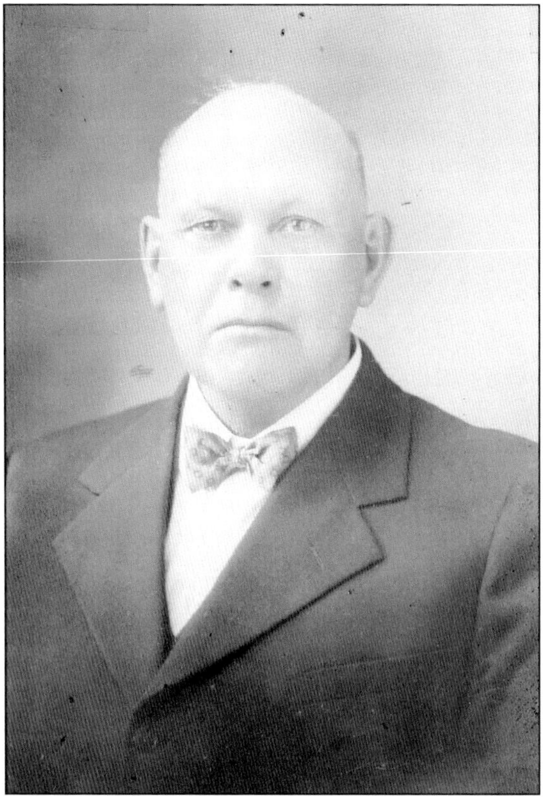

JOHN FRANK SIMPSON. This is a 1929 portrait of a well-known local builder and state representative from Grafton County. Mr. Simpson, pictured at fifty-seven years of age, served on the agriculture committee in the state legislature.

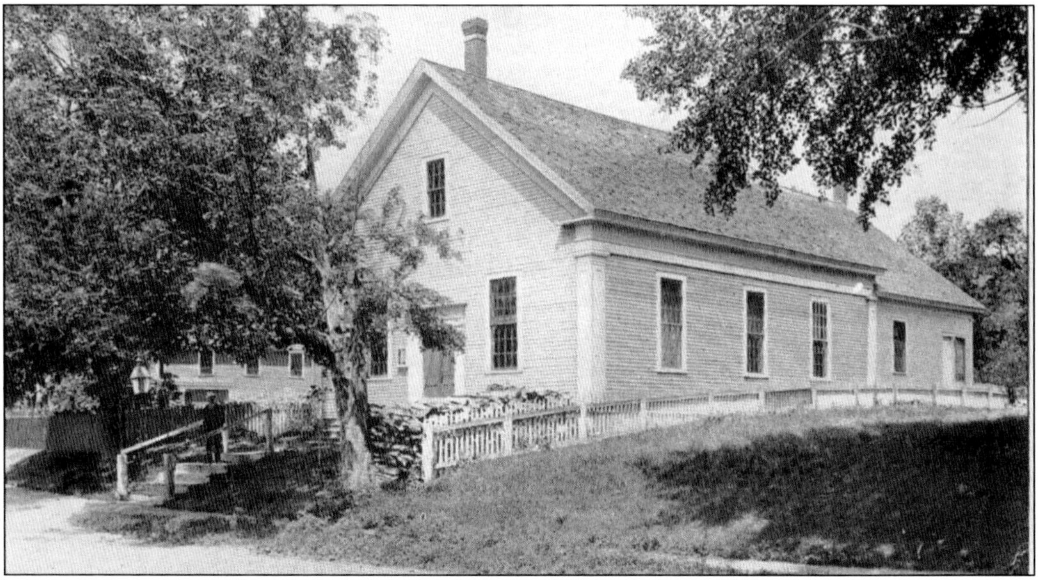

THE TOWN HALL, C. 1910. The town hall was built in 1863 at a total cost of $1,009.48. The Piermont Grange, organized in 1897, also met in this building.

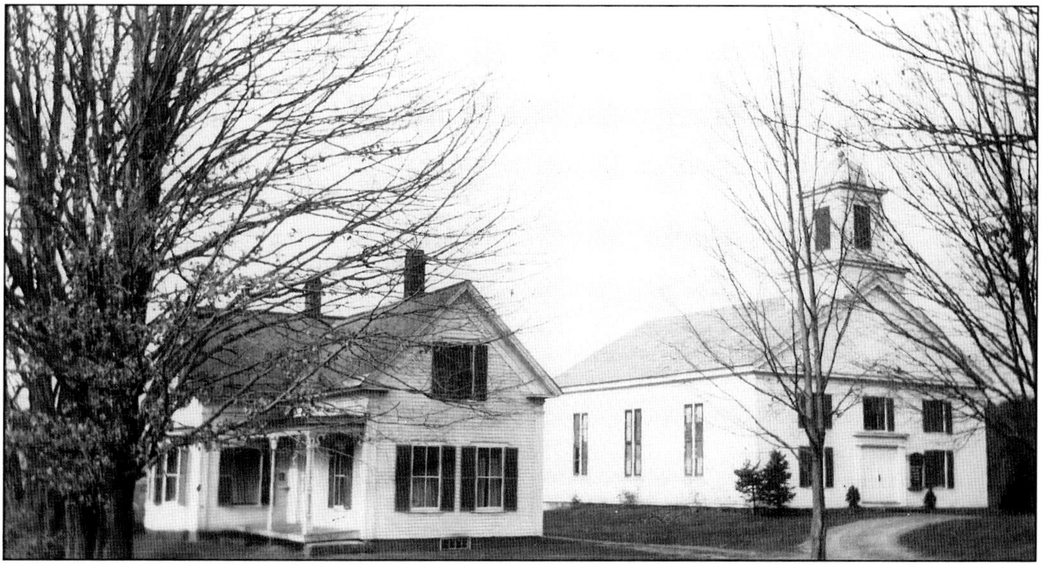

PIERMONT CONGREGATIONAL CHURCH, 1930s. The parsonage is on the left. This church was built in 1837 on what is now Church Street.

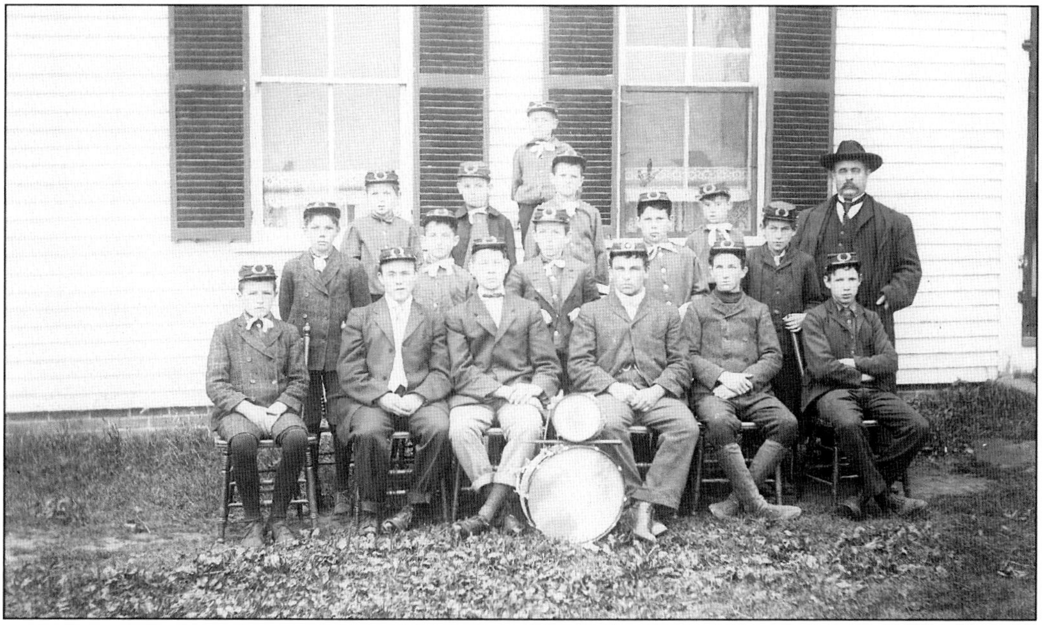

BOYS BAND. The Reverend A. Reginald Crewe, pastor of the Congregational church, is pictured beside the parsonage in 1907 with a group assumed to be a band. The only boy identified is twelve-year-old John Ralph Simpson (second row, third from the right).

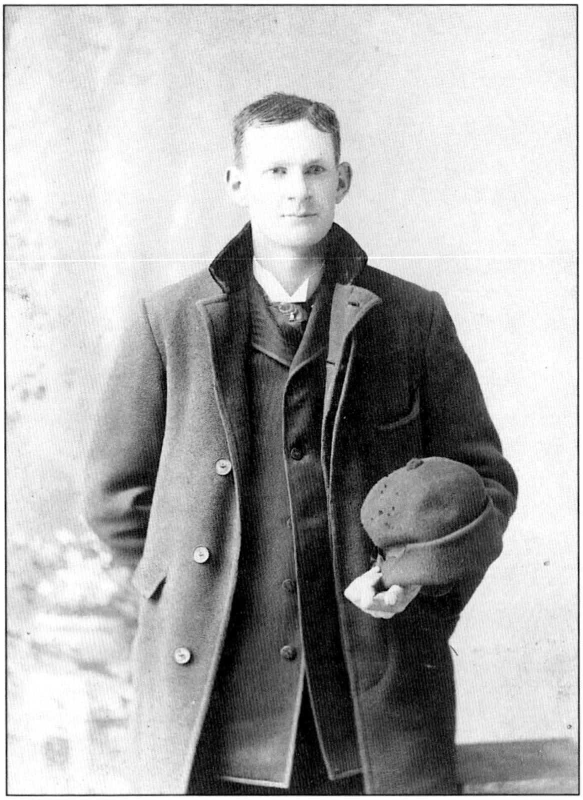

CHARLES BERT FRENCH. Known as Bert in Piermont, Charles French was born in 1871 and died in 1936. He is pictured here around the turn of the century. In 1907 he purchased a blacksmith shop on Brook Road and was the town smithy for a number of years.

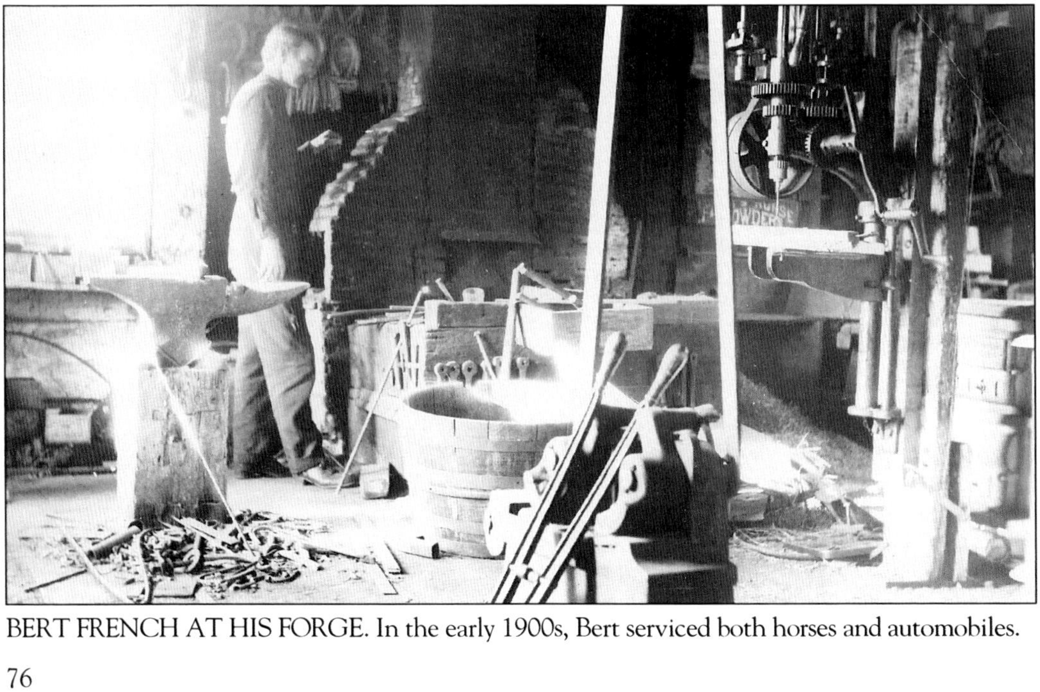

BERT FRENCH AT HIS FORGE. In the early 1900s, Bert serviced both horses and automobiles.

THE MORRISON FAMILY IN EARLY 1900. Eugene Morrison, daughter Christie, and wife Ida Grimes were photographed in Bradford, Vermont. Mr. Morrison owned a sawmill on Eastman Brook and established the Piermont Telephone Company in 1902. He was also involved in a number of other commercial enterprises.

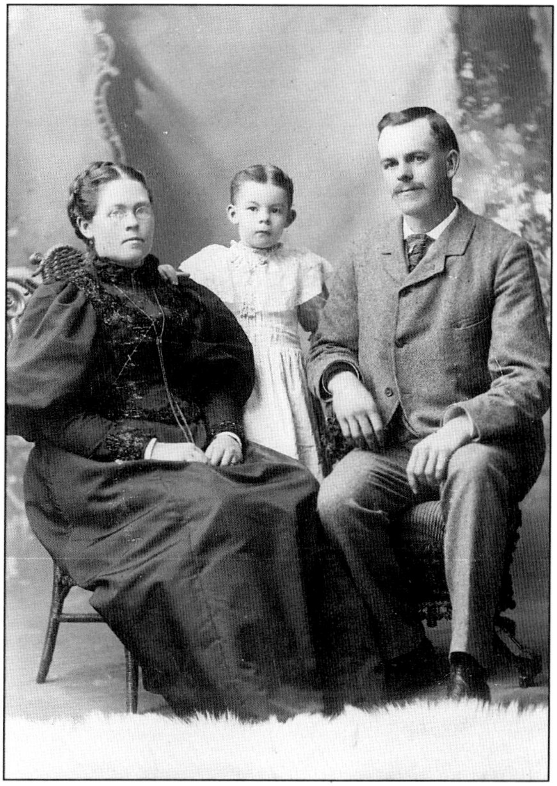

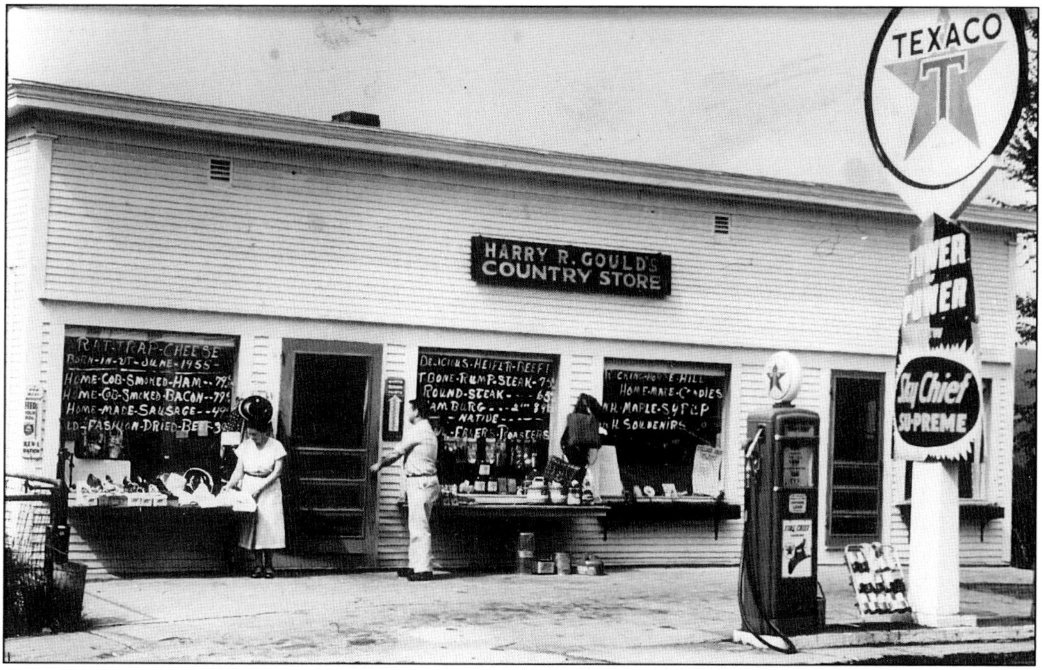

GOULD'S COUNTRY STORE. The store was established by Harry R. Gould in Piermont in 1921 and rebuilt after the 1934 fire that almost destroyed downtown Piermont. Note the food prices chalked on the store windows in the mid-1950s photograph.

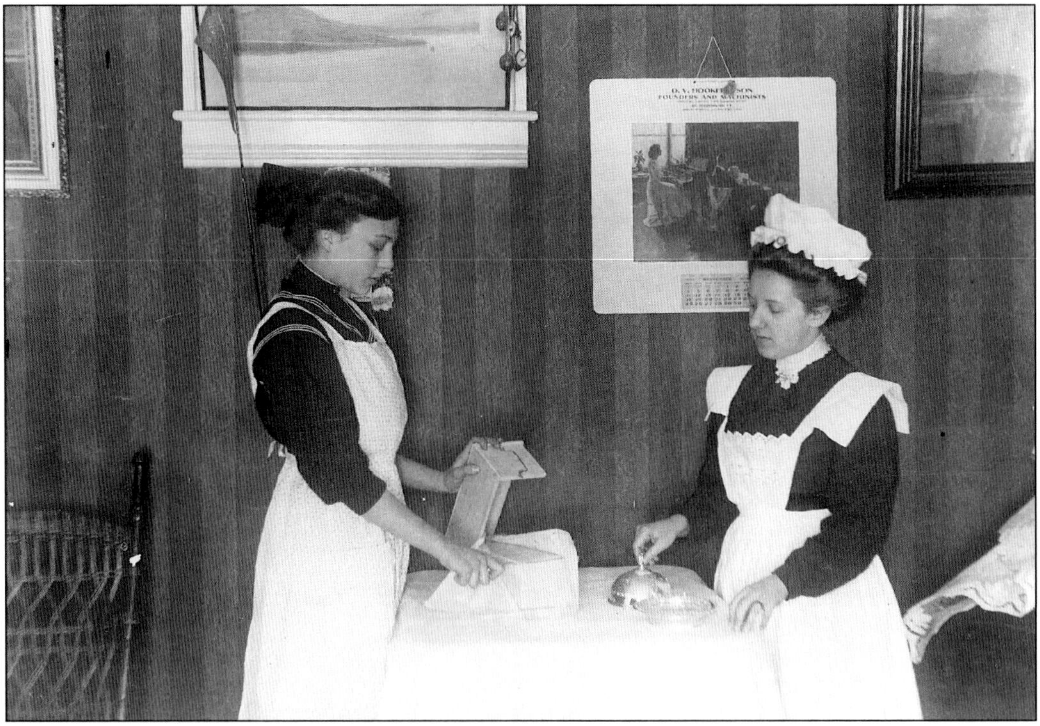

BUTTER BOX ADVERTISEMENT, 1910. Waitresses at the Lake Tarleton Club in Piermont are shown preparing butter for the club's dining room. The butter box was made by the Piermont Manufacturing Company. On the left is Menta Ames. On the right is Myrtie Robie, mother of Alfred Stevens. Alfred served the community as a selectman for many years.

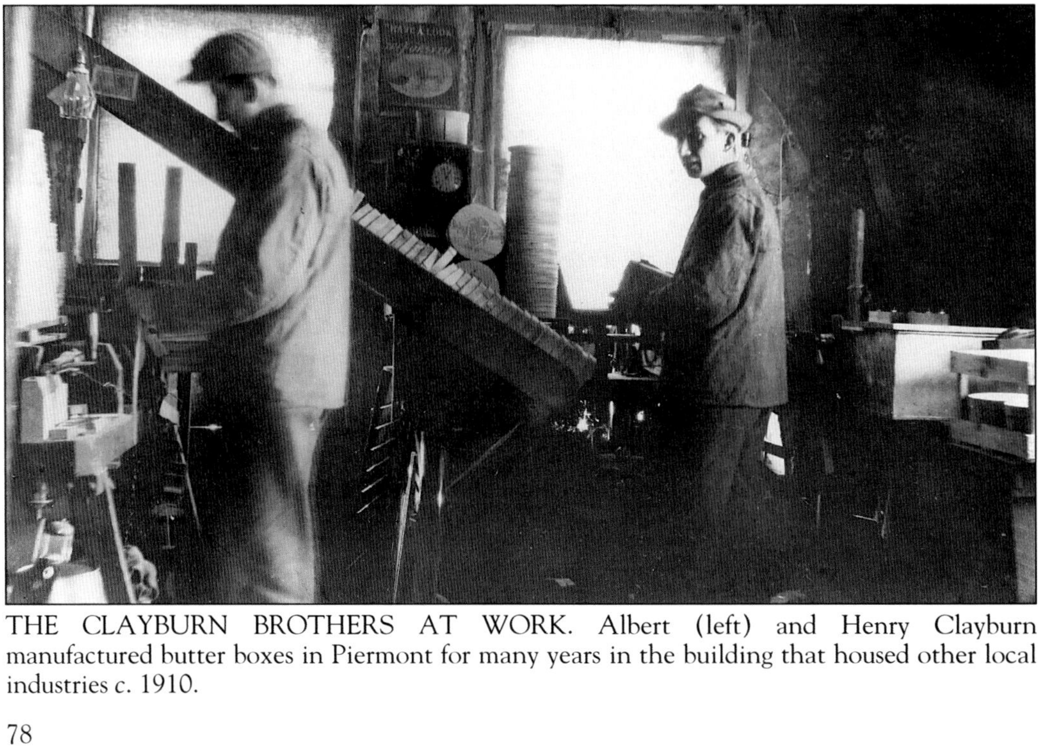

THE CLAYBURN BROTHERS AT WORK. Albert (left) and Henry Clayburn manufactured butter boxes in Piermont for many years in the building that housed other local industries c. 1910.

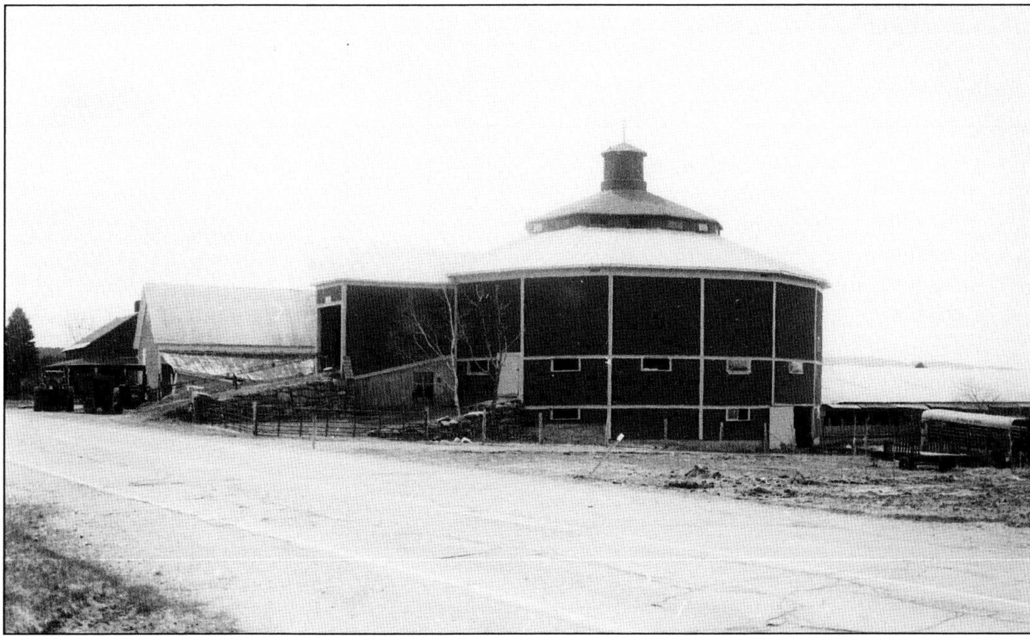

ROUND BARN, FLATLANDER FARM. Actually sixteen-sided, this barn was built in 1906 by Ernest Stevens on Route 10. The present owners brought their dairy business to this location in 1968.

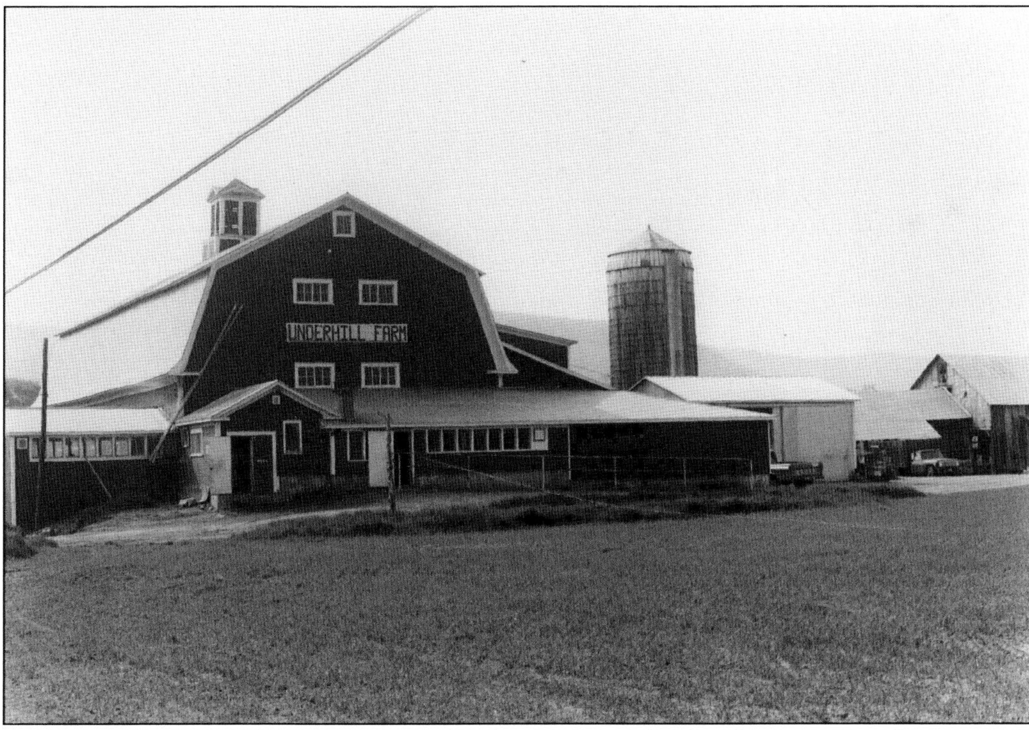

THE UNDERHILL DAIRY BARN. A familiar Route 25 landmark since it was built in 1905 by John Frank Simpson, the barn was the center of the Underhill family's dairy operation. Buildings at the right once housed Ernest Underhill's Fairview Farm Canning Company.

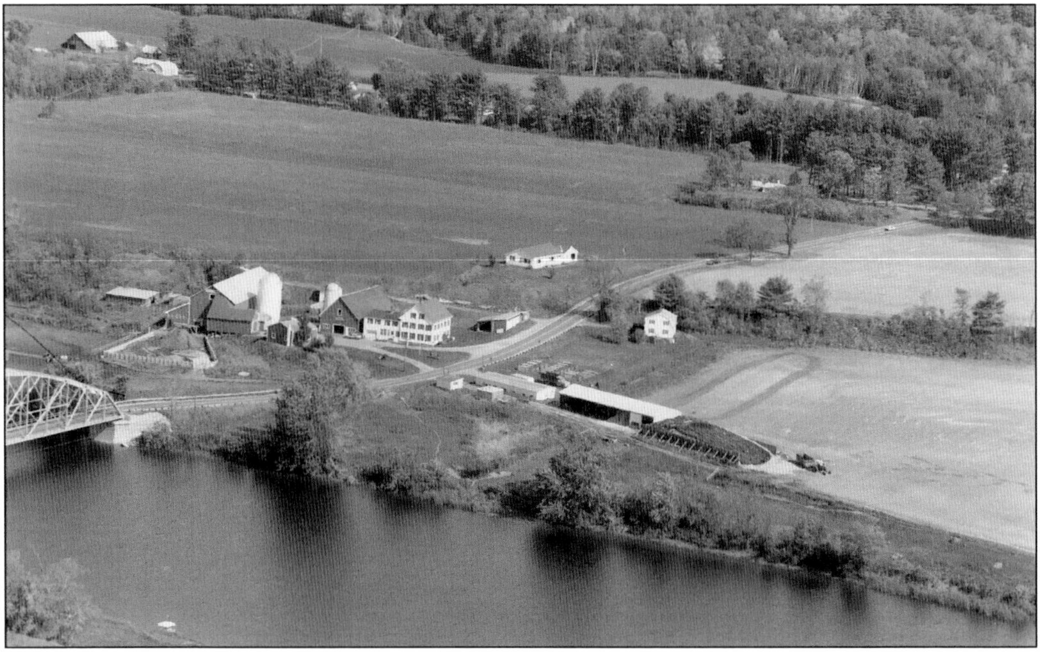

AERIAL VIEW OF THE PUTNAM DAIRY FARM. The farm, pictured in the 1980s, includes 300 acres bisected by Route 25 and bordered by the Connecticut River. The main house was built in 1857. In 1918, the Putnams bought the farm from the Chandler family. At the left is the Piermont/Bradford bridge spanning the Connecticut River.

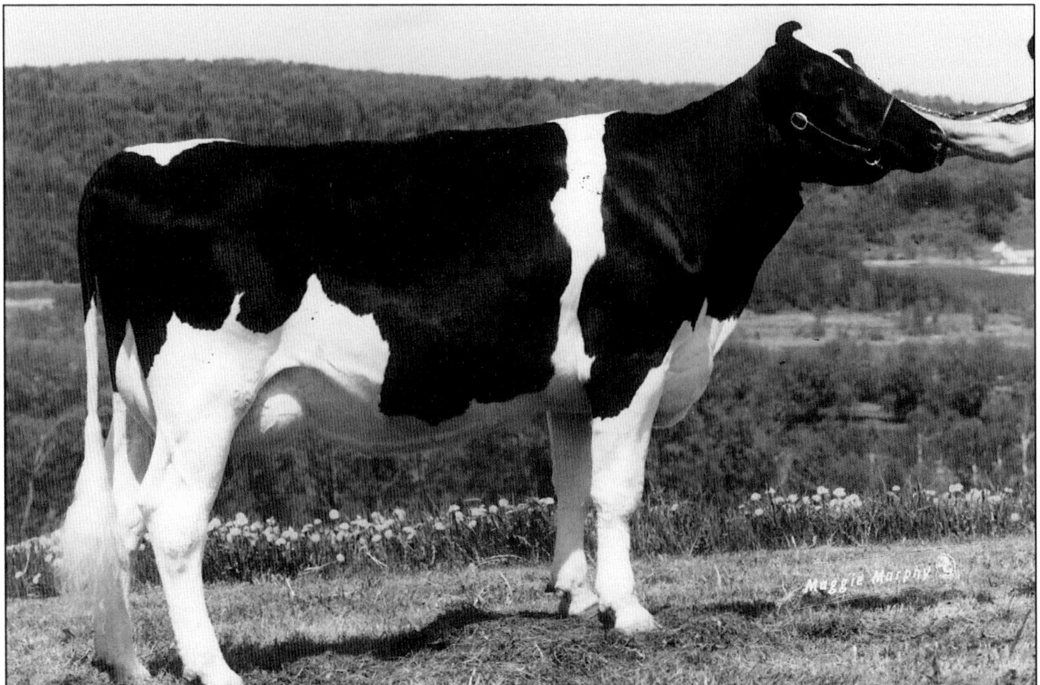

PRIZE-WINNING HOLSTEIN "MARK ILLUSION." Dream and Do Farm's registered cow represents dairying— a major agricultural business in Piermont in the past and present.

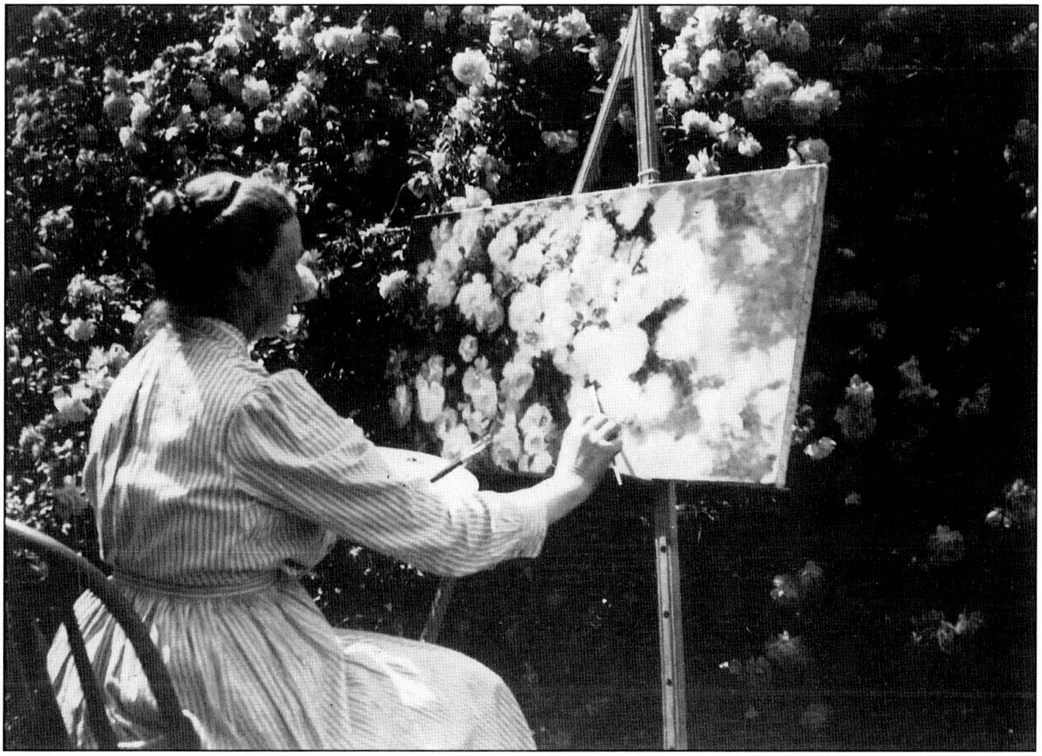

ADELAIDE PALMER, ARTIST. Adelaide Palmer, a painter and art instructor, worked locally and in Boston. She returned to Piermont to tend her ailing parents in the early twentieth century.

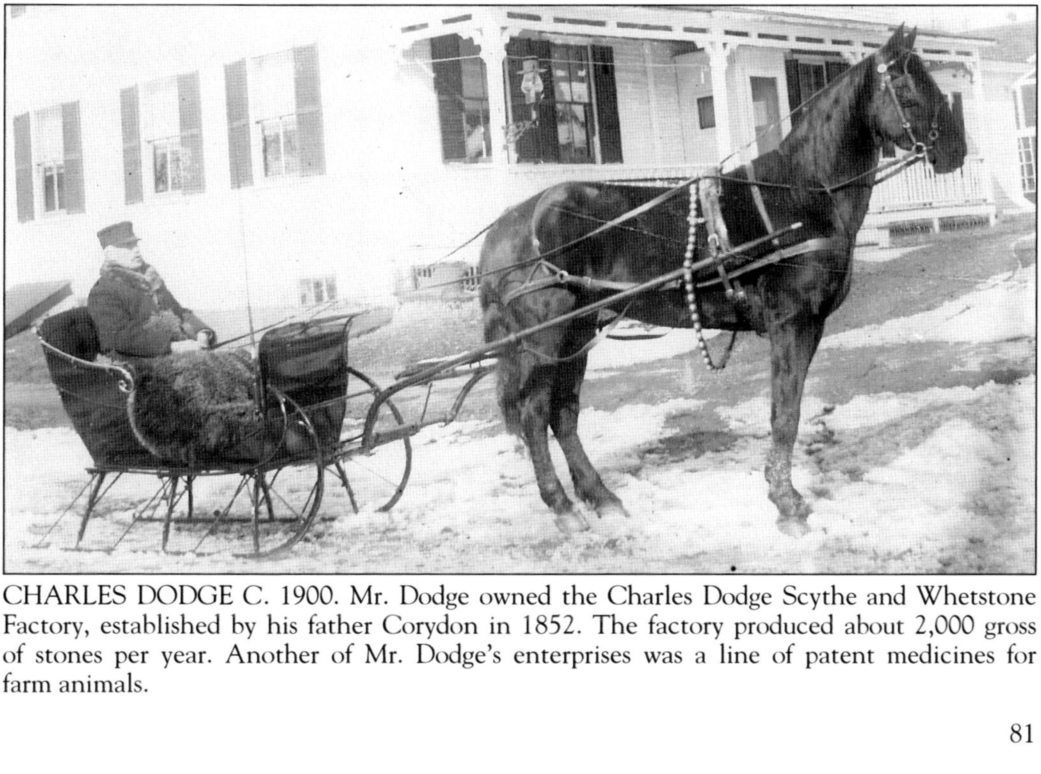

CHARLES DODGE C. 1900. Mr. Dodge owned the Charles Dodge Scythe and Whetstone Factory, established by his father Corydon in 1852. The factory produced about 2,000 gross of stones per year. Another of Mr. Dodge's enterprises was a line of patent medicines for farm animals.

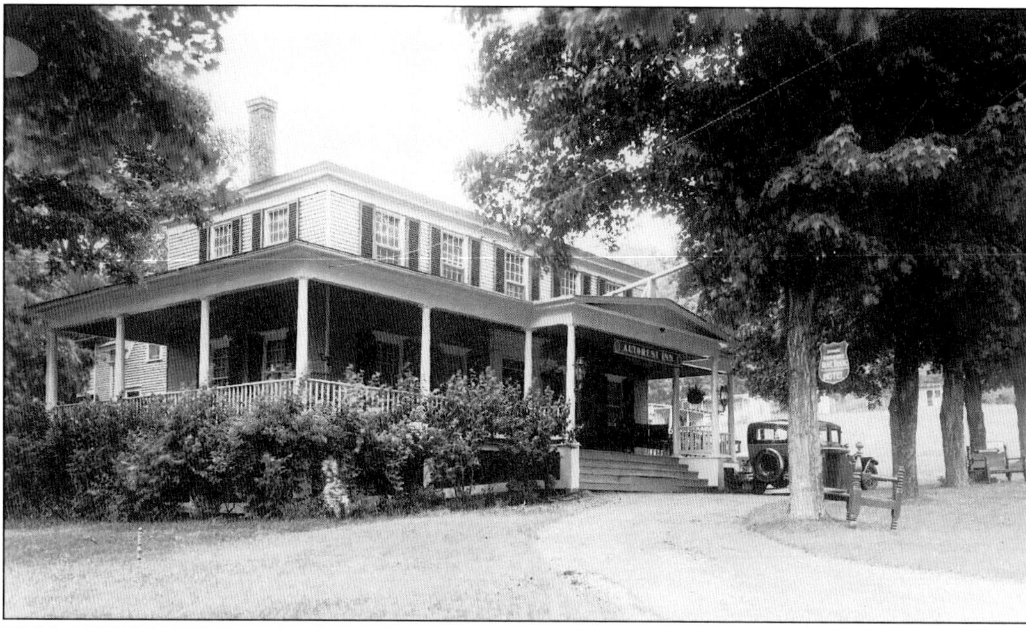

THE AUTOREST INN. Early in the century, this inn opened in Piermont on Church Street, which at the time was a state highway. The original house was built as a private residence in 1812.

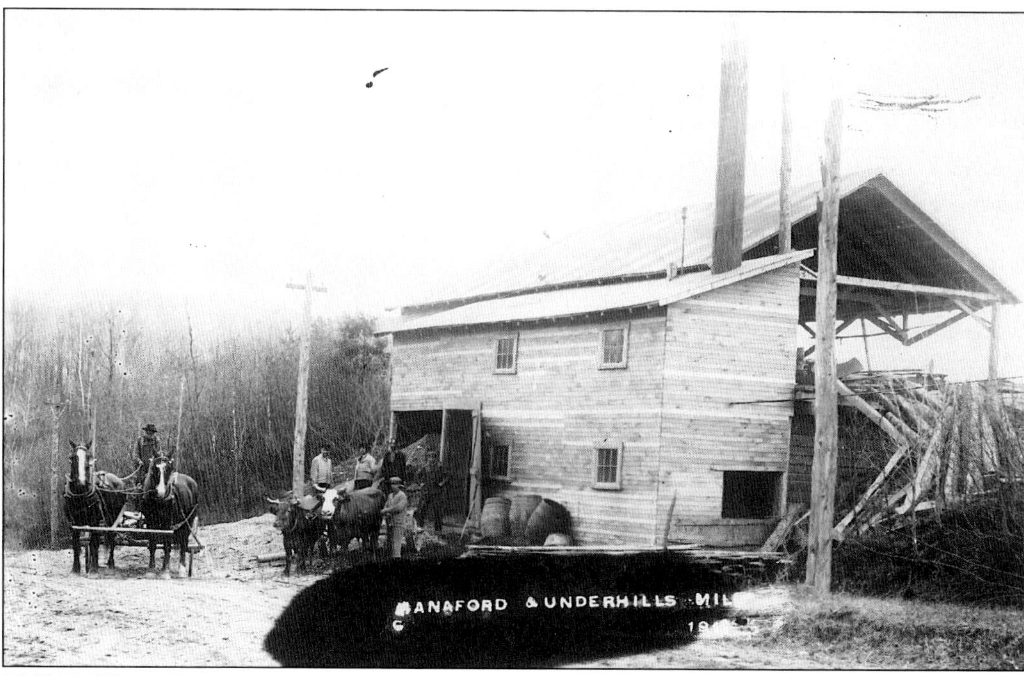

TURN-OF-THE-CENTURY LUMBER DELIVERY, C. 1910. Horses and oxen were used for heavy hauling at the Hannaford & Underhill sawmill. This mill was one of a number located in Piermont in the late nineteenth and early twentieth centuries.

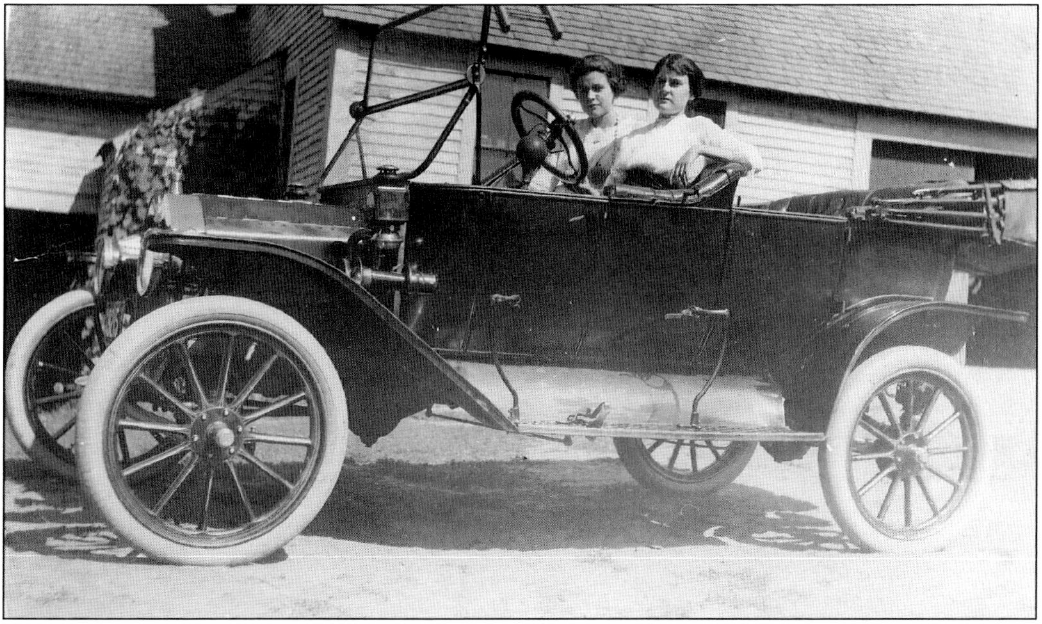

HORSELESS BUGGY ARRIVES IN PIERMONT, C. 1915. Mildred Stewart and Maude French proudly pose in an early Model-T Ford.

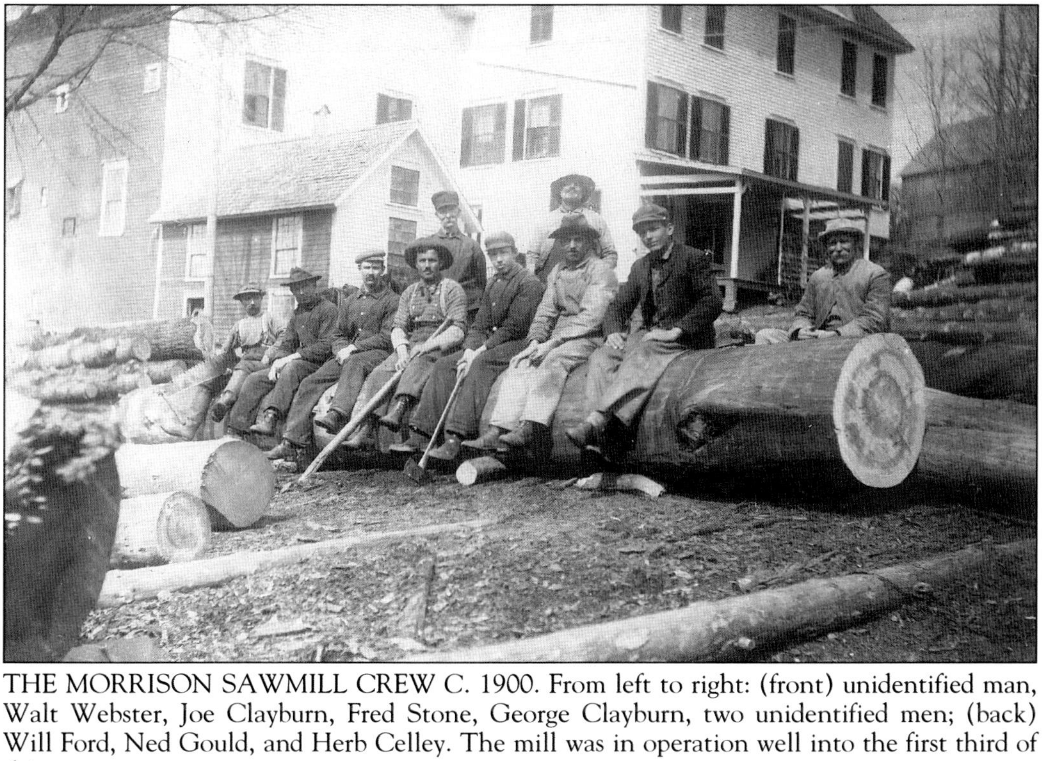

THE MORRISON SAWMILL CREW C. 1900. From left to right: (front) unidentified man, Walt Webster, Joe Clayburn, Fred Stone, George Clayburn, two unidentified men; (back) Will Ford, Ned Gould, and Herb Celley. The mill was in operation well into the first third of this century.

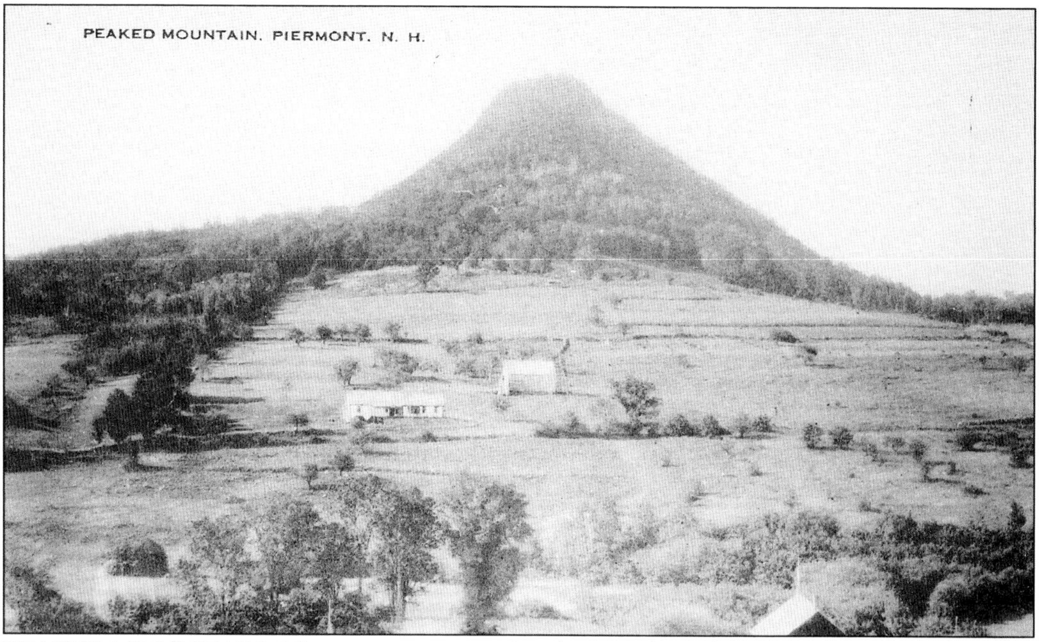

PEAKED MOUNTAIN. This mountain is said to be a geological upthrust and is a prominent feature in the Piermont landscape.

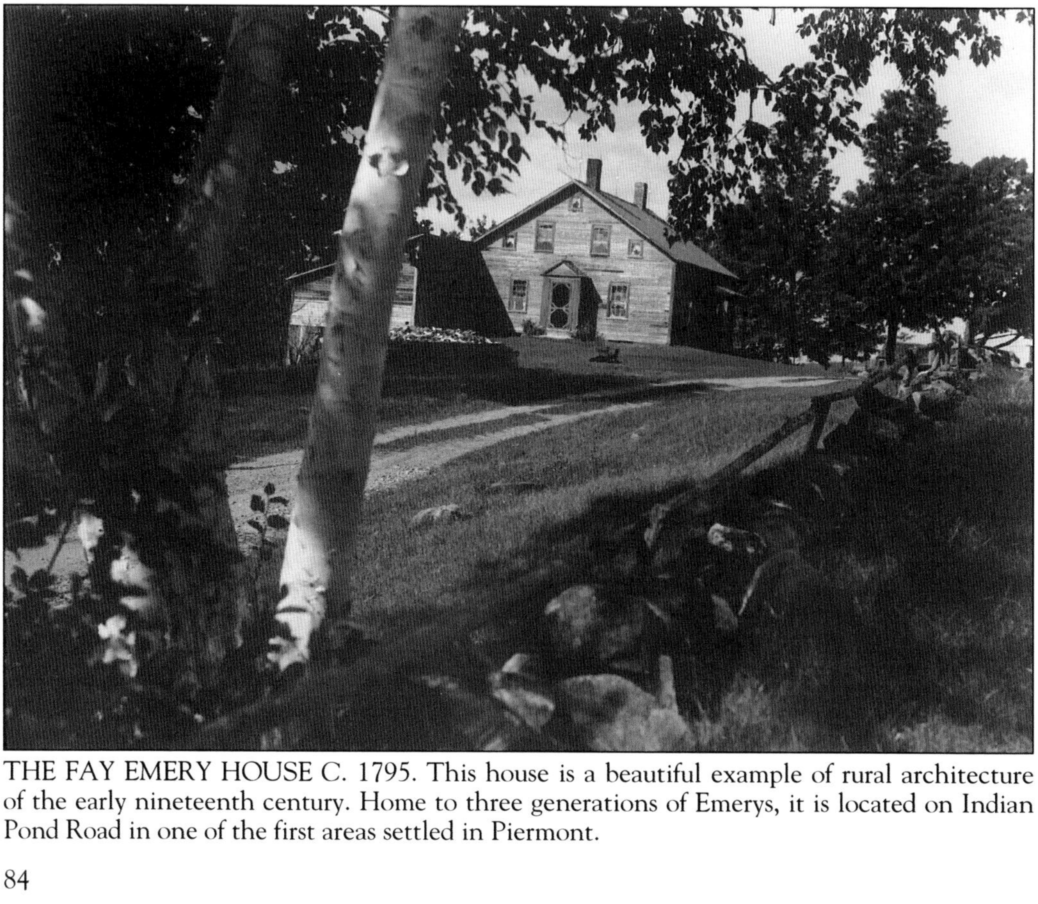

THE FAY EMERY HOUSE C. 1795. This house is a beautiful example of rural architecture of the early nineteenth century. Home to three generations of Emerys, it is located on Indian Pond Road in one of the first areas settled in Piermont.

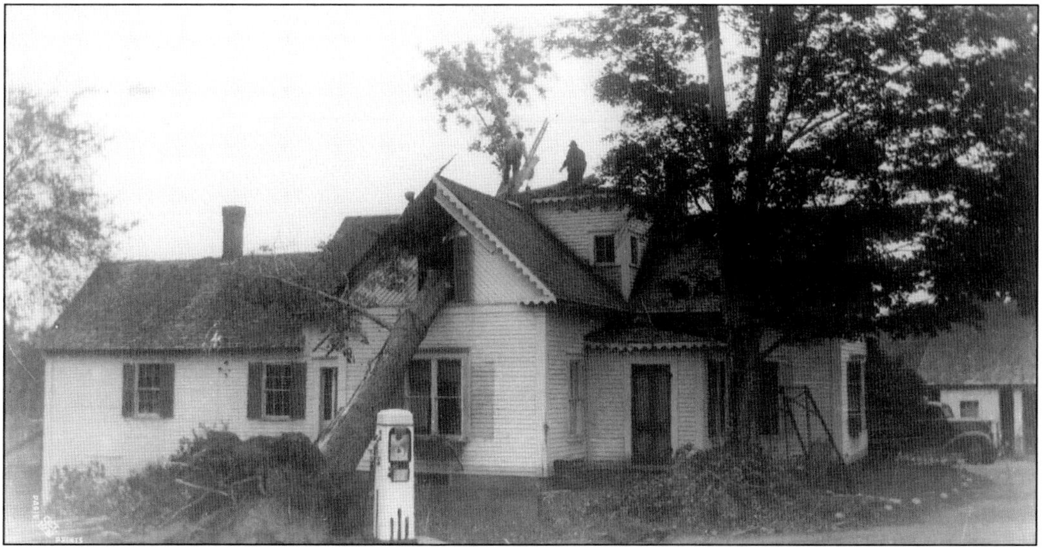

HURRICANE DAMAGE, 1938. The Charles Jewell house was not spared by the hurricane's wrath.

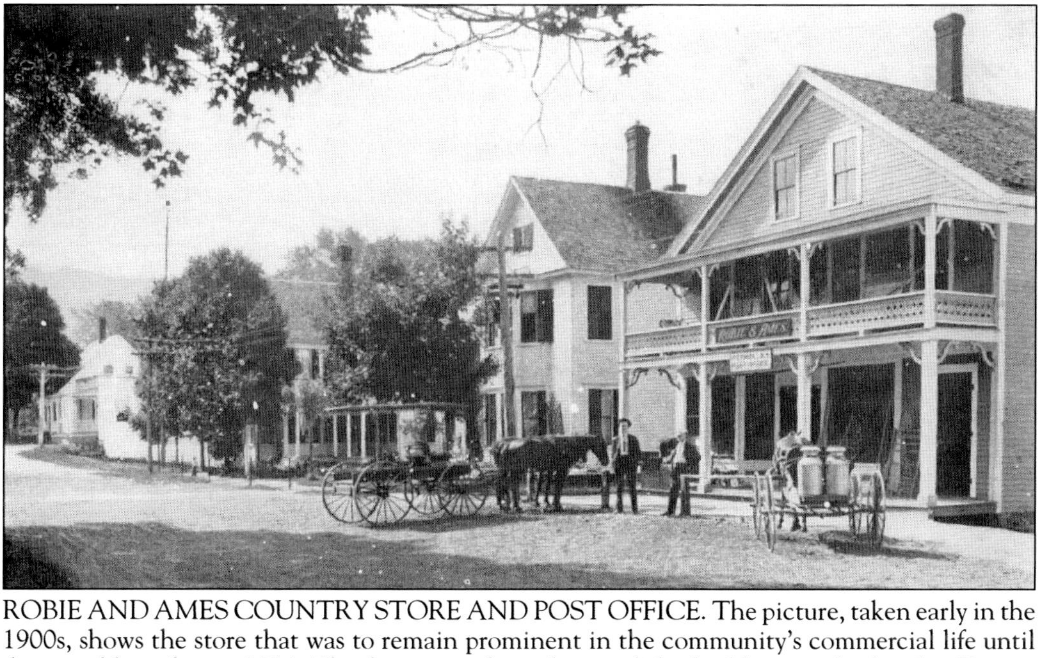

ROBIE AND AMES COUNTRY STORE AND POST OFFICE. The picture, taken early in the 1900s, shows the store that was to remain prominent in the community's commercial life until destroyed by a fire in 1934. The fire swept through it and the buildings on both sides. During those years the store also was known as "Grimes," "J. E. Lee," and "Gould's Country Store."

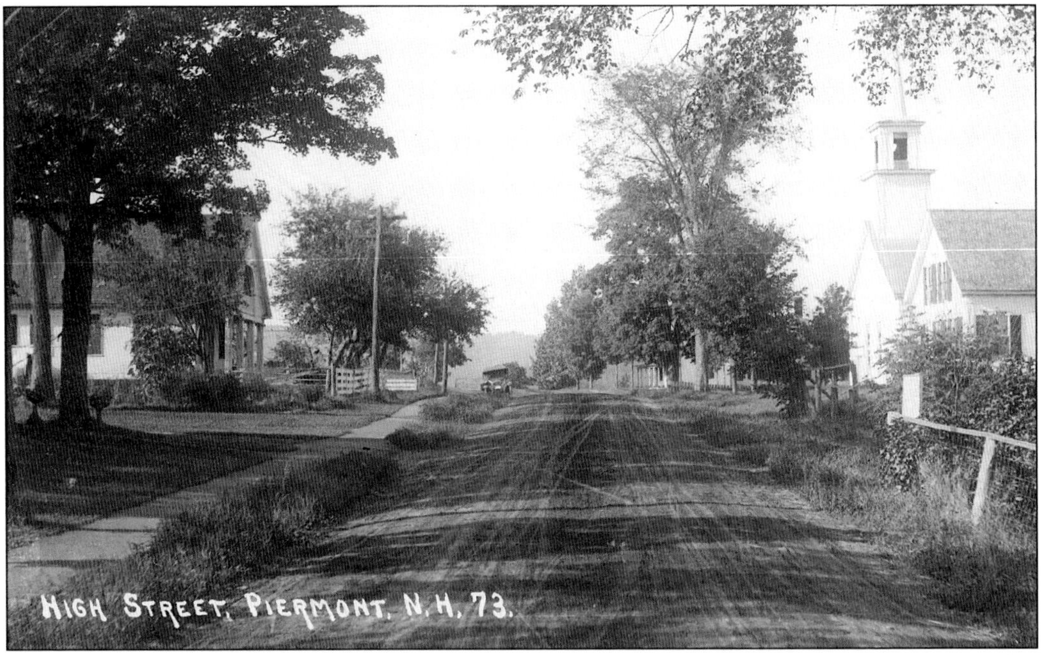

HIGH STREET LOOKING SOUTH C. 1910. This is now State Route 10. The Methodist church and parsonage are on the right. Pictured across the street is the farmhouse which presently contains the town offices, the library, and the historical society.

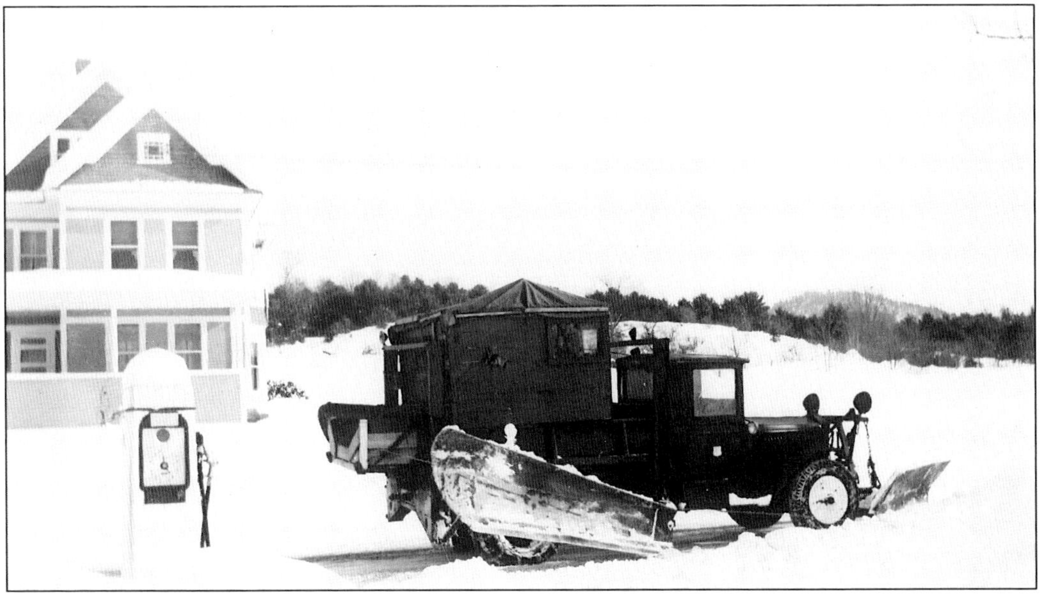

TOWN SNOW PLOW. Road Agent Charles Jewel's plow is parked on Church Street, c. 1920. Notice the gasoline pump. The house on the left was built around 1893 by John Frank Simpson.

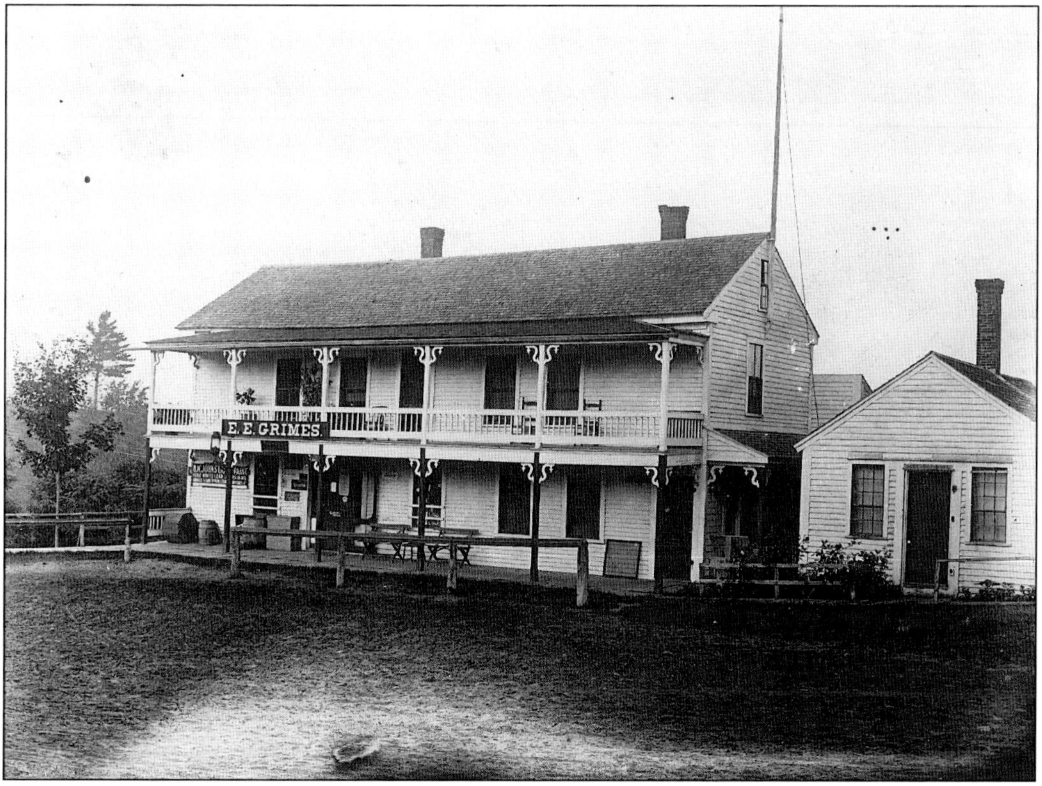

E. E. GRIMES COUNTRY STORE. This store also was operated as "J. E. Lee" and as "Howard Bros." and was the location of the town post office. The building pictured burned in 1927. It was rebuilt and later converted to apartments.

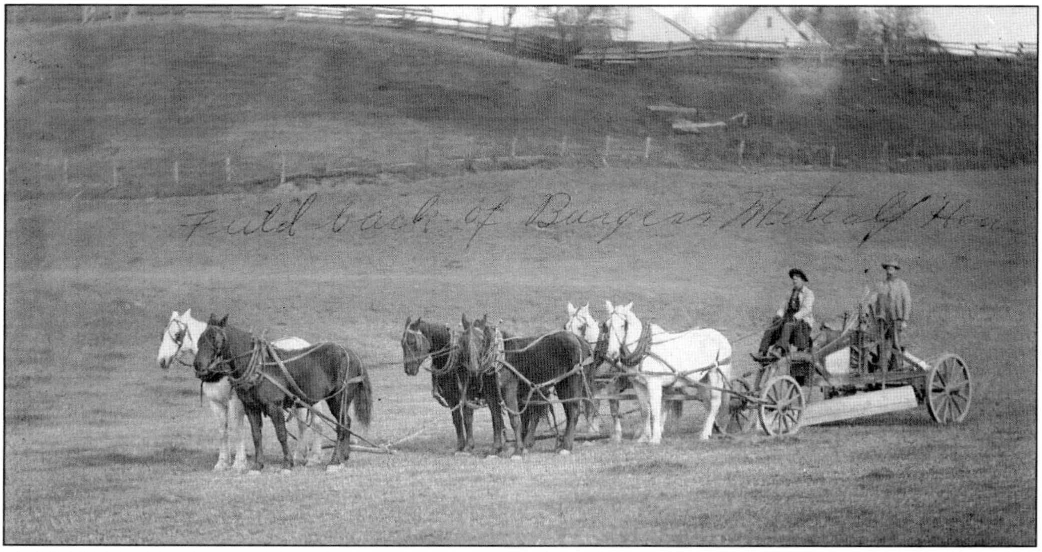

TOWN ROAD GRADER. The grader is pictured in the early 1900s in Burgess Metcalf's field. George Webster is driving and Road Agent Ned Gould is on the right.

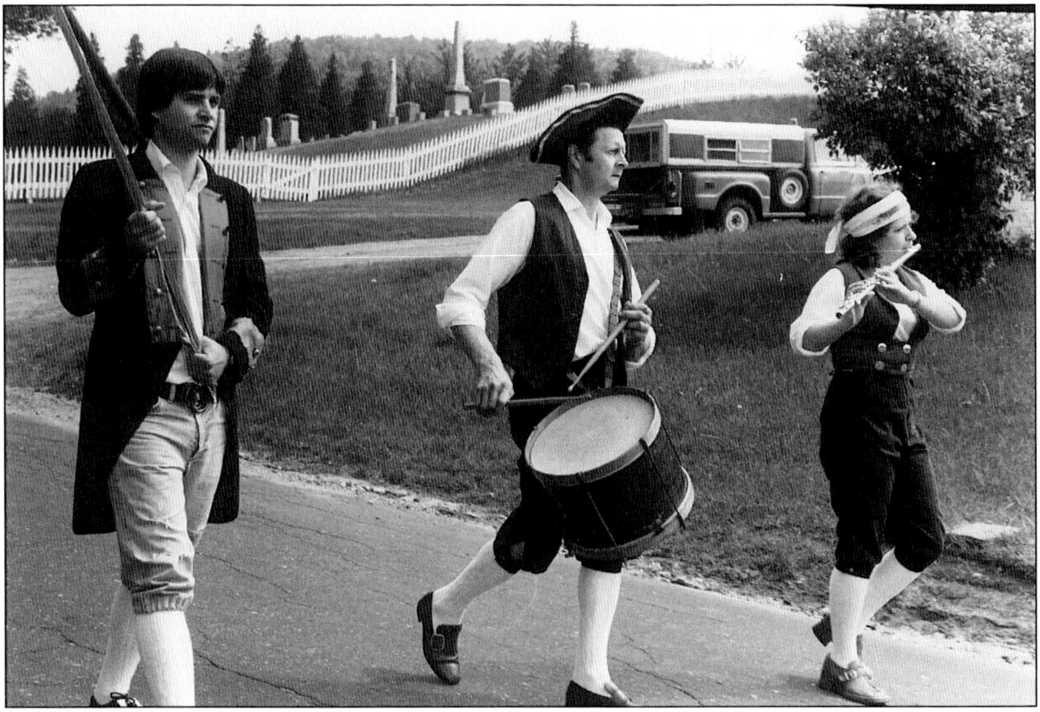

BICENTENNIAL IN PIERMONT, 1976. Richard Waterman is at the center, with his son, Michael, and daughter, Holly.

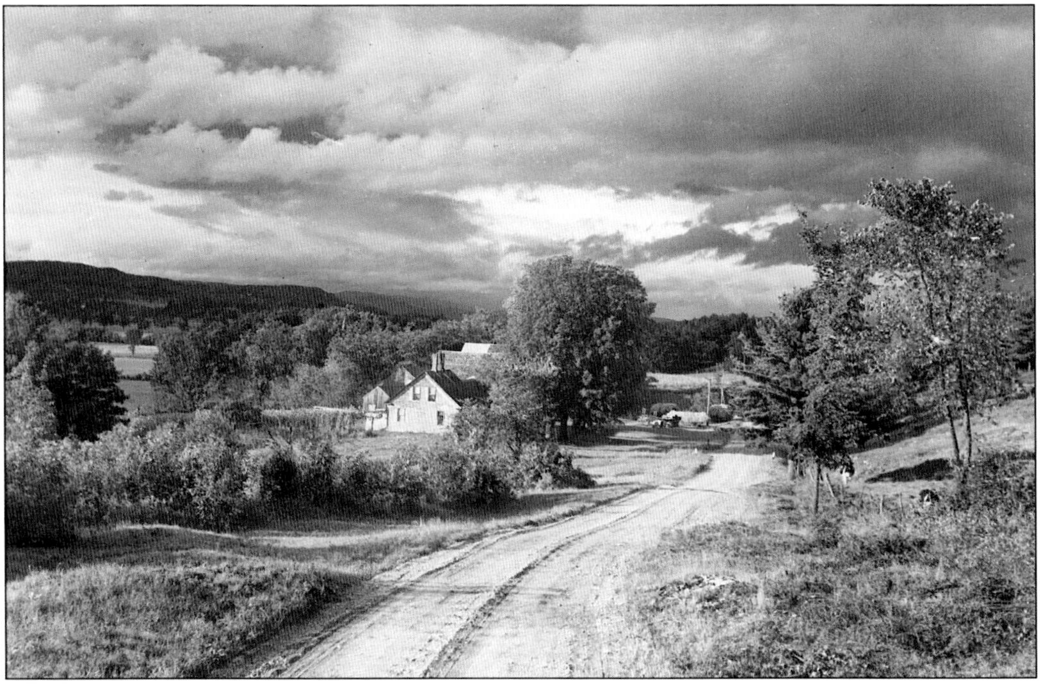

PASTORAL NEW ENGLAND. The Phil Dearth Farm, once owned by Joseph Lawrence, stands today at the north end of River Road in Piermont. The photograph was taken in midsummer at the turn of this century.

Five

Newbury

VERMONT
Orange County
First Settled: 1762
Chartered: 1763
Population in 1990: 1,986
Area: 57 square miles
Principal Settlements: Newbury Village, West Newbury, Wells River

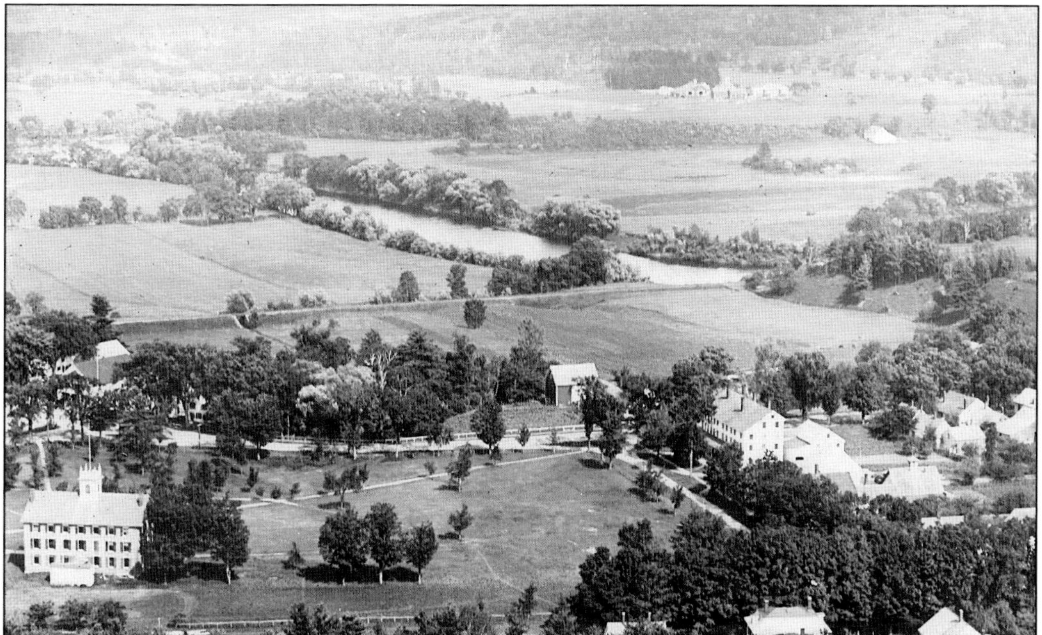

NEWBURY VILLAGE, C. 1898. Newbury Seminary and Newbury Village are seen from Mount Pulaski, looking east to the Oxbow. The south end of the common shows the hotel and Route 5.

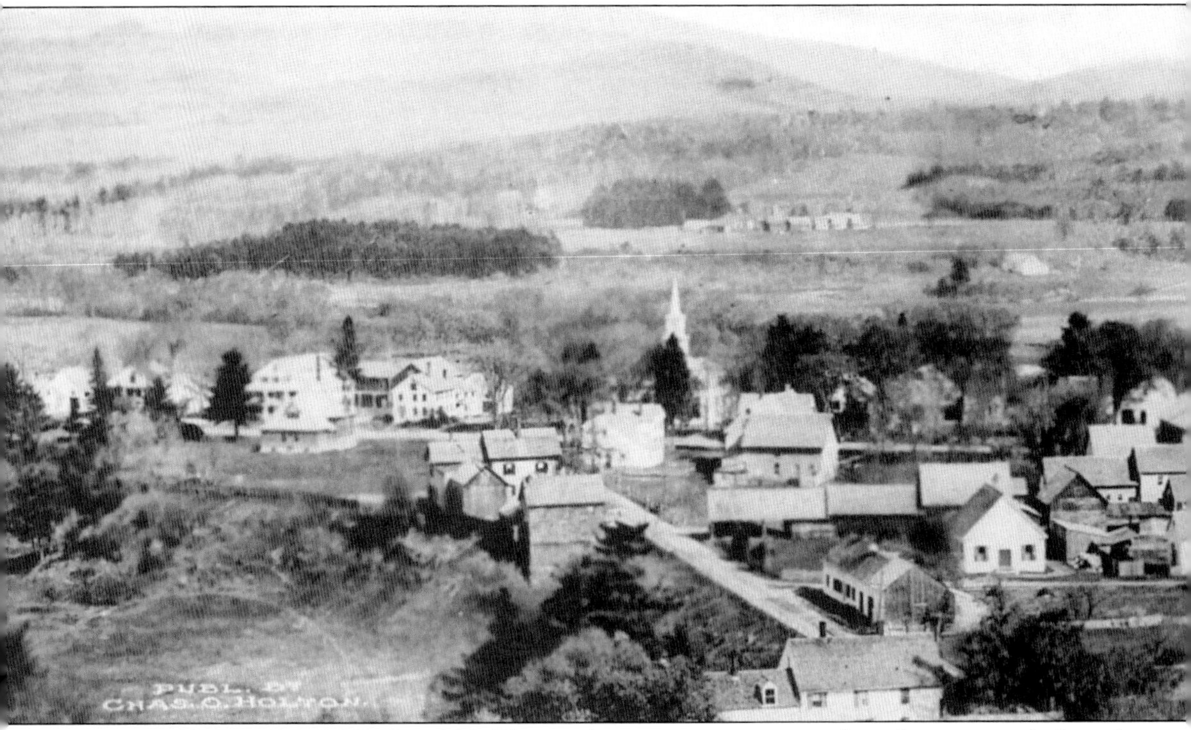

NEWBURY VILLAGE, C. 1900. This is the town as it appeared in the era just before the devastating fire that almost destroyed the village. The lower picture shows the fire damage of June 14, 1913. Note the smoke still rising from the embers. The Methodist church was spared,

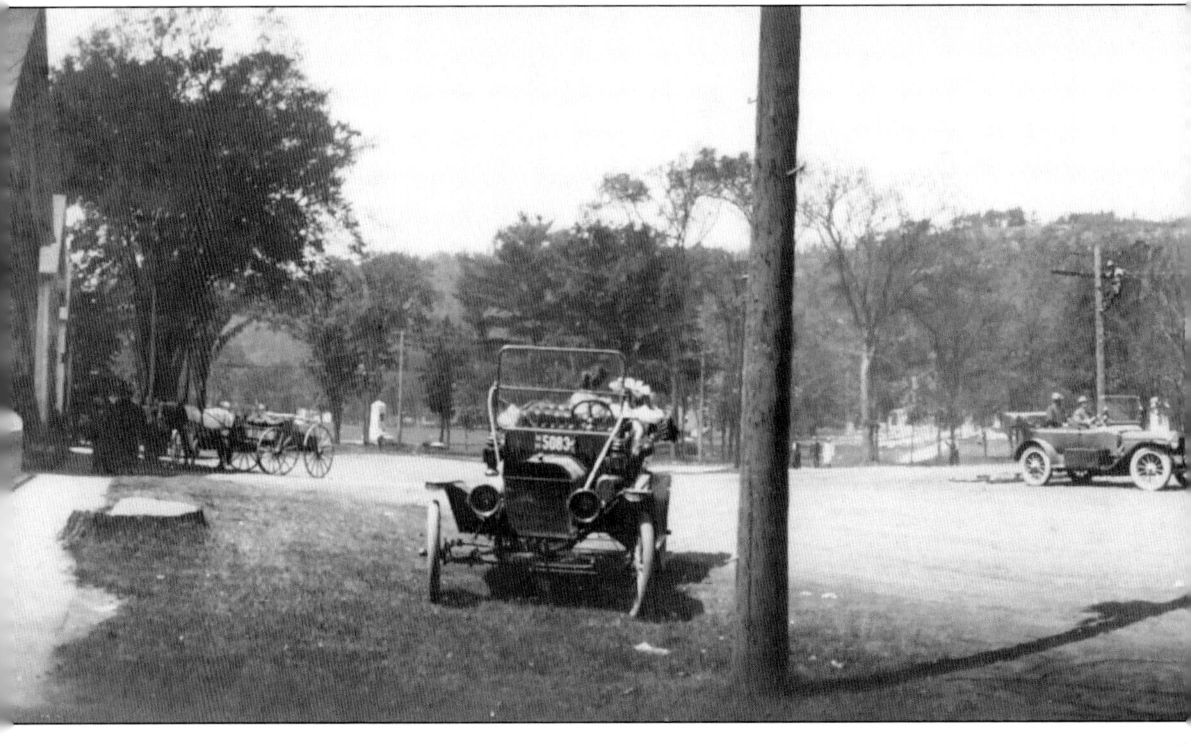

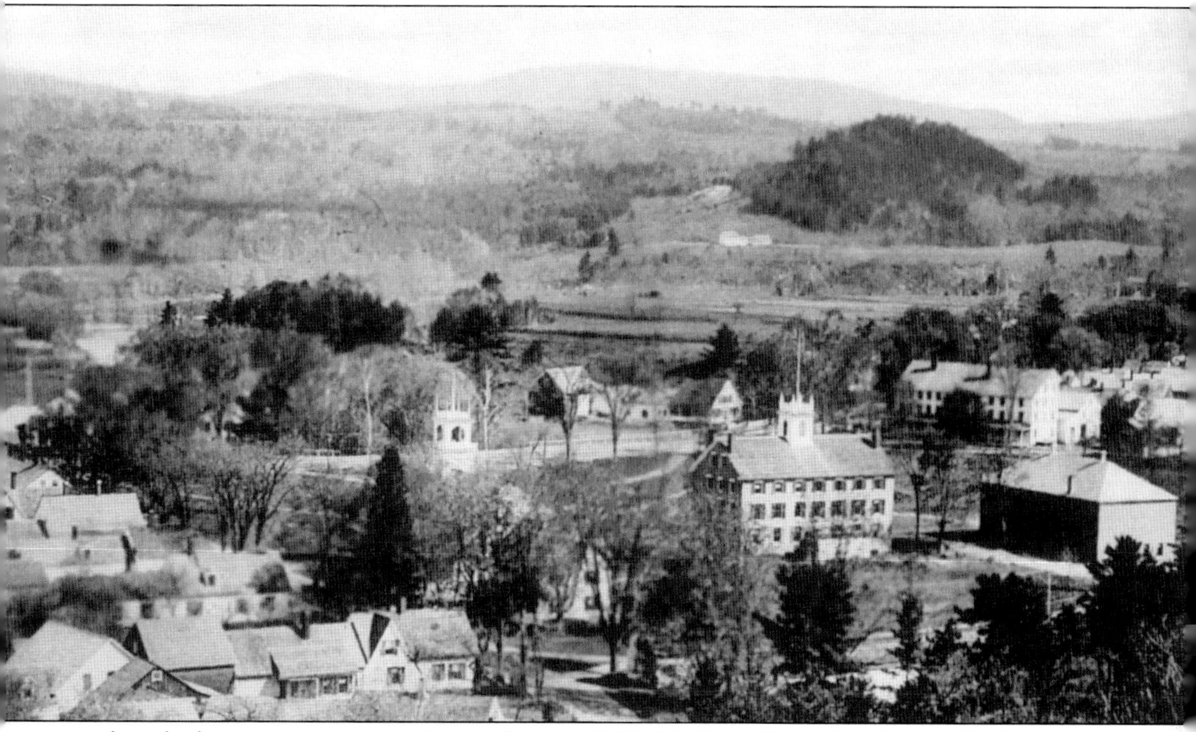

even though the seminary next to it was destroyed! Hale's Store burned and was rebuilt soon after with bricks. It is now the location of the Newbury Town Offices. The little brick town office next to Hale's is now a bank.

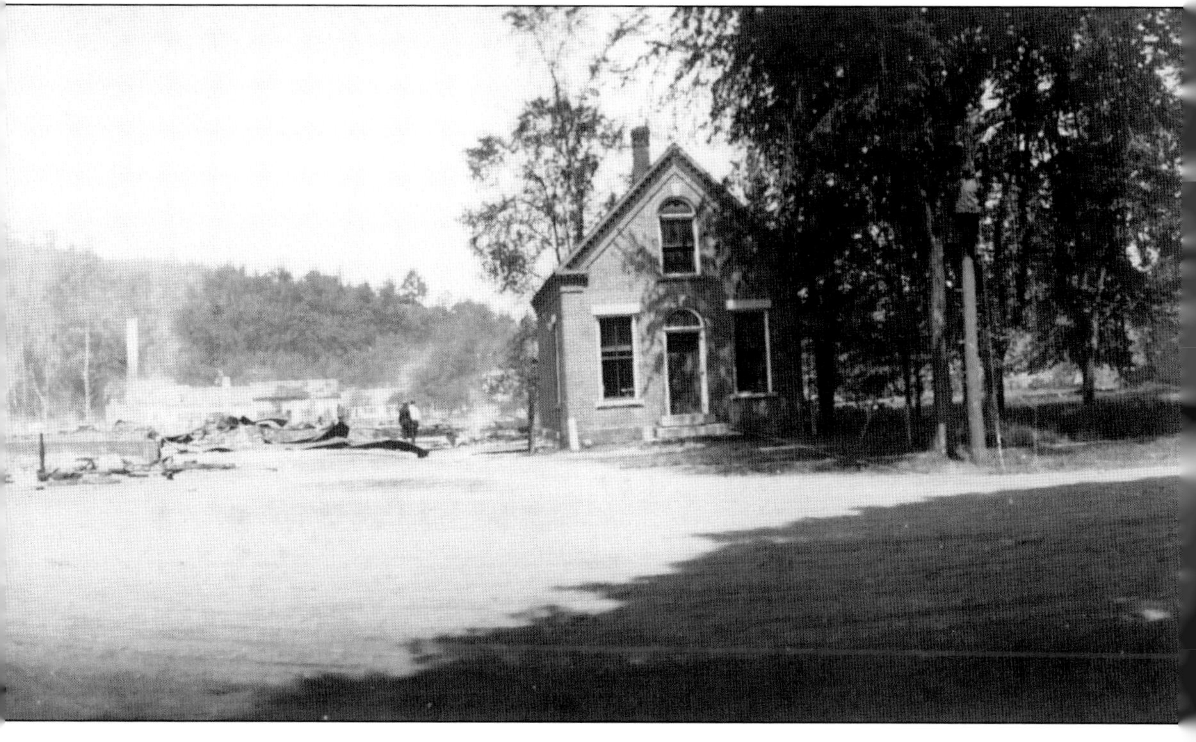

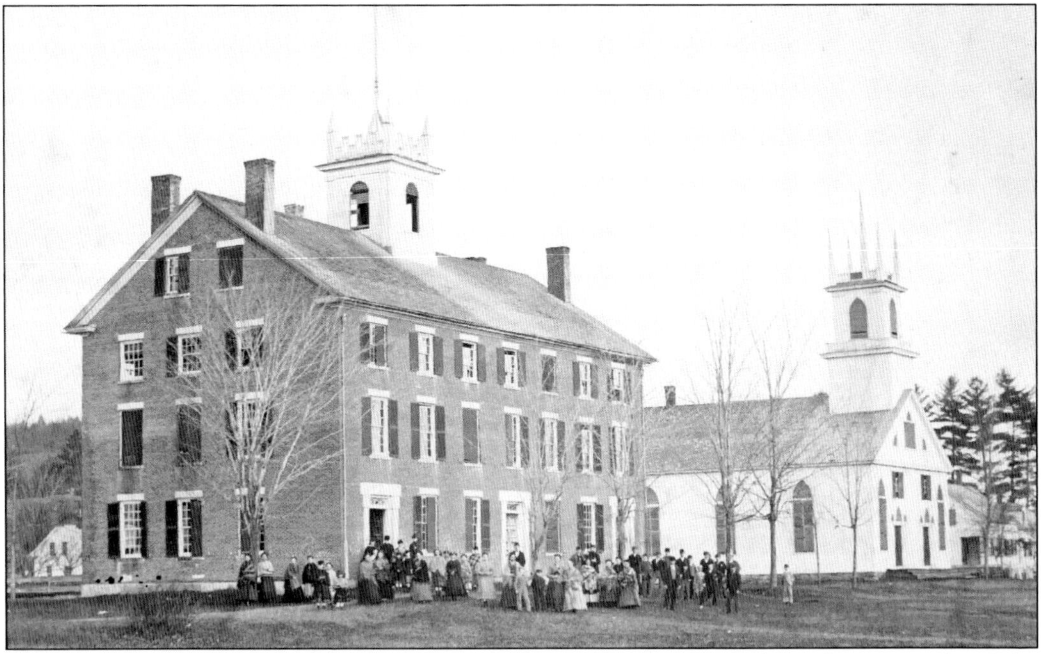

OLD NEWBURY SEMINARY, C. 1911. The seminary was located on the west side of the Newbury Common before being burned in the 1913 fire. At the time this photograph was taken, the steeple on the Methodist church was beginning to tilt slightly. The steeple was taken down in 1994, and the base was strengthened, completely rebuilt, and repositioned on the church thanks to the efforts of the Newbury Women's Club, many benefactors, and a state grant.

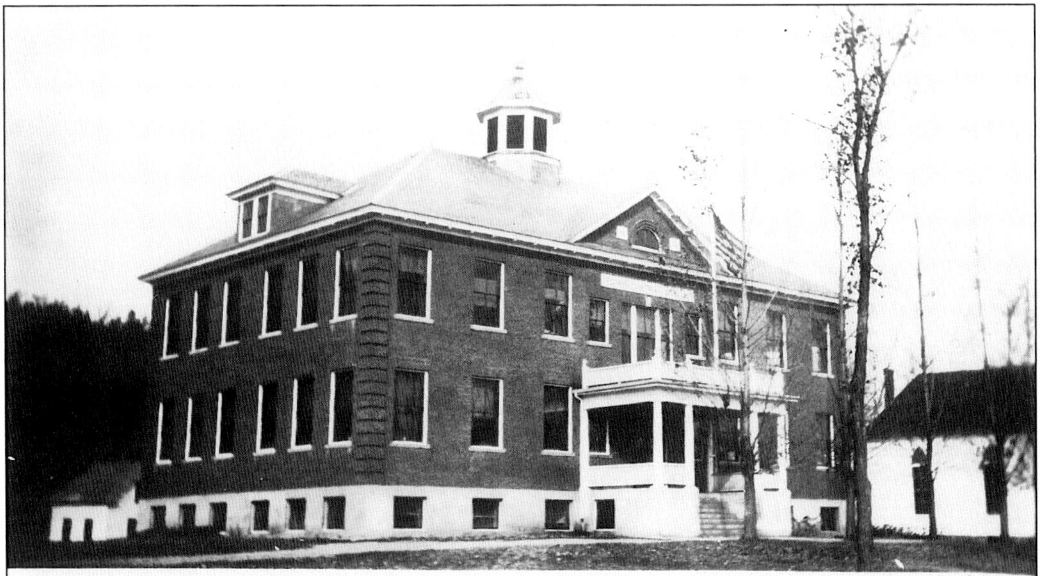

NEWBURY CENTRAL SCHOOL, C. 1920. This academic institution was constructed on the site of the old seminary building, next to the Methodist church. The school was later rebuilt and attached to the town hall building, also completely modernized by the taxpayers of Newbury in 1994.

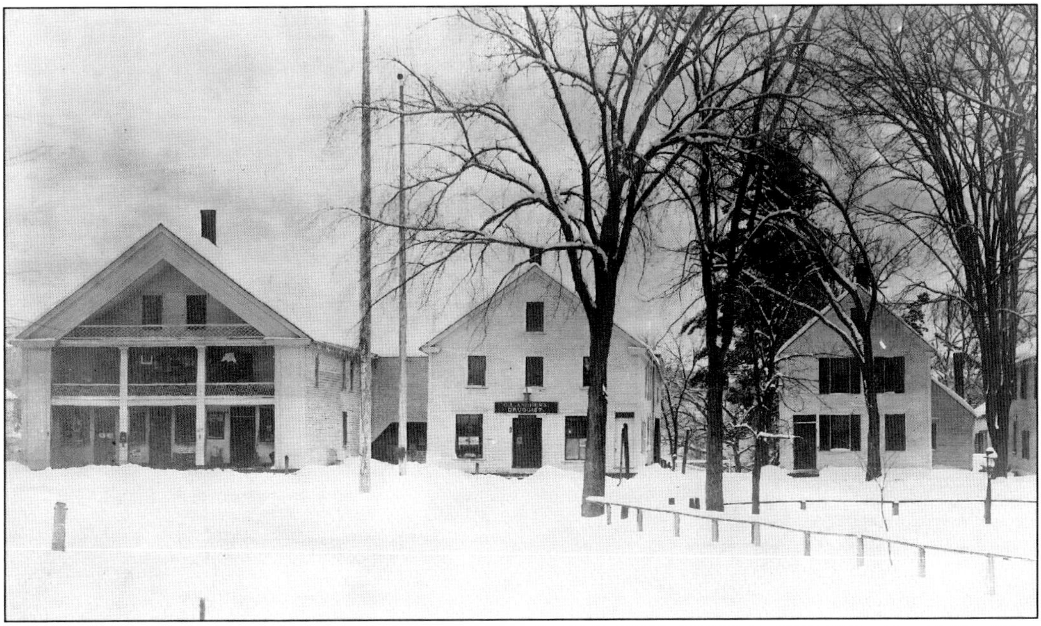

NEWBURY VILLAGE STORE AND G. L. ANDREWS DRUG STORE, C. 1915. The northeast corner of the Village Green (Route 5) shows a gas lamp and double flagpoles on the triangle.

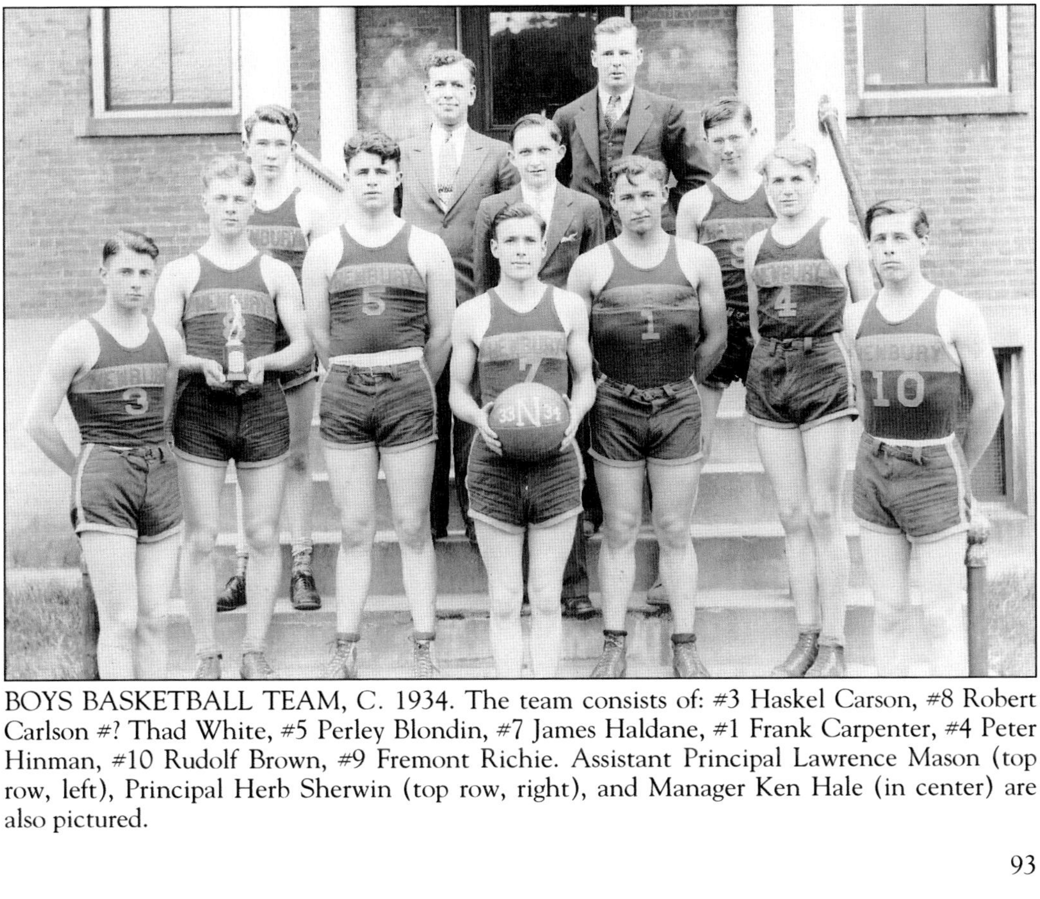

BOYS BASKETBALL TEAM, C. 1934. The team consists of: #3 Haskel Carson, #8 Robert Carlson #? Thad White, #5 Perley Blondin, #7 James Haldane, #1 Frank Carpenter, #4 Peter Hinman, #10 Rudolf Brown, #9 Fremont Richie. Assistant Principal Lawrence Mason (top row, left), Principal Herb Sherwin (top row, right), and Manager Ken Hale (in center) are also pictured.

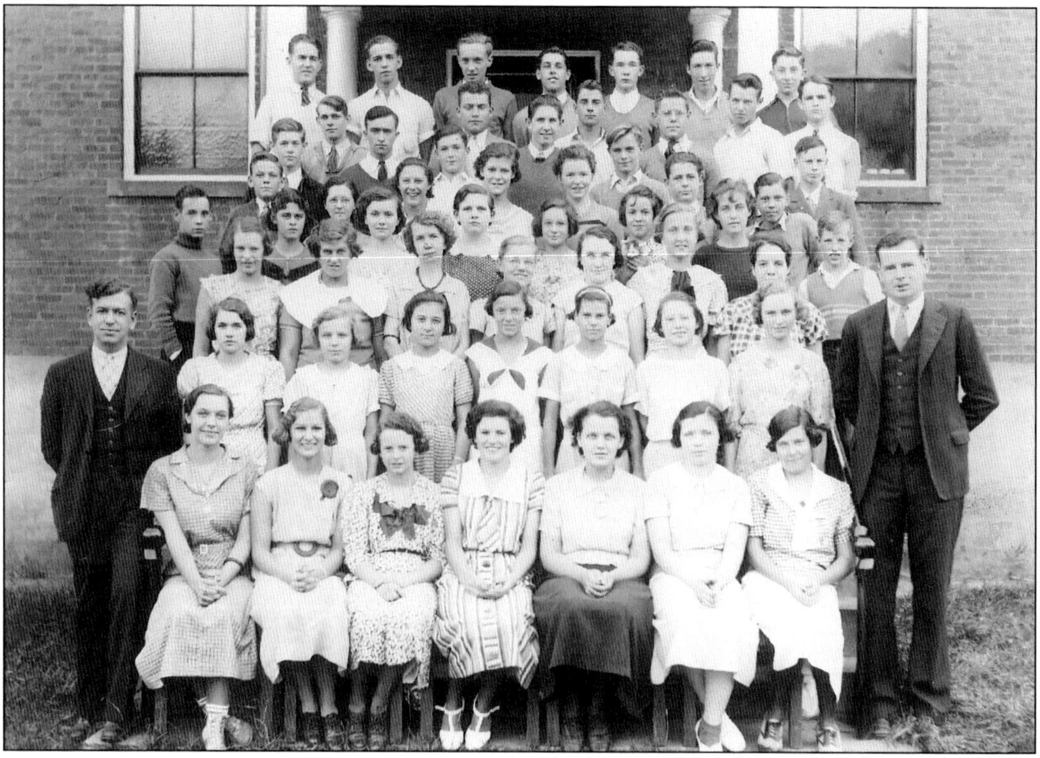

NEWBURY TOWN CENTRAL SCHOOL, AROUND OCTOBER 1935. Are *you* here? Some names are: George Demick, Thad White, Henry Rollins, Junie Hebb, John Renfrew, Olive Young, Margaret Meserve, Barbara Thompson, Jean Tyler, Hazel Henderson, and Ethel Putnam.

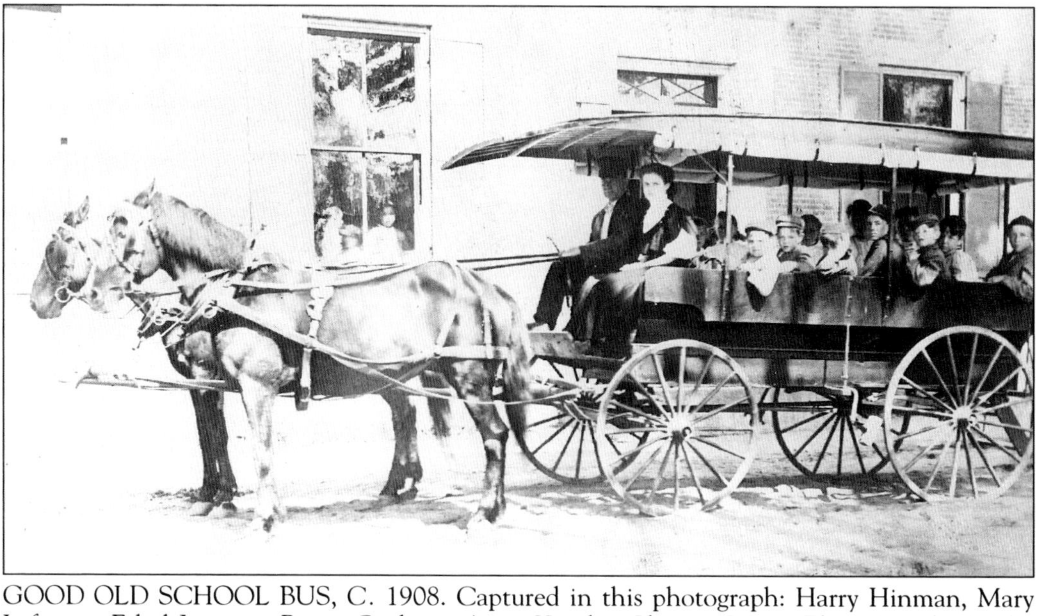

GOOD OLD SCHOOL BUS, C. 1908. Captured in this photograph: Harry Hinman, Mary Lafrance, Ethel Jessman, Bessie Gorham, Artur Knight, Chester Stone, Elmer Knight, Leslie Hildreth, Clarence Stone, Olean Lafrance, and two friendly, reliable horses!

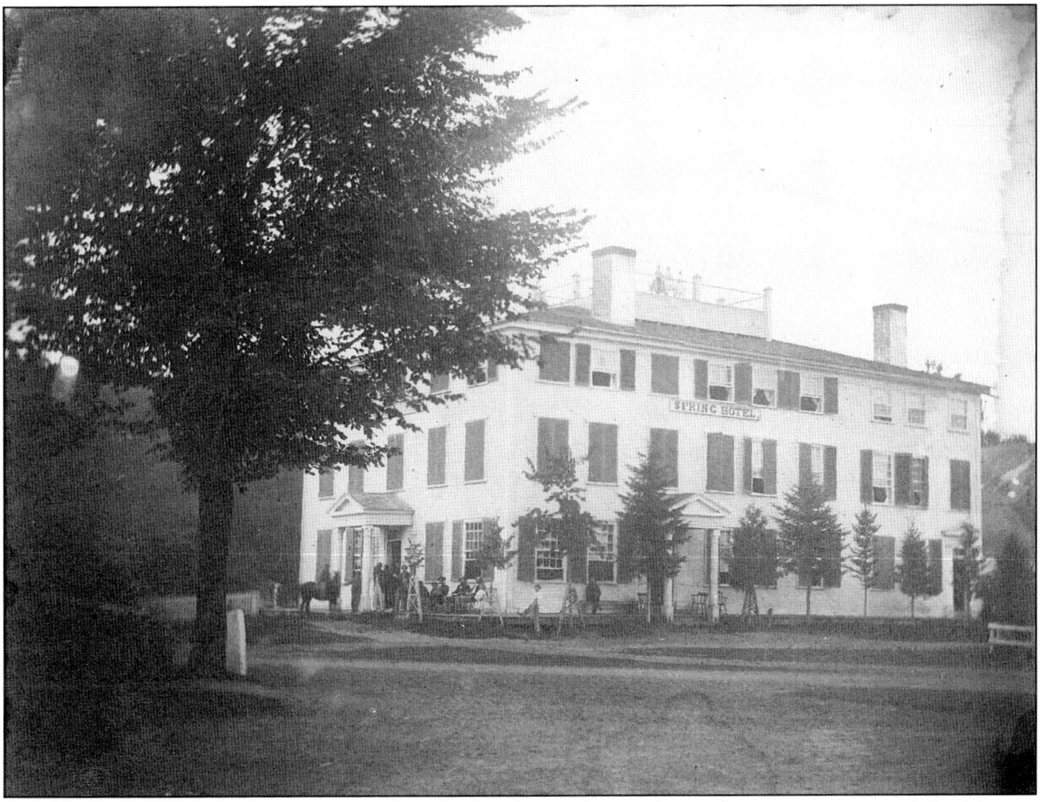

SPRING HOTEL, C. 1879. The Spring Hotel was located on the present site of the Tenny Library. The hotel was destroyed by a fire on September 5, 1879.

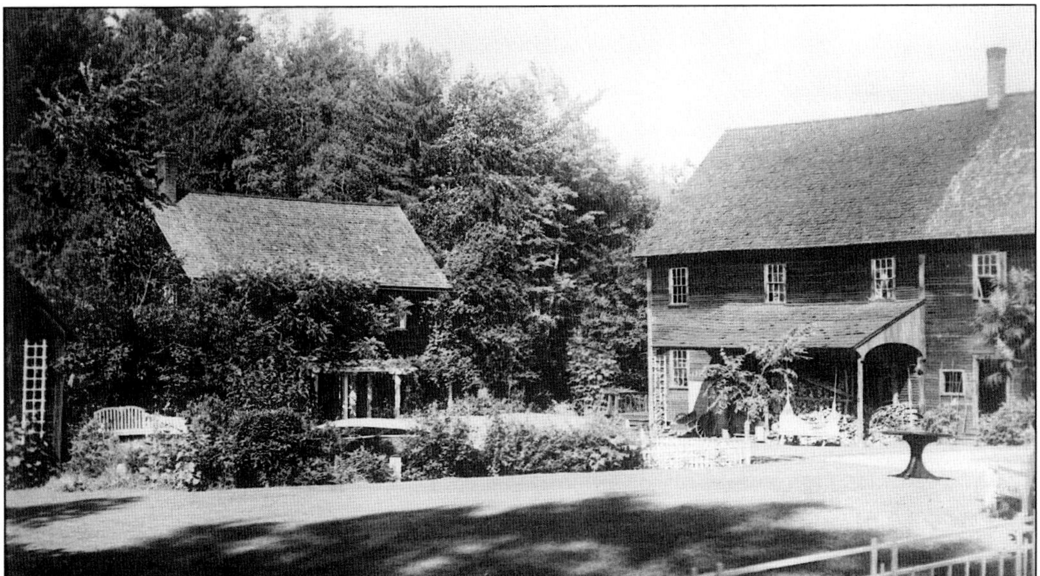

"TWINFLOWER," C. 1900. This is the famous Tea House Restaurant on Snake Road in South Newbury with its beautiful gardens, paths, arbors, boat pond, and waterfalls along the brook. It is currently the home of Bob and Margaret Erickson.

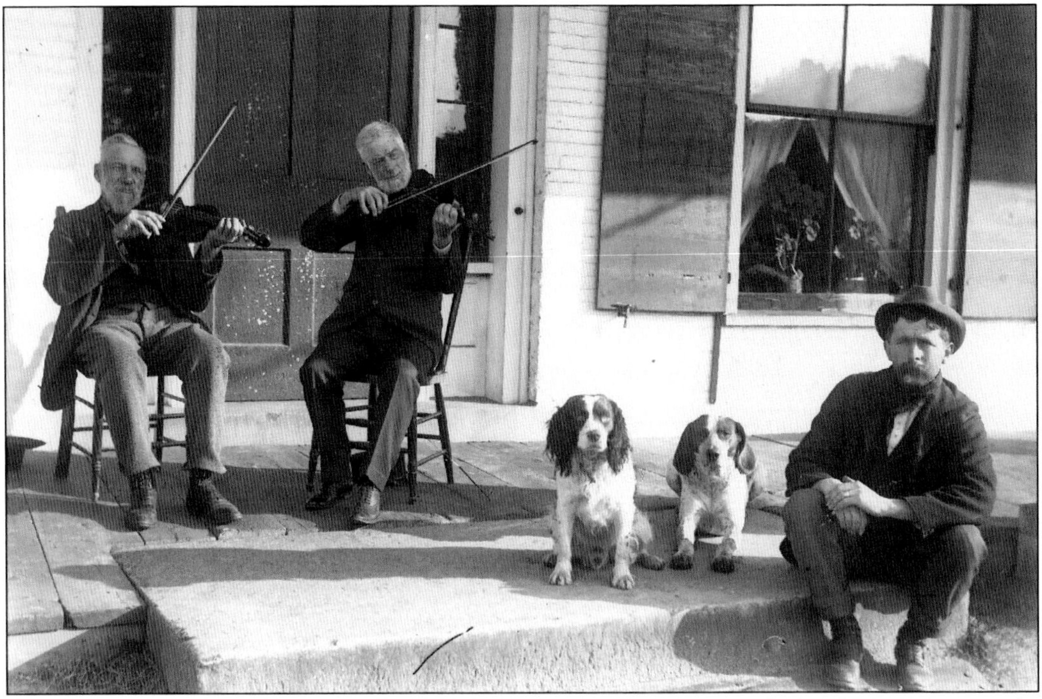

SUNDAY FIDDLERS, C. 1890. Two fiddlers play on the front porch for their audience of a pair of beagle hounds and a friend.

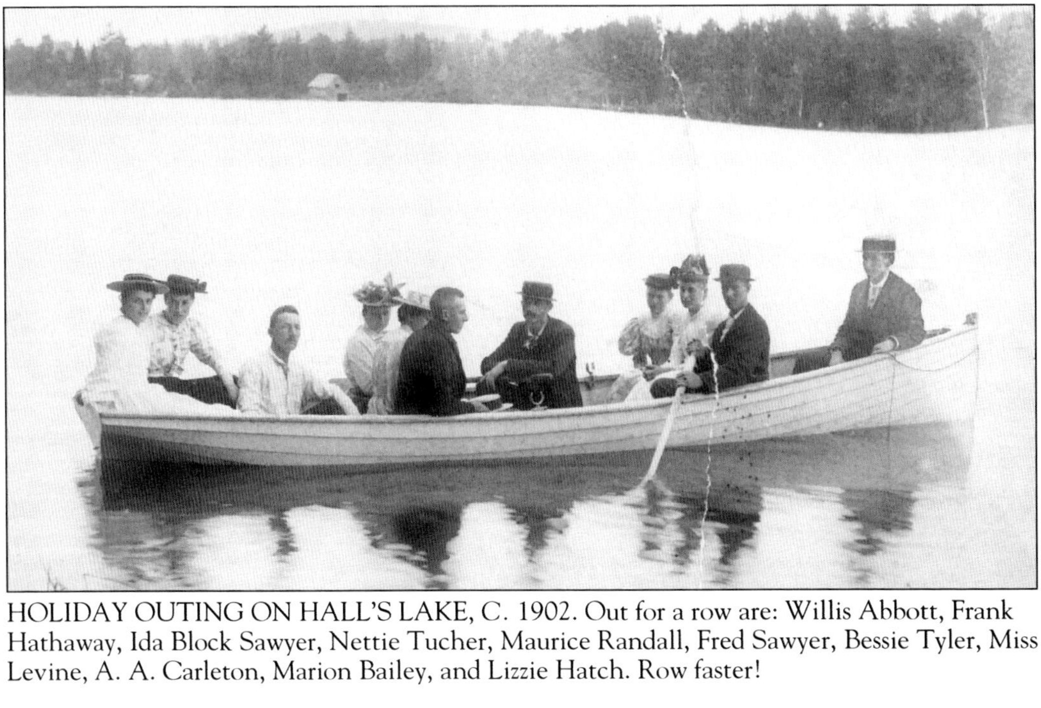

HOLIDAY OUTING ON HALL'S LAKE, C. 1902. Out for a row are: Willis Abbott, Frank Hathaway, Ida Block Sawyer, Nettie Tucher, Maurice Randall, Fred Sawyer, Bessie Tyler, Miss Levine, A. A. Carleton, Marion Bailey, and Lizzie Hatch. Row faster!

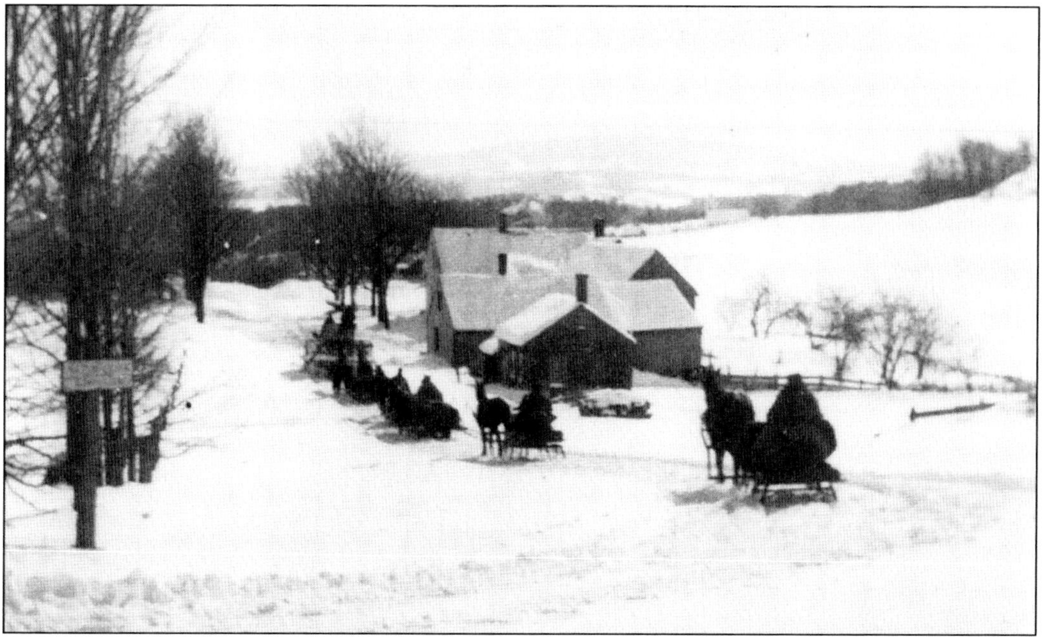

SNOWROLLER, C. 1900. The town snowroller leads local sleds through West Newbury from North Road and Tucker Mtn. Road down Snake Road, past the old blacksmith's shop, and down into town.

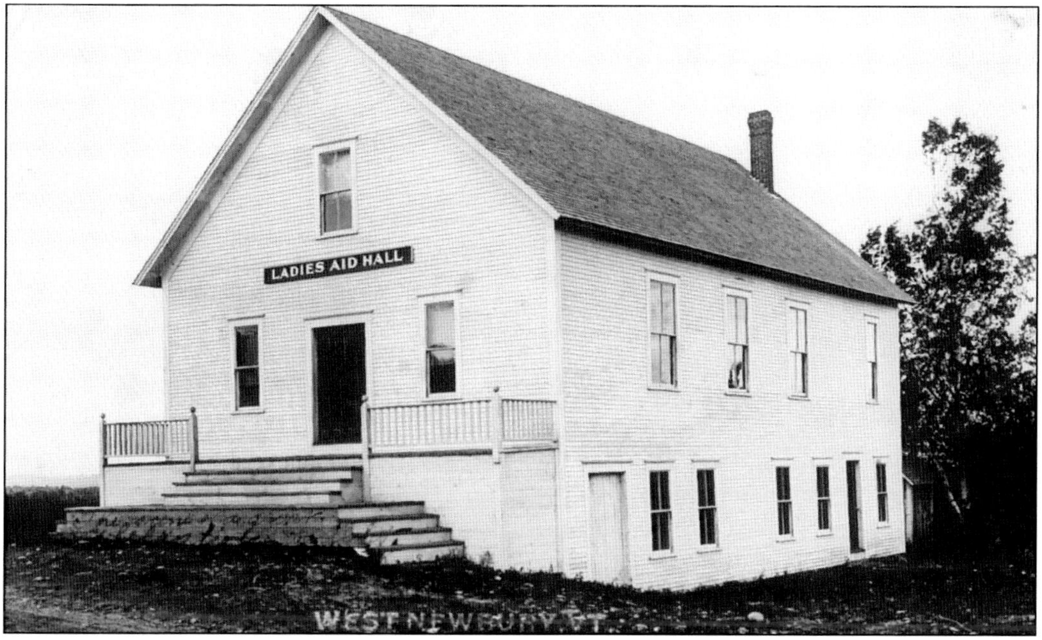

LADIES AID HALL, C. 1910. This is the old hall in West Newbury where the annual famous turkey dinners are served in October by members of the community.

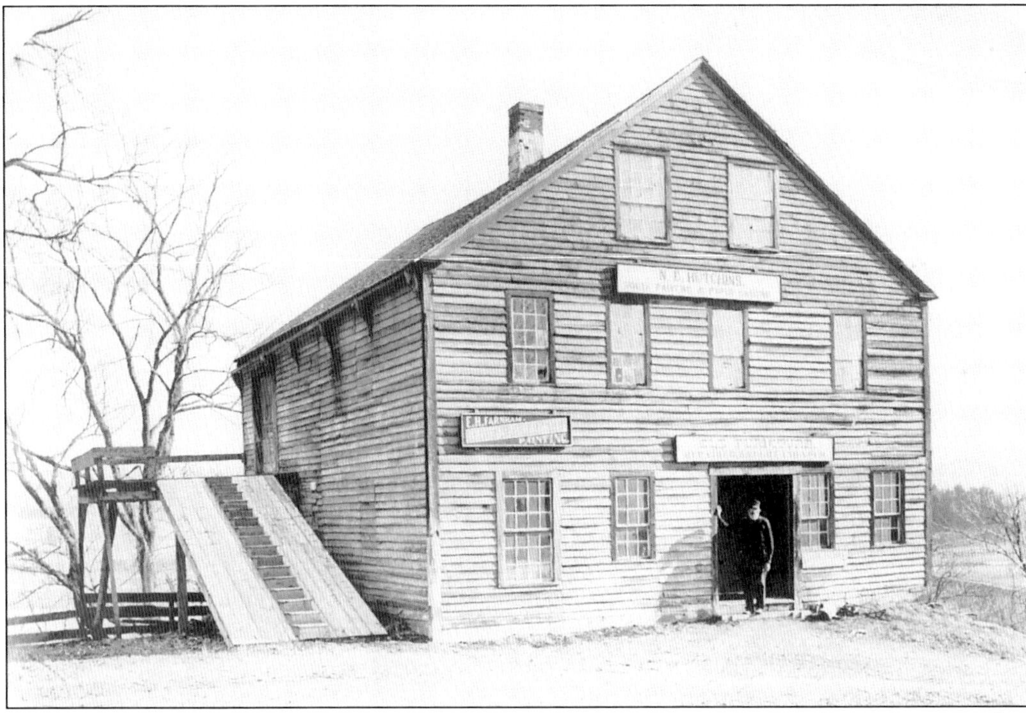

FARNHAM'S SHOP, C. 1900. This painting and old furniture shop was located just south of the Frances Atkinson House, below Mrs. Salter's home.

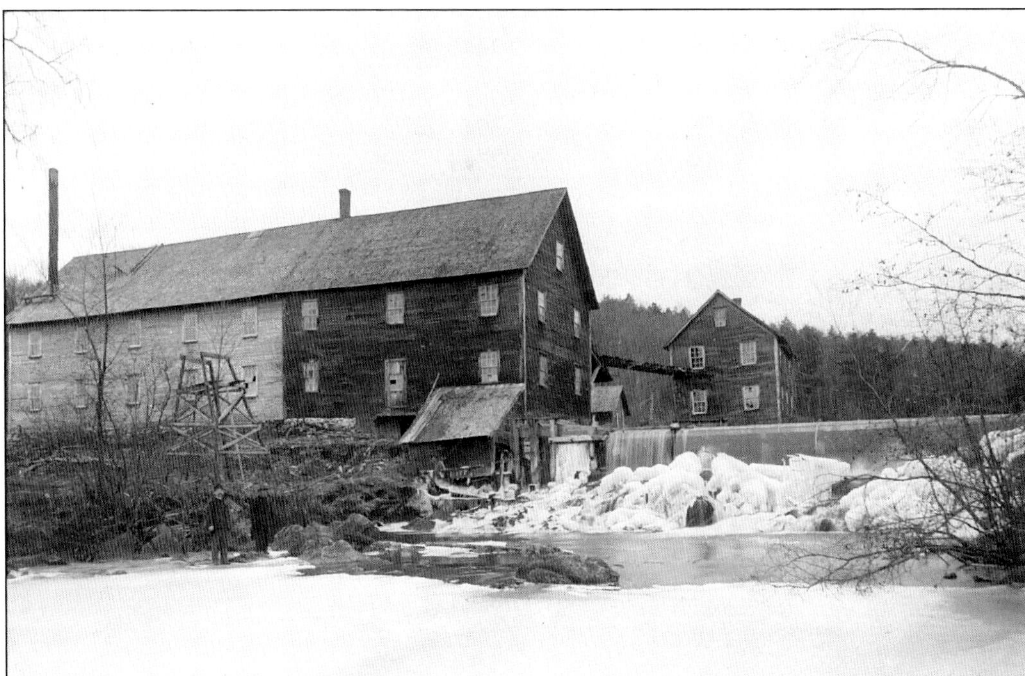

THE A. A. OLMSTEAD SAWMILL, C. 1900. (Dr. Rachel H. Allyn and Evelyn Allyn McDonald photograph.)

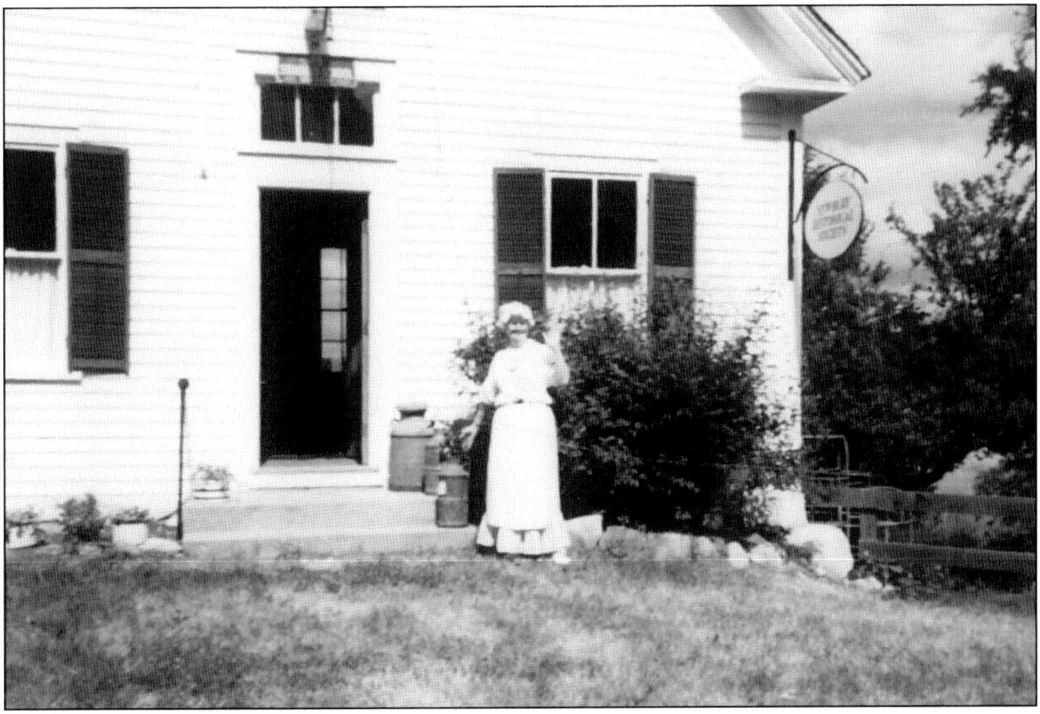

NEWBURY HISTORICAL SOCIETY SCHOOLHOUSE, C. 1884. In 1994 we celebrated the centennial of our rebuilt and refurbished schoolhouse in West Newbury. Here, Mary Marsar, one of the local members, greets guests to the kitchenware display in July 1995.

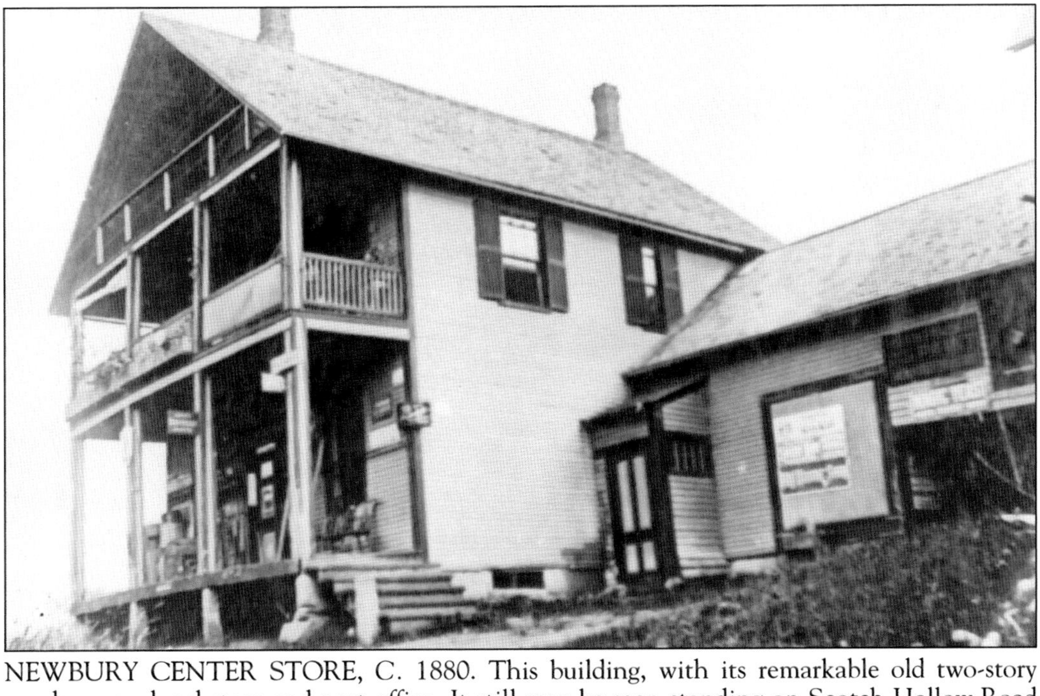

NEWBURY CENTER STORE, C. 1880. This building, with its remarkable old two-story porch, was a local store and post office. It still may be seen standing on Scotch Hollow Road near the Meyette Farm in Newbury Center.

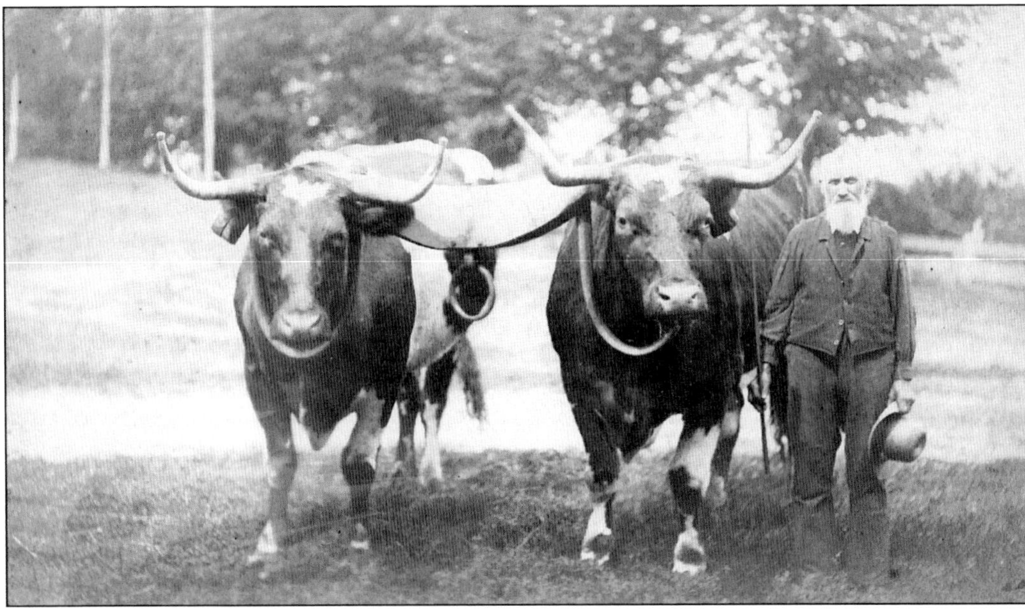

OLDTIME OXEN TEAM, C. 1870. W. C. Carleton drives his team on the West Newbury Maple Grove Farm. This farm has been in the same family for five generations, and dairy products and maple syrup continue to be produced here today.

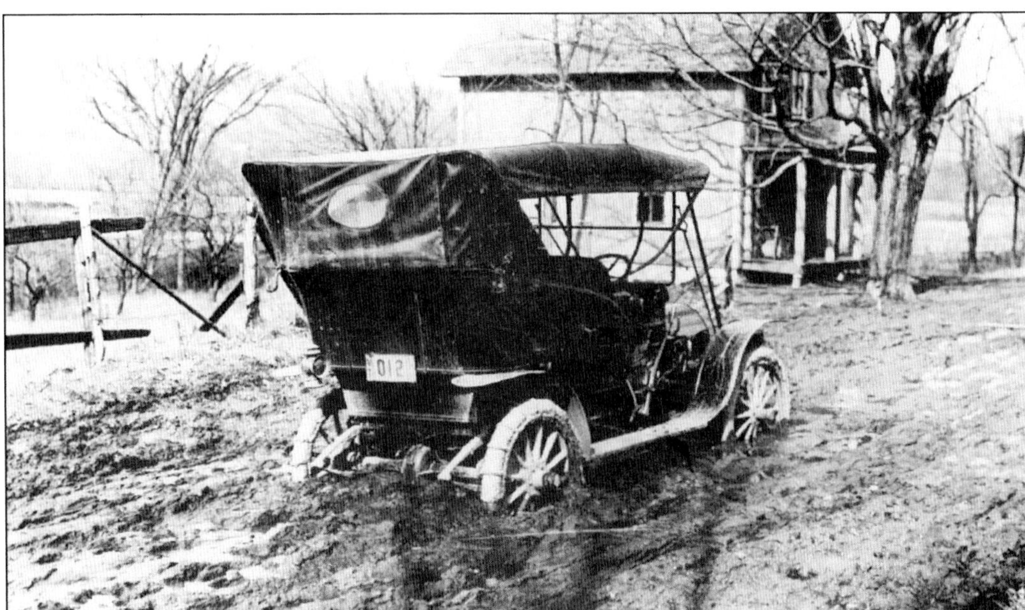

SPRING DRIVE, C. 1913. One of the road hazards of spring touring on old Route 5—"mud season" on Vermont back roads.

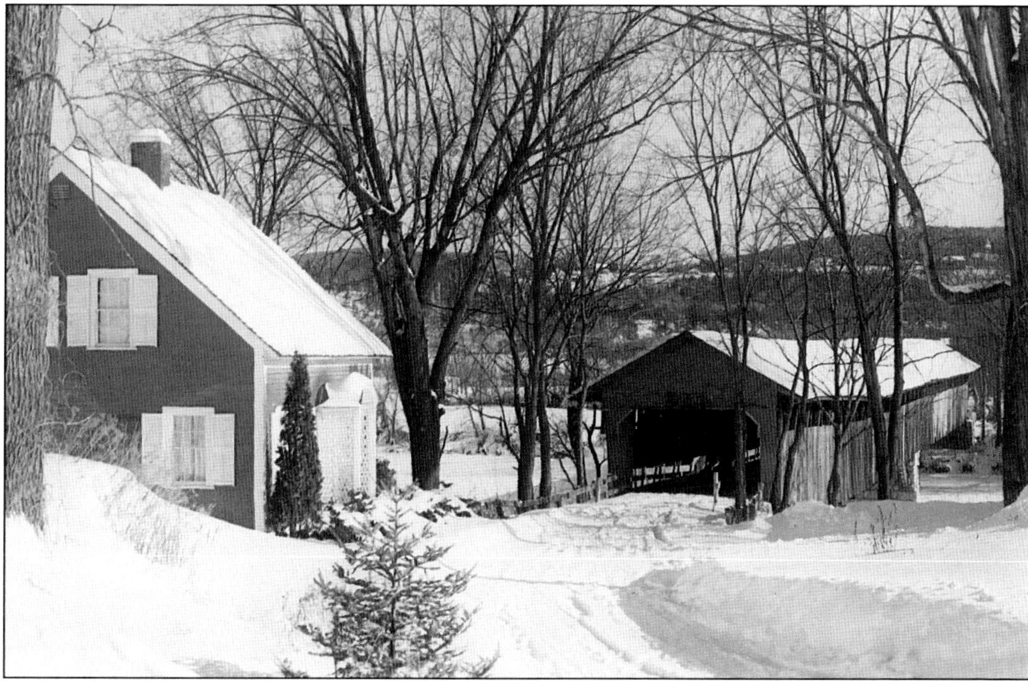

THE BEDELL COVERED BRIDGE, C. 1866. Below, the bridge is pictured during the 1927 flood. Notice that the old flood warning tower is almost underwater itself. The bridge was rebuilt and refitted in 1974 by a twin-state group of concerned citizens. Its design is the famous "Patent Arch Truss" by Theodore Burr, used for many wooden bridges of the era. Its 396-foot length made it the fourth longest in the U.S., and it ran from South Newbury, Vermont, to Haverhill, New Hampshire, over the Connecticut River. Only stone pillars remain where this engineering marvel once stood. It was destroyed by a violent windstorm on September 14, 1979.

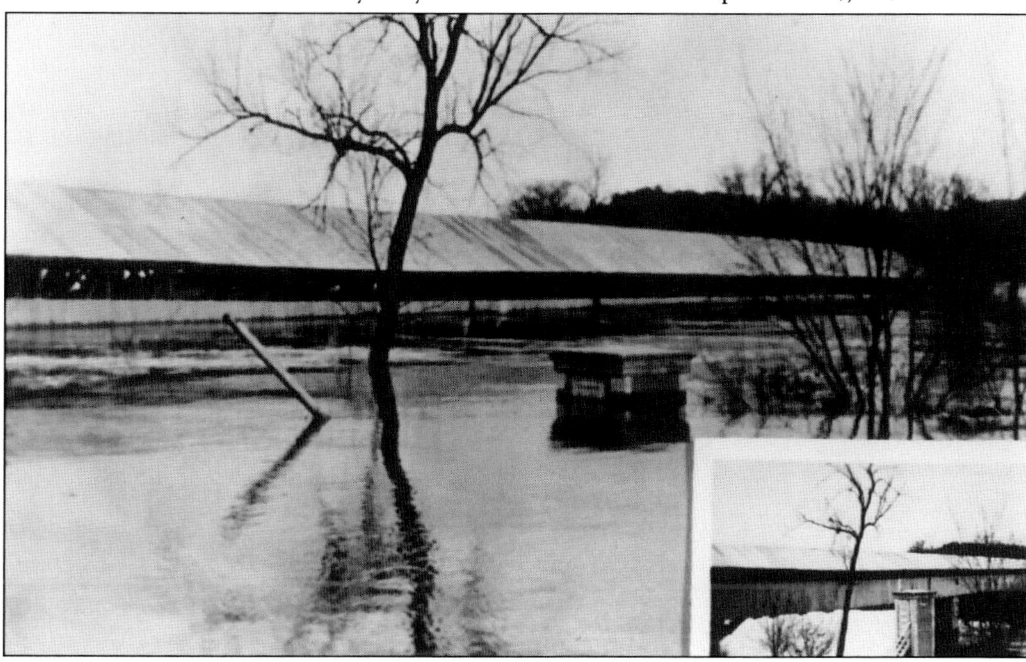

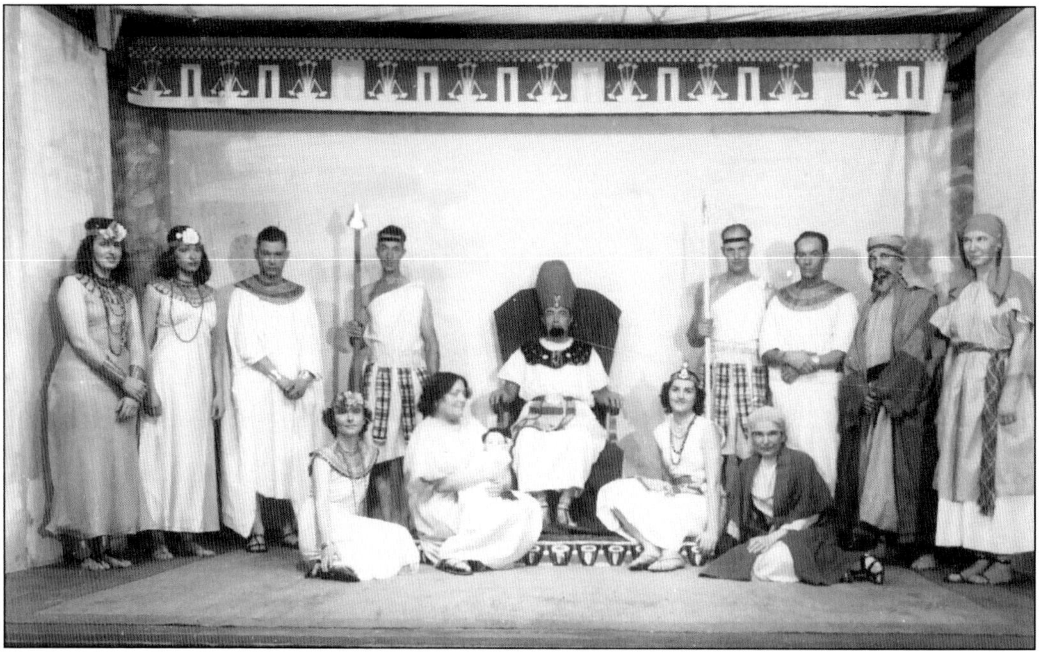

THE PHARAOH'S DAUGHTER, C. 1946. Players in this West Newbury theater group were, from left to right: (seated) Catherine Brock, Lena Staples, Polly Williams, Esther Urquhart, and ?; (standing) Jan Halley, Bea Putnam, Dean Staples, Jim Halley, Carlton Barnett (on throne), Walter Staples, Stanley Brock, Bob Urquhart, and Ruth Barnett.

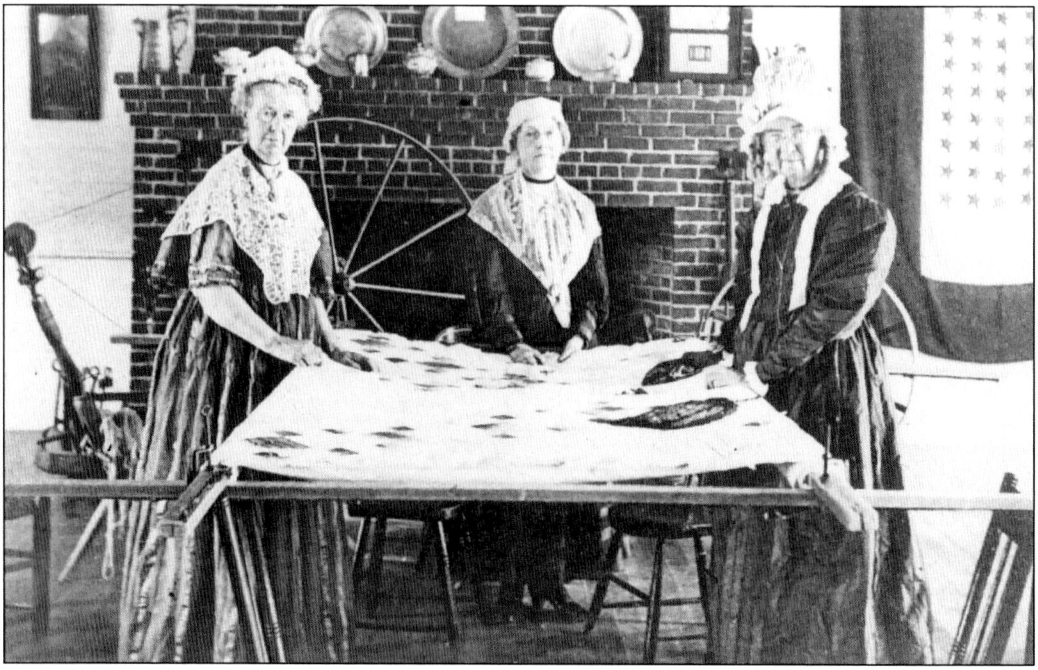

NEWBURY DAUGHTERS OF THE AMERICAN REVOLUTION, C. 1922. Inside the D.A.R. historic building at a quilting are, from left to right: Clara Atkinson, Emma Kimball, and Hattie Keyes.

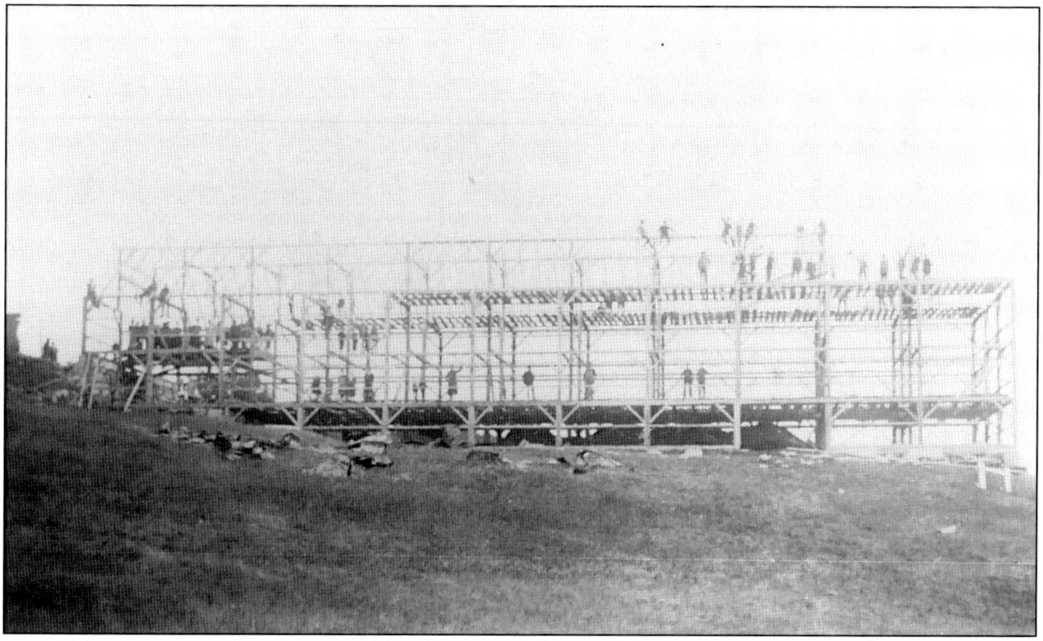

BIG BARN BUILDING, C. 1907. A remarkable shot shows many community men from Newbury during the construction of a huge barn on land near the present West Newbury Post Office. The women were down below preparing on-site meals. The barn was on the Carleton farm.

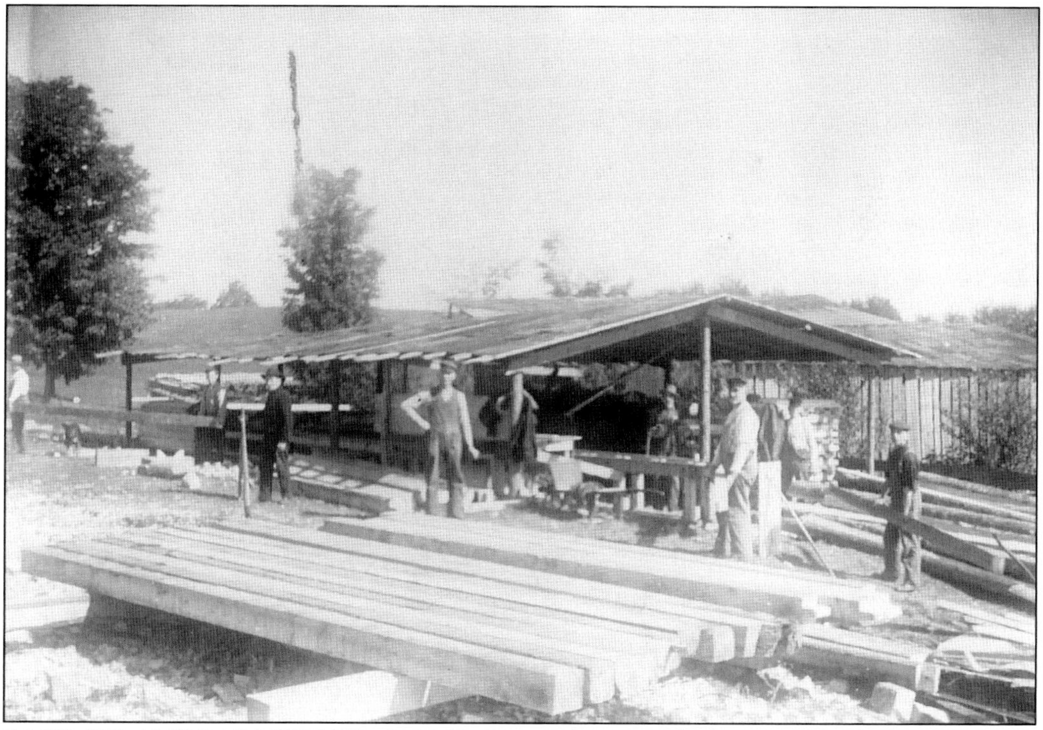

SAWMILL AND BARN WOOD, C. 1907. Cutting beams and other wood for the barn-building was quite an operation and took a lot of trees.

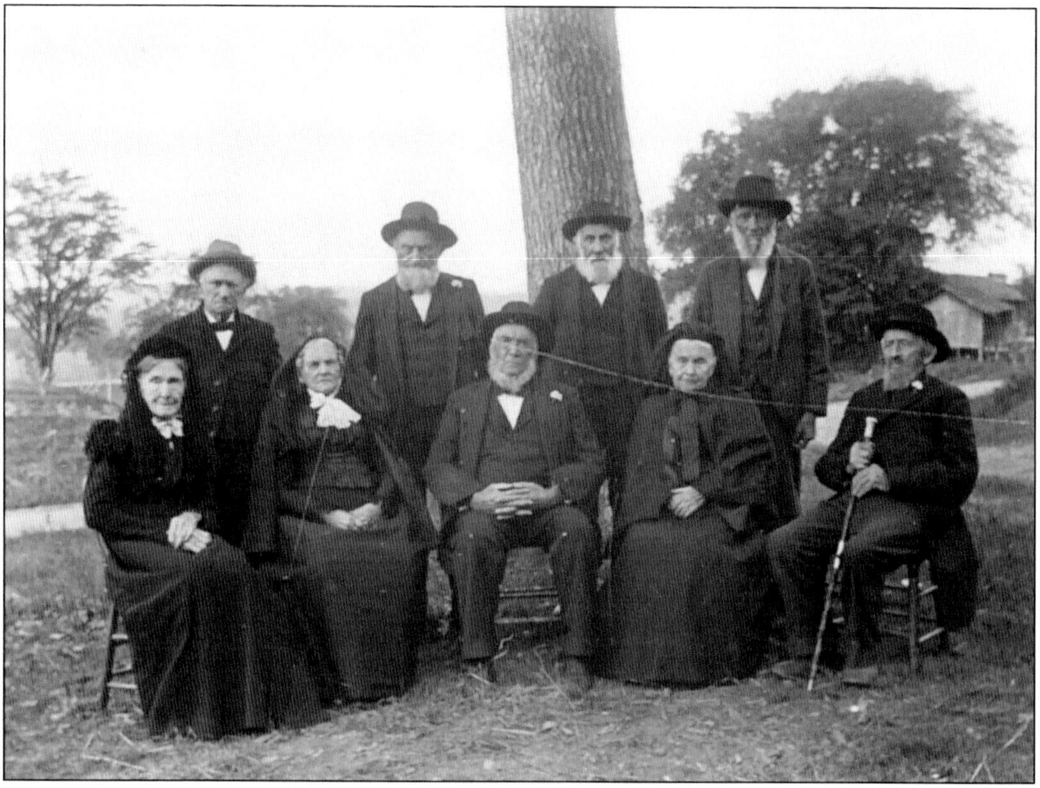

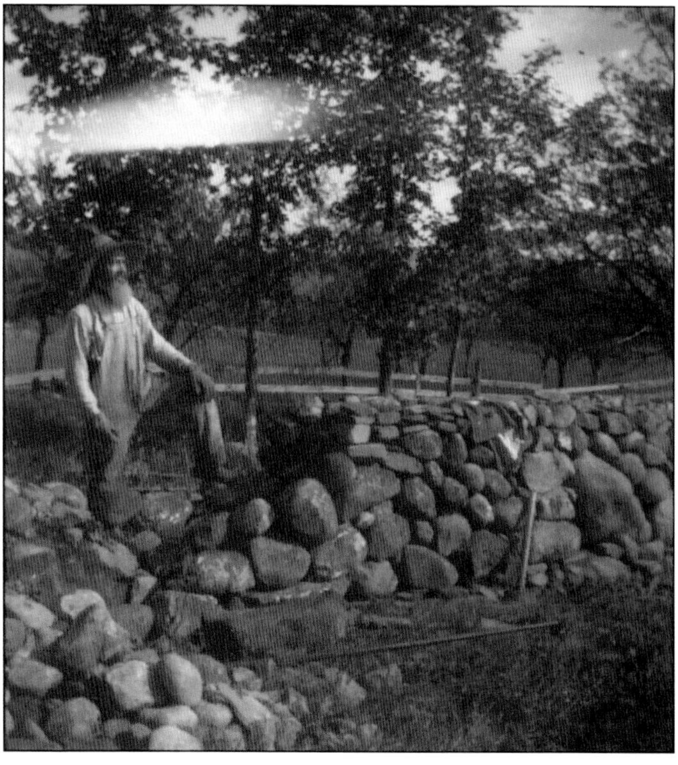

NEWBURY OVER EIGHTY CLUB, C. 1898. These old folks are, from left to right: (standing) Wallace Brock, W. C. Carleton, Israel Willard, Harry Stevens; (seated) Mrs. Severance, Mary Ann Clark Rowe, Moses Rowe (on his eighty-eighth birthday), Mrs. Tewksbury (relative and lookalike of Marjorie Peach), and O. B. Rogers.

MOSES BROCK WALL, C. 1898. Moses Brock is shown constructing a farm stone wall, often seen as a work of art, left to future generations. Today we marvel at these oldtimers' great strength and abilities.

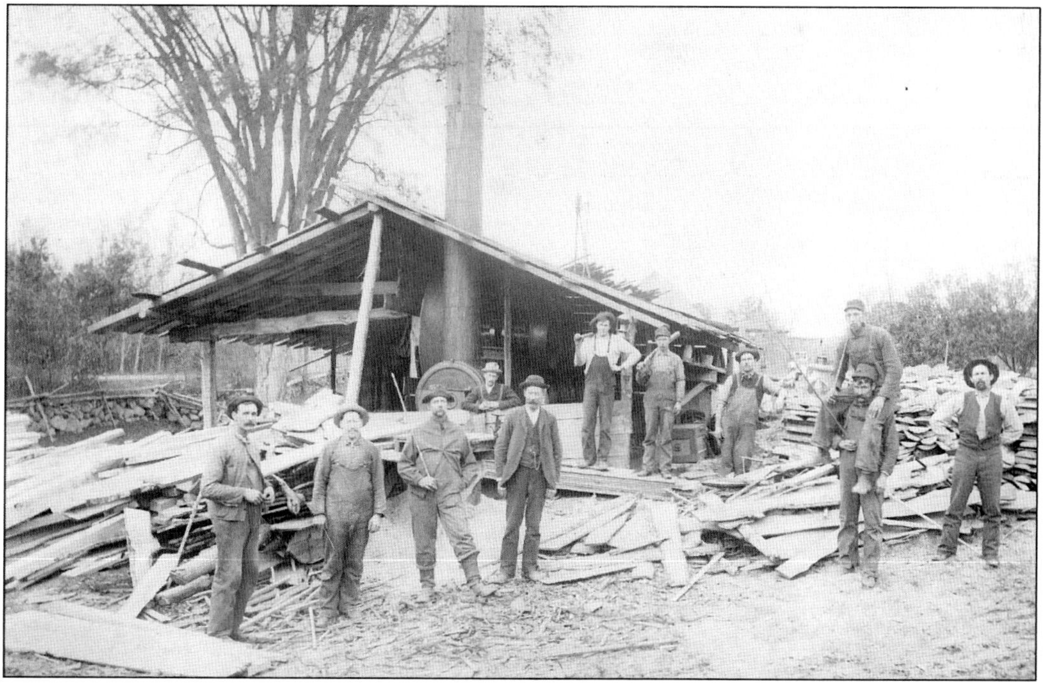

SAWMILL BUSINESS, C. 1905. The William Bailey Sawmill operated in Newbury Center, cutting much of the timber for local homes and farms. (W. C. Rideout photograph.)

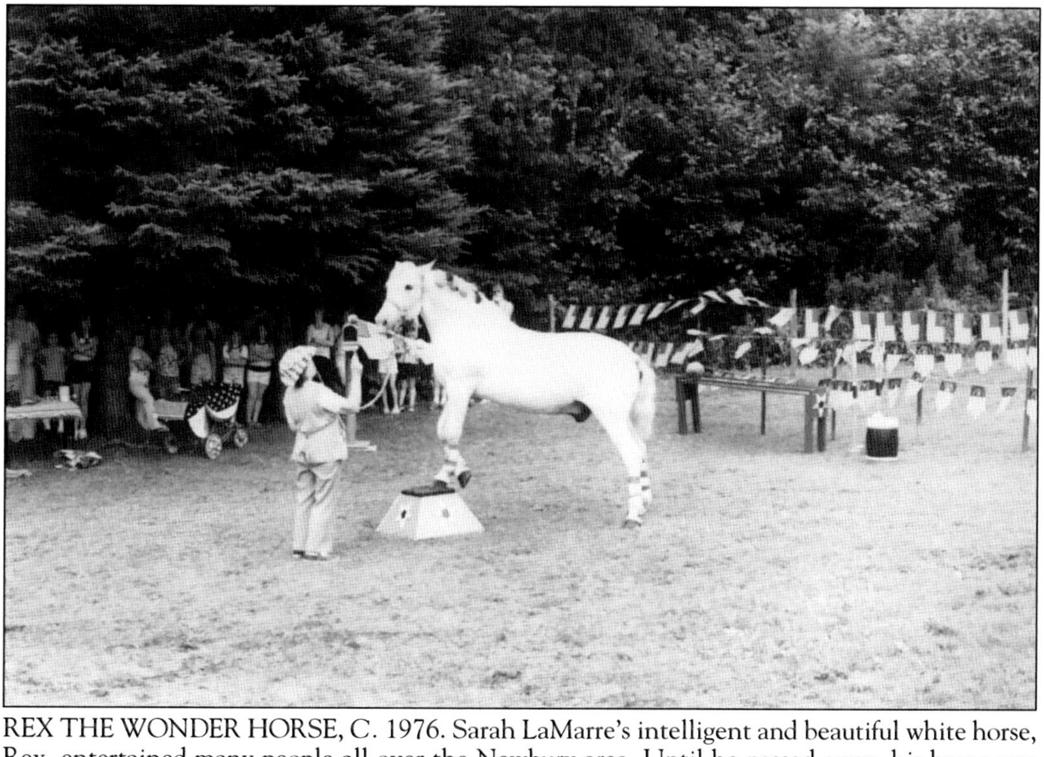

REX THE WONDER HORSE, C. 1976. Sarah LaMarre's intelligent and beautiful white horse, Rex, entertained many people all over the Newbury area. Until he passed away, his home was in Wells River on Route 302 .

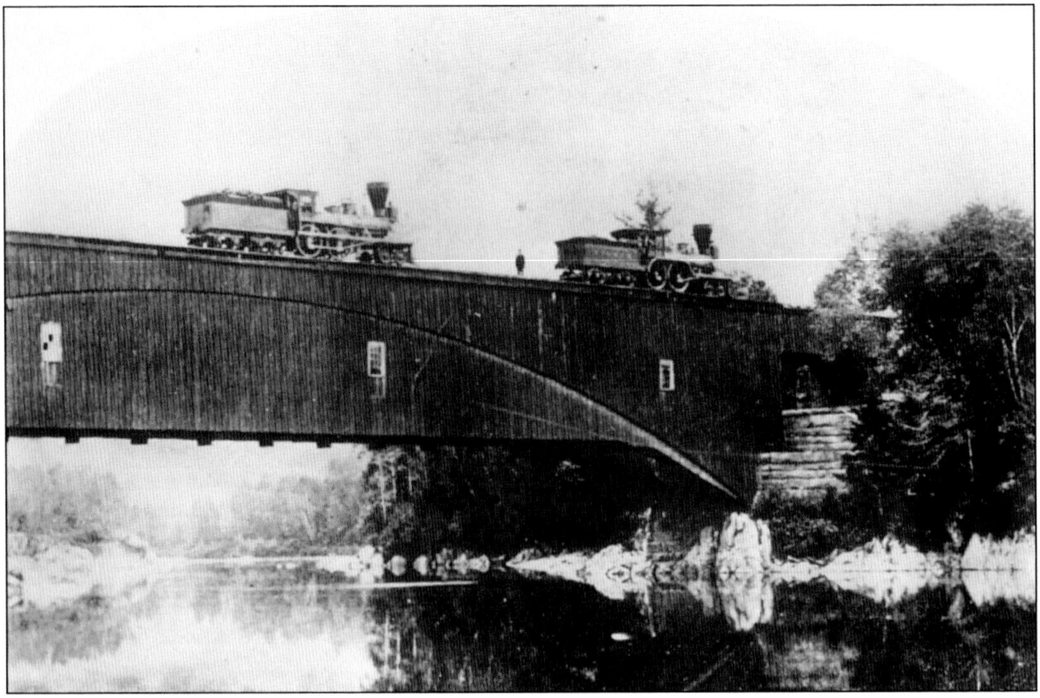

RAILROAD AND HIGHWAY BRIDGE, C. 1920. BC & M engines (possibly the Granite State and McDuffee) and trains chugged overhead as cars and wagons moved along inside from Wells River to Woodsville, New Hampshire.

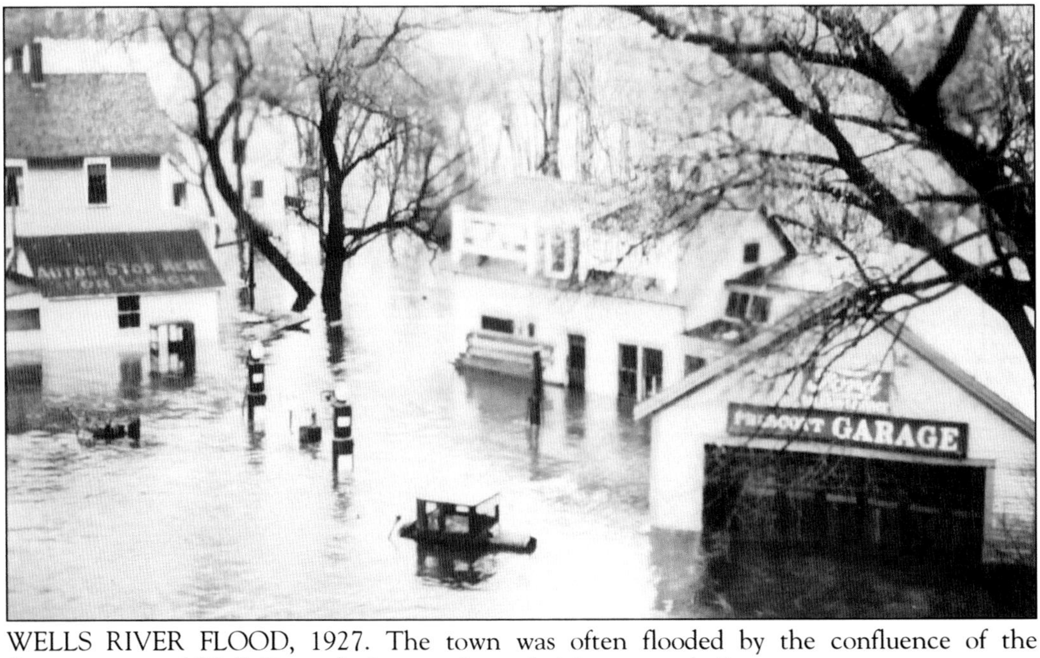

WELLS RIVER FLOOD, 1927. The town was often flooded by the confluence of the Connecticut and Wells Rivers before much-needed dams were built.

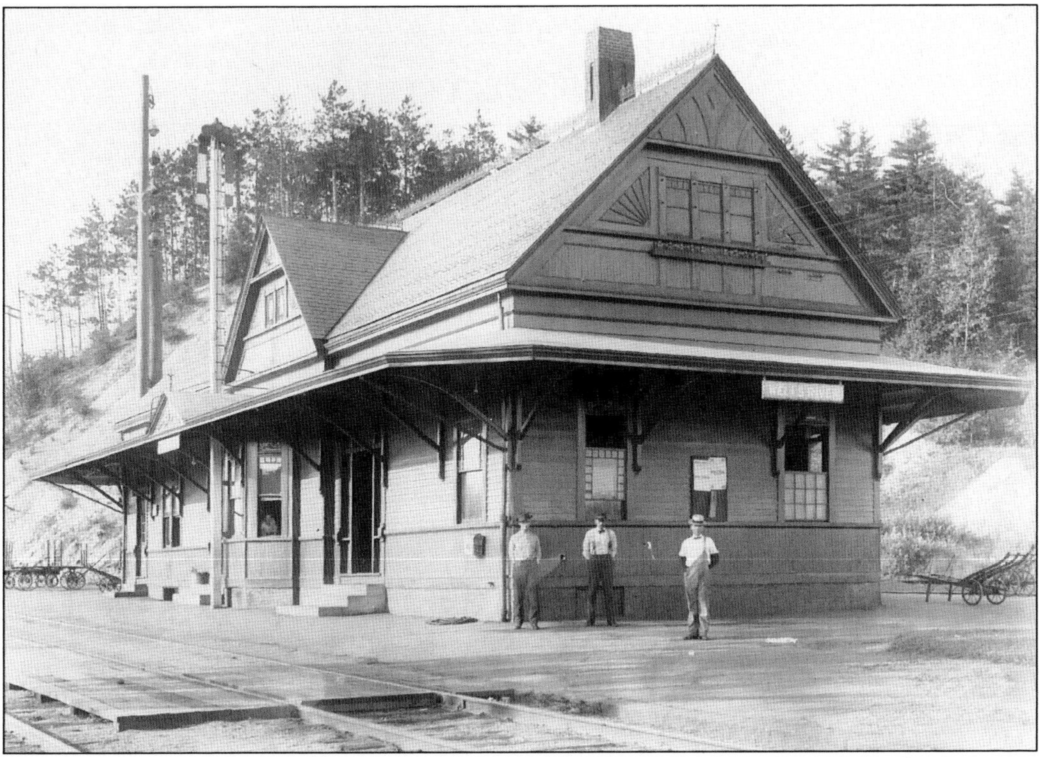

RAILROAD STATION, C. 1920. Wells River Station is shown, with Dean Gochey, George Leonard, and Ed Donahue in attendance. The station was lost to fire in 1974.

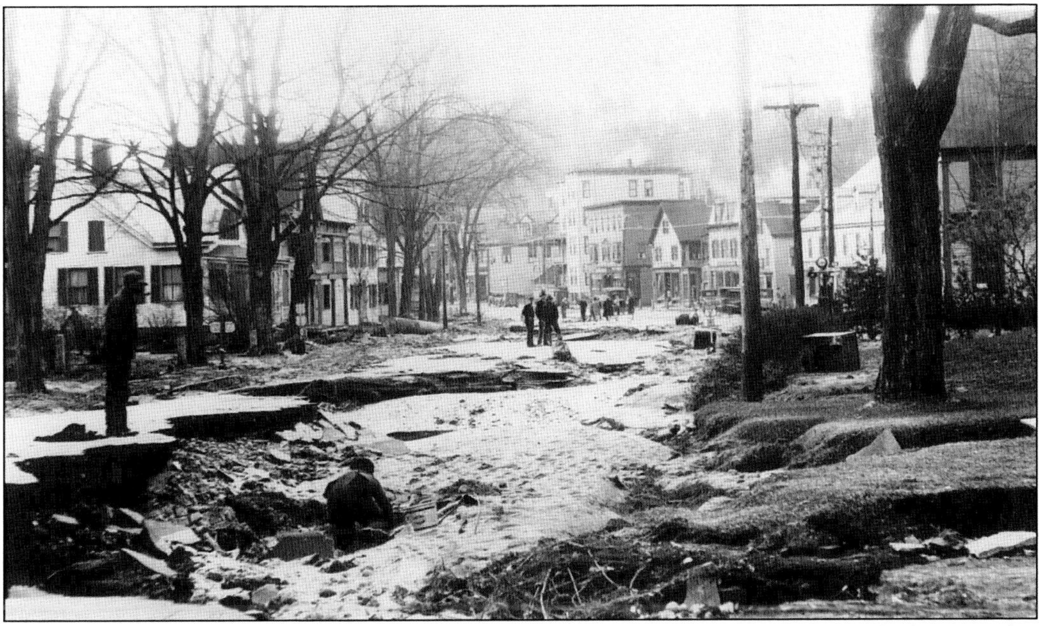

WELLS RIVER FLOOD, 1927. This is Main Street, as it looked after the flood of 1927. This flood devastated roads in many town areas.

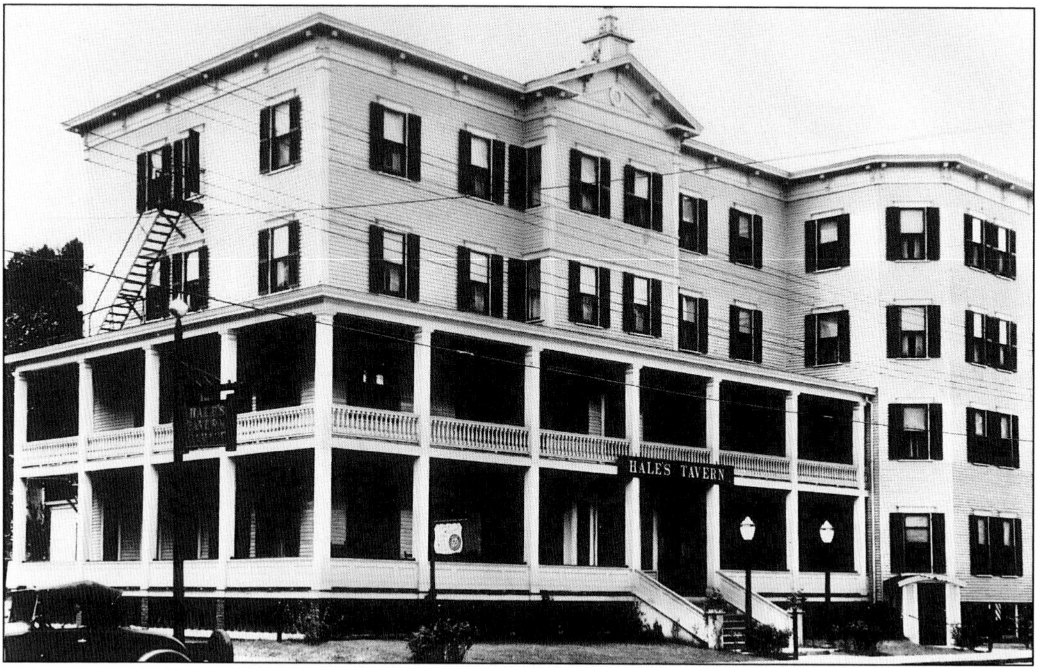

HALE'S TAVERN, C. 1900. Hale's was a popular meeting place for travelers and members of area clubs, including the New England Fat Men's Club, where you had to be 200 pounds or over to be a member in 1903.

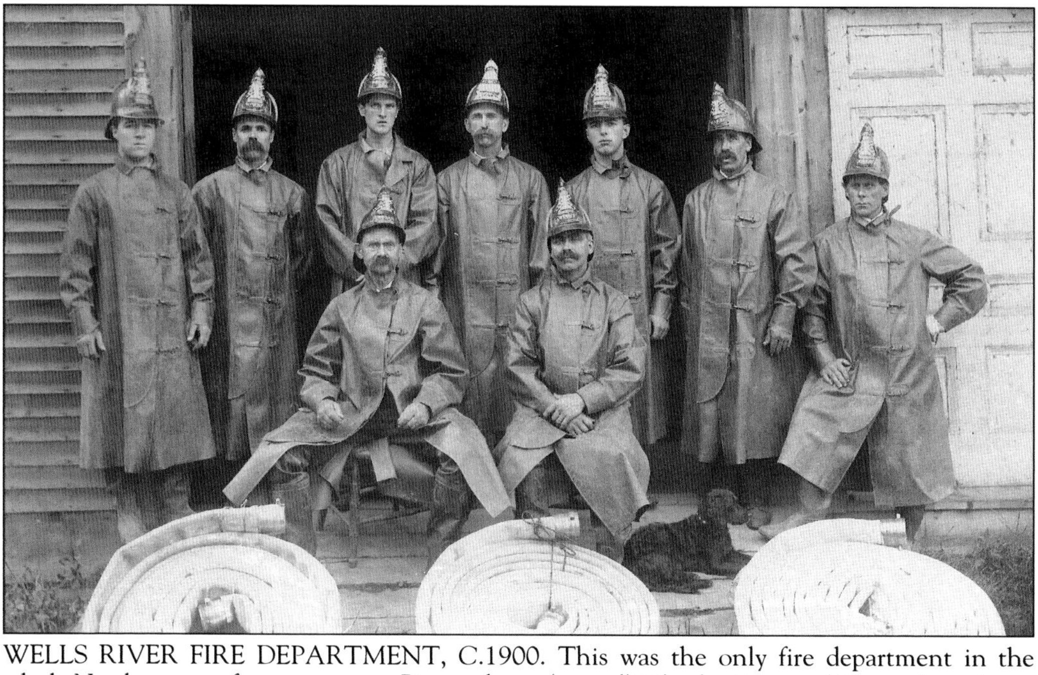

WELLS RIVER FIRE DEPARTMENT, C.1900. This was the only fire department in the whole Newbury area for many years. Pictured are: (seated) Charles Page and Heney Lamphare; (standing) Beanie Vincent (third from left), George Tiedeman (second from right), Freeman Lyons (center), and unknown others. The building was located behind the bank and had a jail room.

Six

Haverhill

NEW HAMPSHIRE
Grafton County
First Settled: 1761
Chartered: May 18, 1763
Population in 1990: 4164
Area: 52.11 square miles
Principal Settlements: Woodsville, North Haverhill, Haverhill Corner

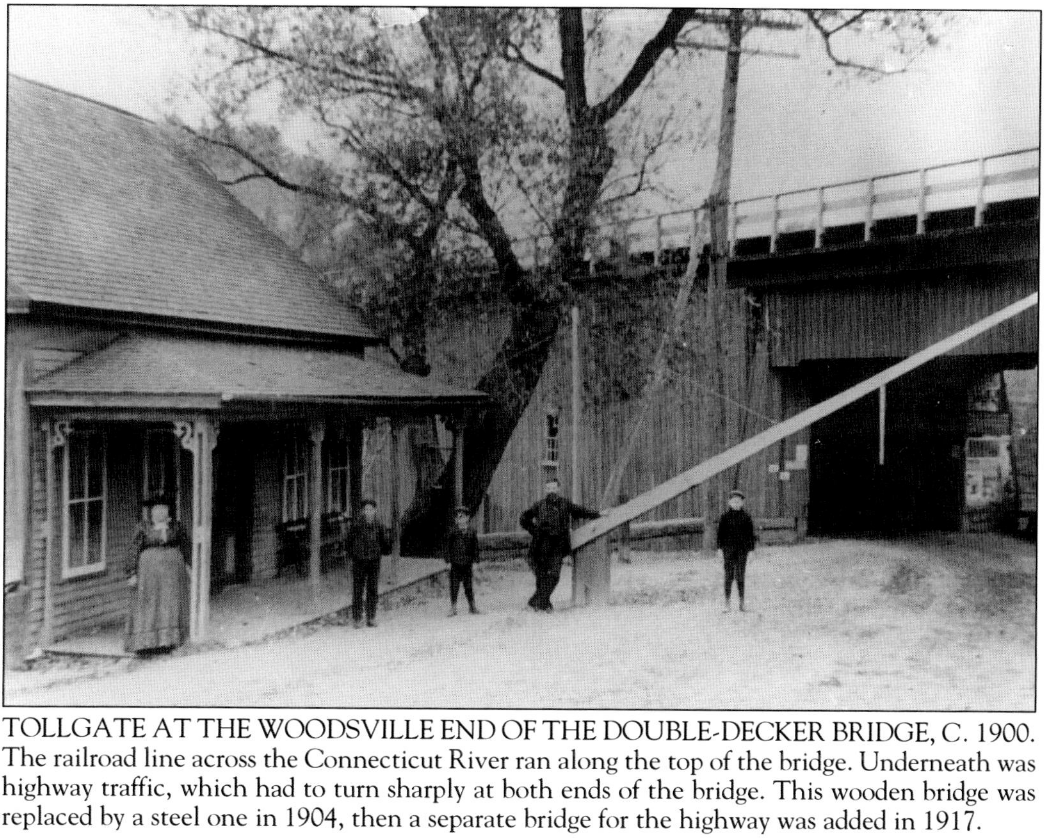

TOLLGATE AT THE WOODSVILLE END OF THE DOUBLE-DECKER BRIDGE, C. 1900. The railroad line across the Connecticut River ran along the top of the bridge. Underneath was highway traffic, which had to turn sharply at both ends of the bridge. This wooden bridge was replaced by a steel one in 1904, then a separate bridge for the highway was added in 1917.

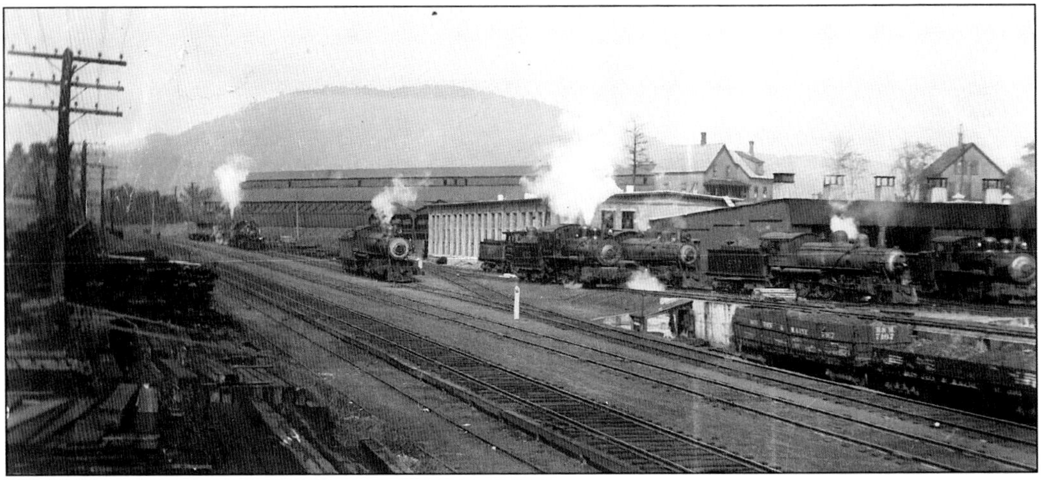

BUSY RAILROAD YARD IN WOODSVILLE. Until the 1950s, railroad lines came into Woodsville-Wells River from five directions. Railroad service was hard-hit by the Depression. It recovered somewhat during World War II, but afterwards increasingly lost business to trucks and automobiles.

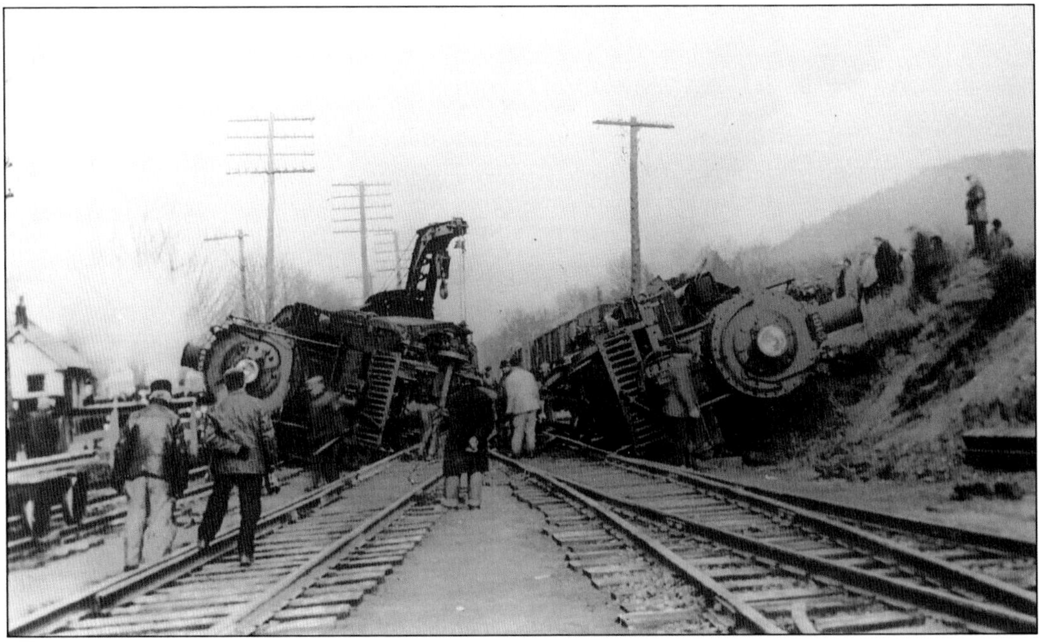

WOODSVILLE RAILROAD COLLISION, 1931. Two locomotives backed into the same cross-over, near the coal sheds. Everyone was able to jump free except engineer Edward Buckley, who was scalded to death by steam.

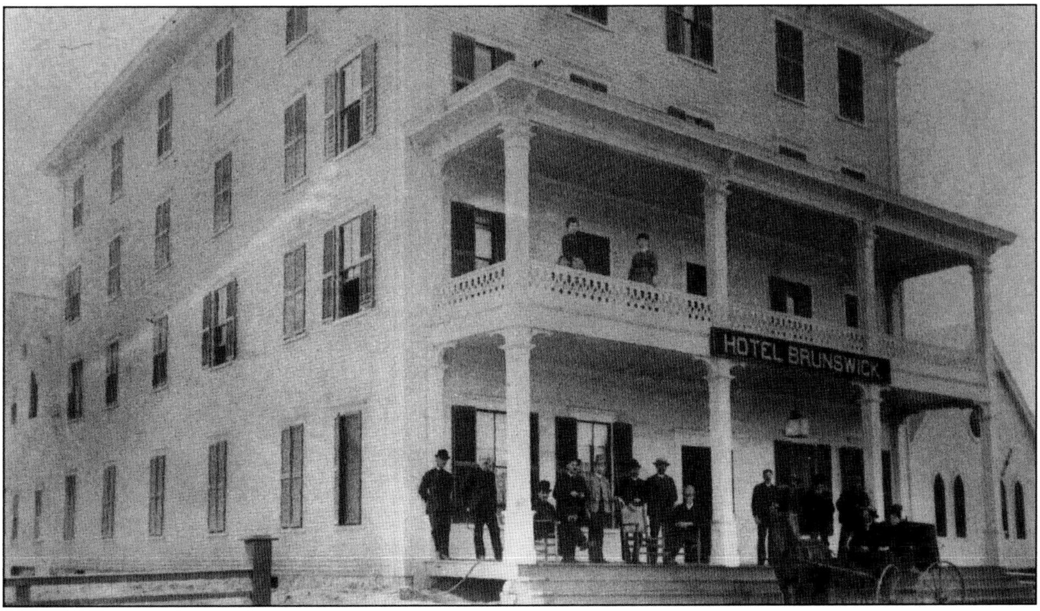

HOTEL BRUNSWICK, CENTRAL STREET, WOODSVILLE, C. 1889. At various times, this was also known as the Hotel Johnson, Tremont House, Wright's Tavern, and the New Orrington. It burned in 1912 and was replaced by the Rowden Block, with two stores, which burned in 1950. Chamberlin's flower shop is in this location now. At the right in the photograph is the Methodist church, which was moved to its present location on Maple Street in 1890.

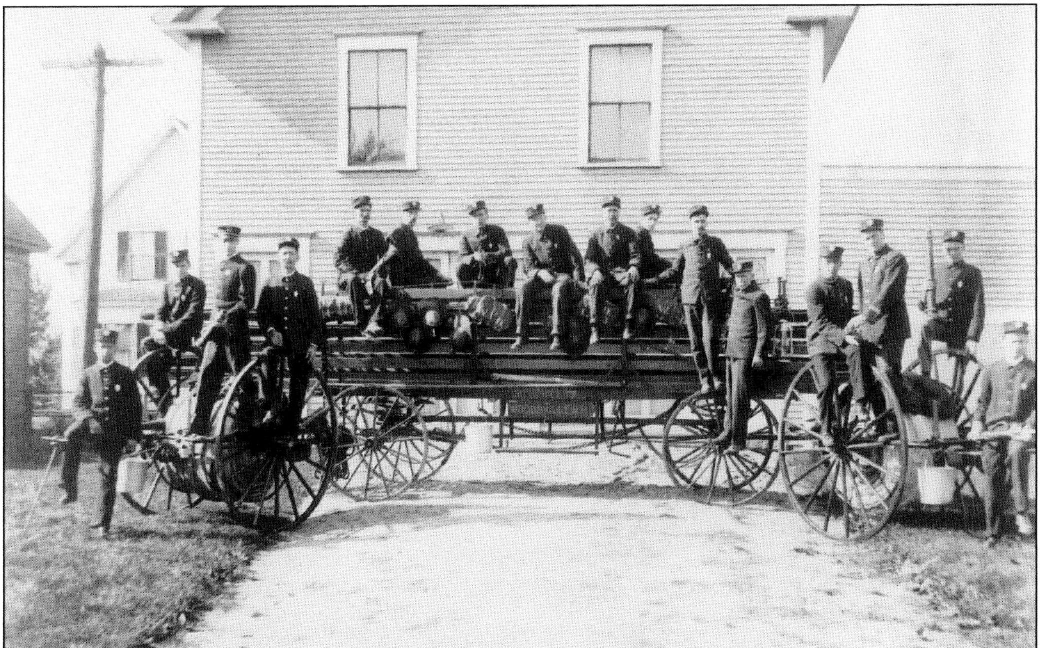

WOODSVILLE FIREMEN AND FIRE STATION, EARLY 1900s. The original hose house was built on School Street in 1887, then moved to Central Street in 1899. The large annex on the front was added in 1973. The move to the new fire station on Route 10 was made in 1995.

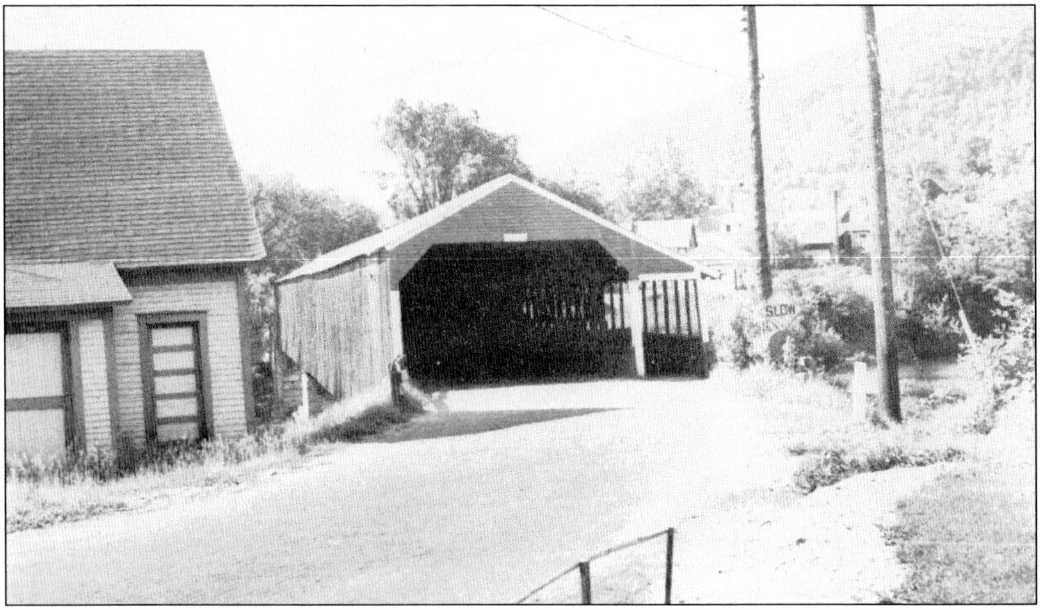

HAVERHILL-BATH COVERED BRIDGE AT WOODSVILLE. Built across the Ammonoosuc River in 1829, this is the oldest covered bridge still standing in New Hampshire. To our knowledge, it is the oldest authenticated one in the country. On the left was the Woodsville creamery, built in 1900.

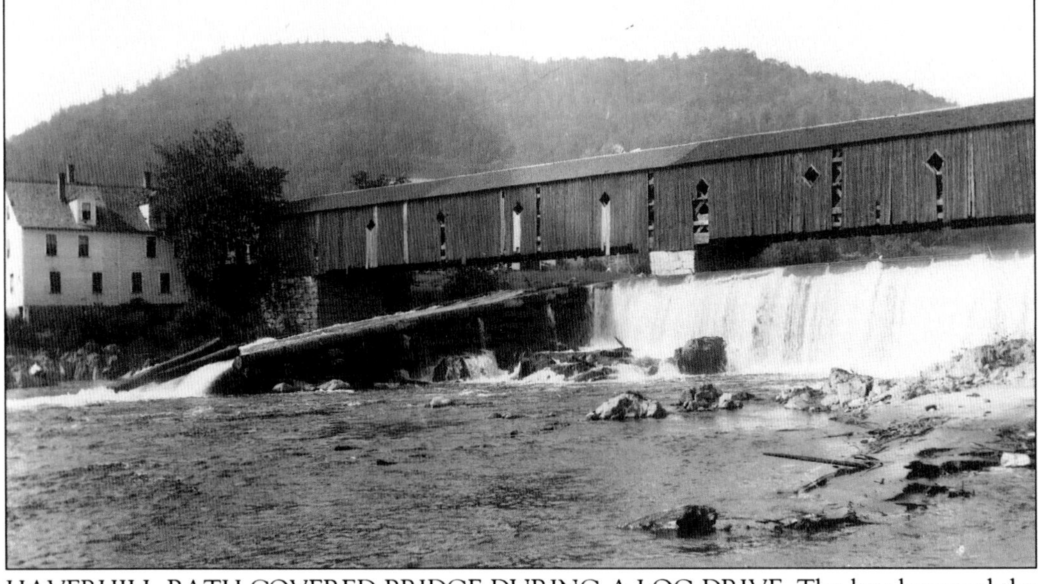

HAVERHILL-BATH COVERED BRIDGE DURING A LOG DRIVE. The logs bypassed the local power dam by means of a sluice. In the early 1900s, the bridge still had windows on the west side.

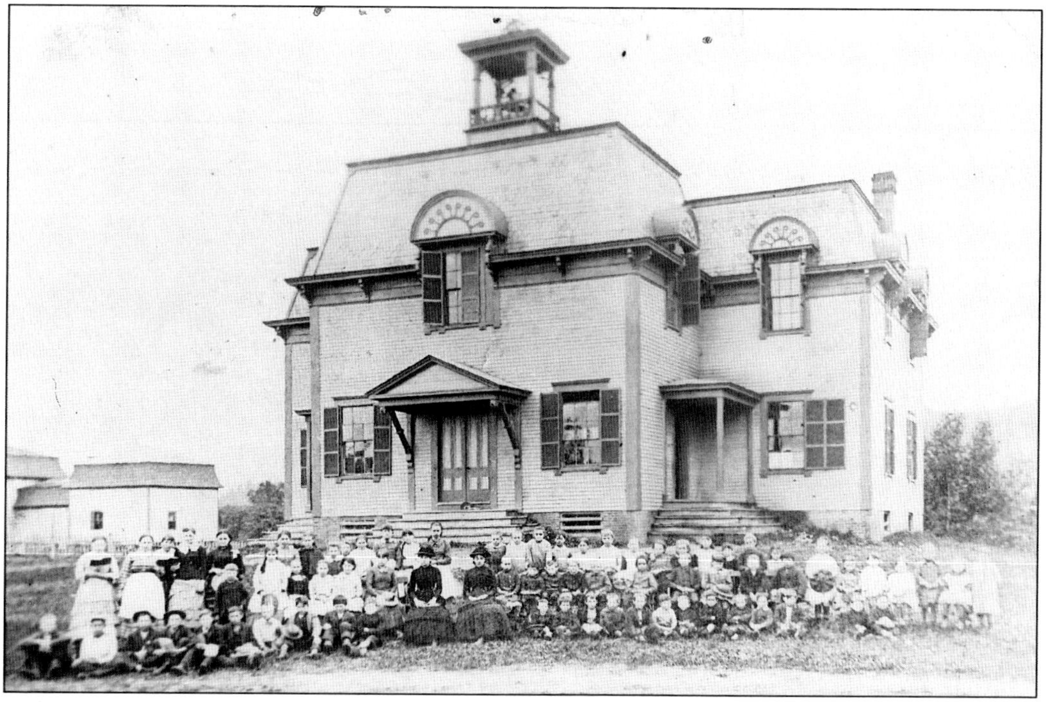

WOODSVILLE SCHOOLHOUSE, THE FIRST ON SCHOOL STREET, BUILT IN 1872. A section of the schoolhouse was partitioned off for the high school in 1885. The building was outgrown by 1899, when it was sold and moved to the C. N. Davison property. There it was used for many years as a bakery, among other businesses, and as a public hall, until it was torn down in 1936.

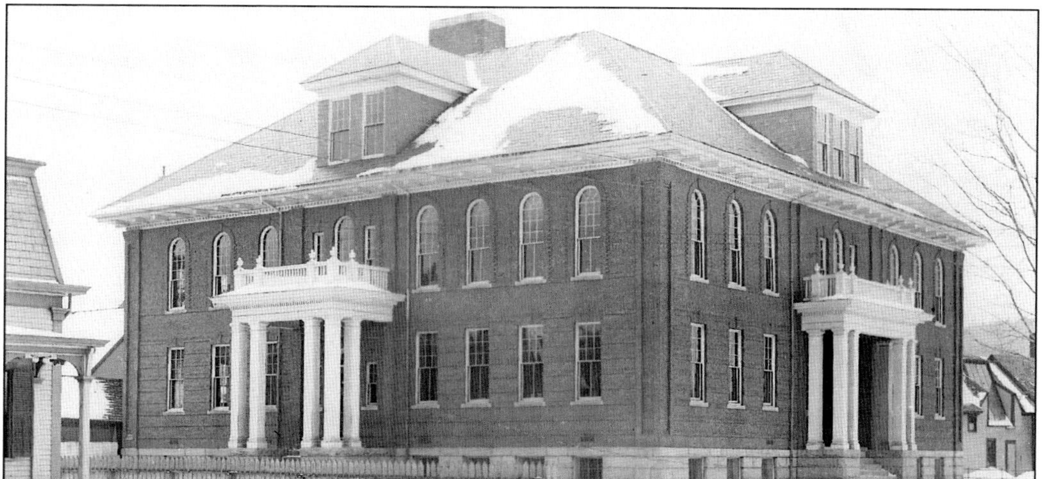

WOODSVILLE'S "NEW" SCHOOL, BUILT ON THE SAME LOT, 1899. The children moved in after Christmas vacation, but Woodsville was growing so fast that by May the lower grades were crowded again. Finally, the high school moved into the present building on King's Plain in 1914. The elementary school burned in 1961.

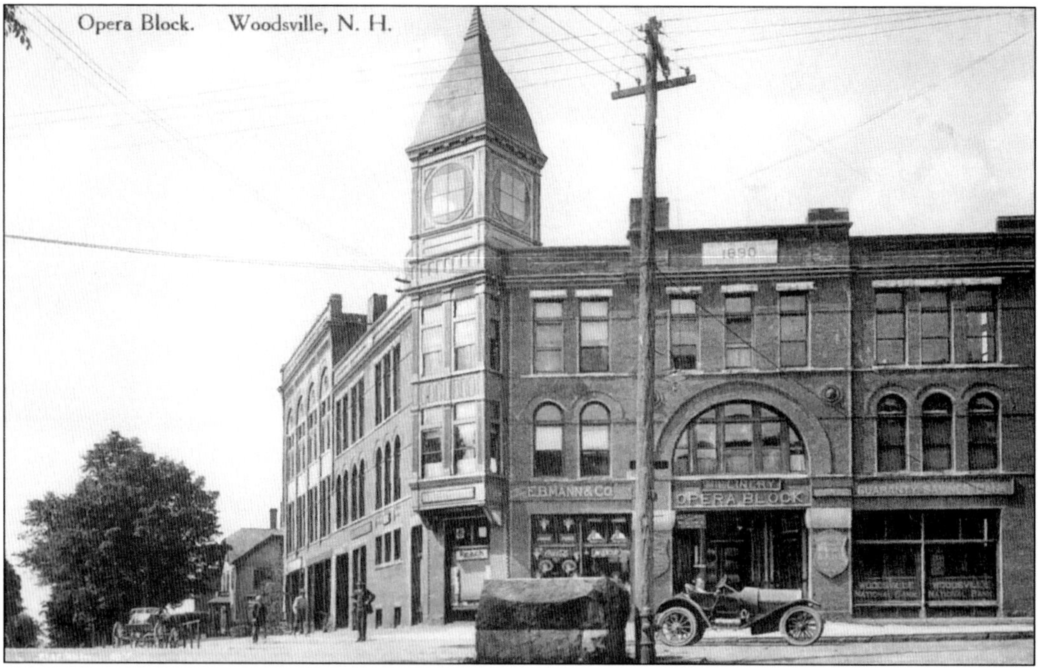

OPERA BLOCK BEFORE THE CLOCK WAS ADDED IN 1923. In front is the stone water trough, installed in 1897. When its location became hazardous for auto traffic, it was moved to the front of the American Legion home. At the left, beyond the Opera Block, stands the Railroad YMCA.

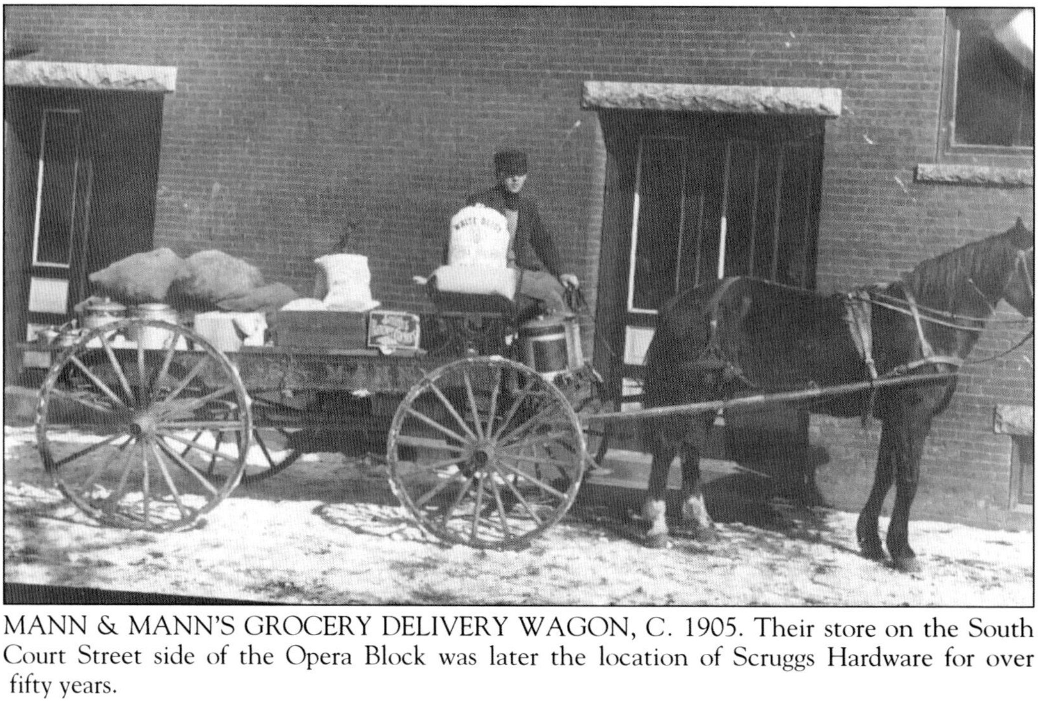

MANN & MANN'S GROCERY DELIVERY WAGON, C. 1905. Their store on the South Court Street side of the Opera Block was later the location of Scruggs Hardware for over fifty years.

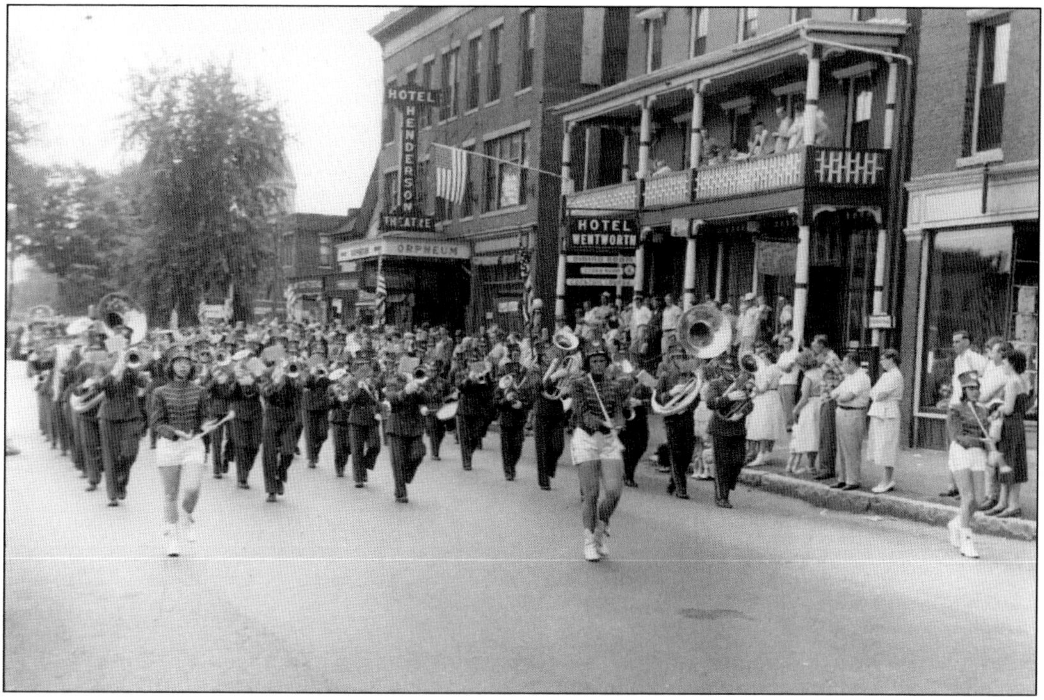

FOURTH OF JULY PARADE ON CENTRAL STREET, C. 1957. Marching along smartly past the Henderson and Wentworth hotels is McLure's Student Band, led by drum major Ann Sherwin.

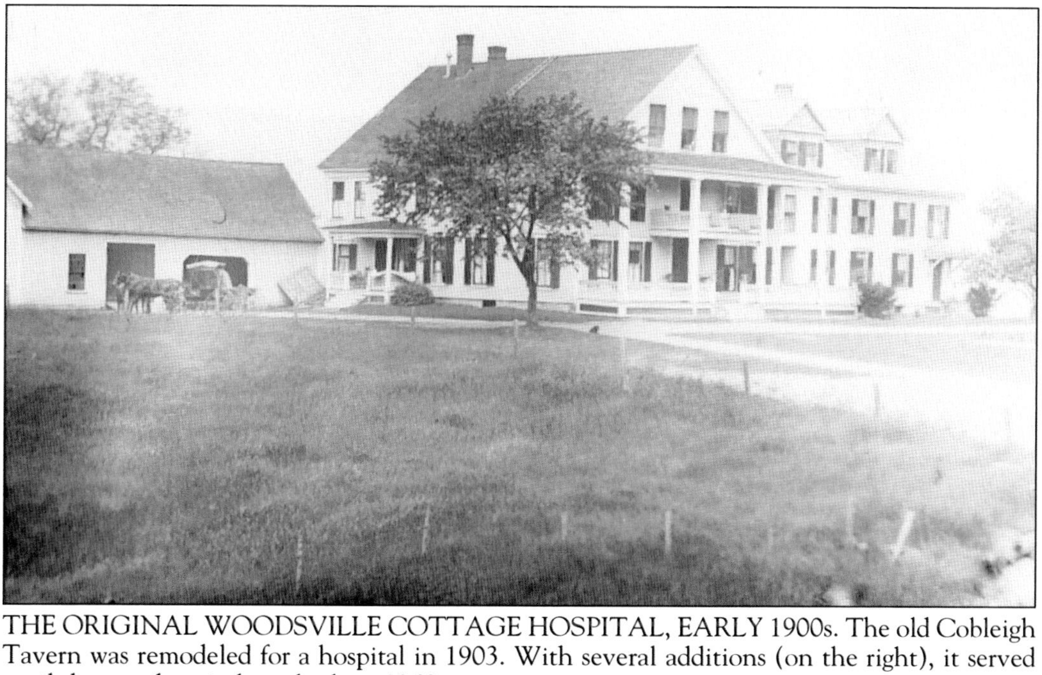

THE ORIGINAL WOODSVILLE COTTAGE HOSPITAL, EARLY 1900s. The old Cobleigh Tavern was remodeled for a hospital in 1903. With several additions (on the right), it served until the new hospital was built in 1960.

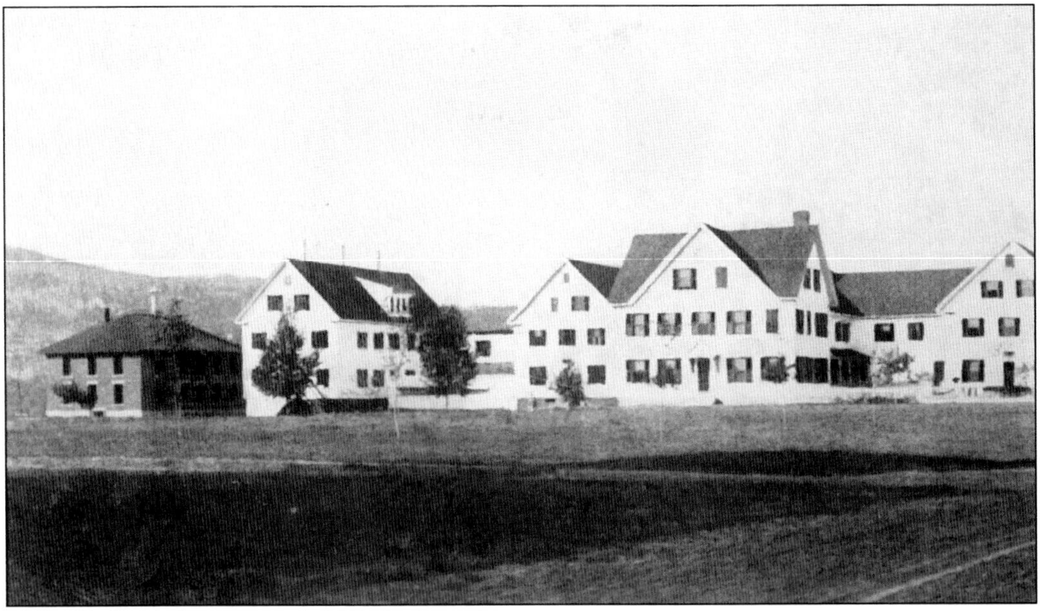

GRAFTON COUNTY HOME ON HORSE MEADOW, NORTH HAVERHILL. When the facility began in 1866, the first wooden buildings were in a line at a right-angle to the highway. The first brick building was erected in 1930, and the hospital wing was added in 1969.

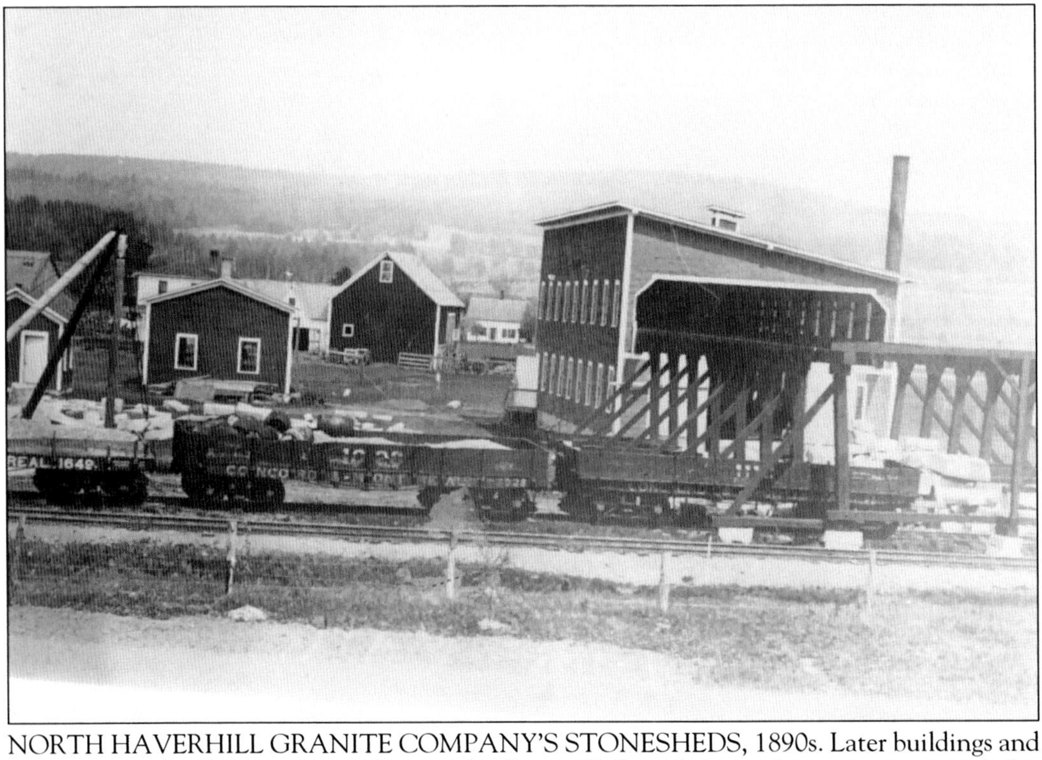

NORTH HAVERHILL GRANITE COMPANY'S STONESHEDS, 1890s. Later buildings and businesses in this location were those of the Forest Hills and Ames discount stores, and also Grossman's building supplies. A large boarding house, barns, blacksmith shop, and derricks were at the granite company's quarries on Briar Hill.

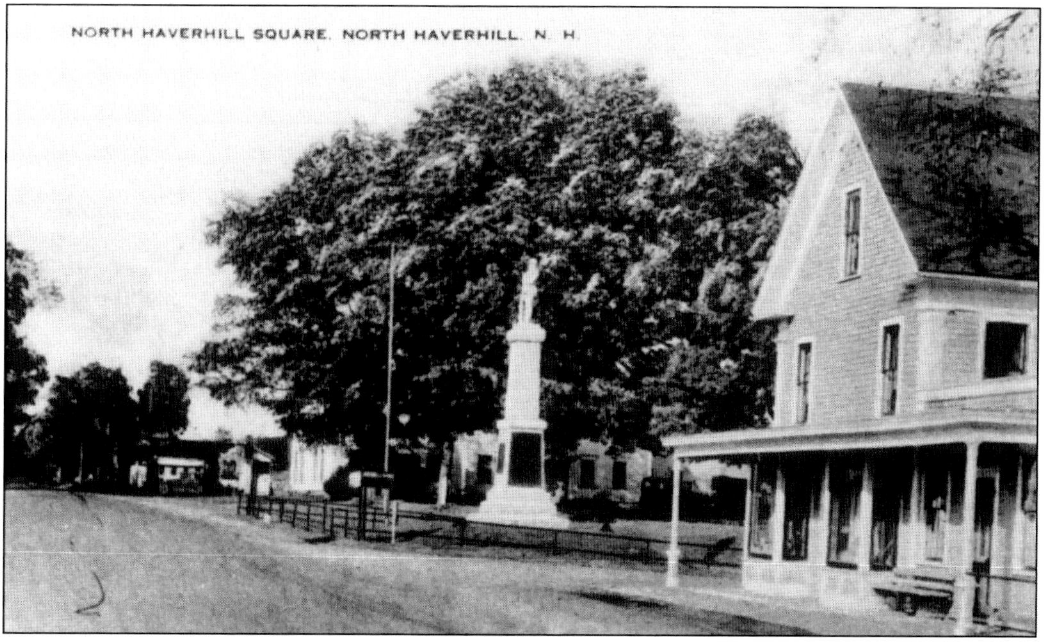

NORTH HAVERHILL, C. 1940. On the right is the corner store, built in 1887 and now converted to apartments. The soldiers' monument was erected in 1912 by the town and the Women's Relief Corps. Behind the big tree is Marcia Lackie's house, a tavern in the old days. Just beyond was Rintha Church Nutter's gas station and lunch room.

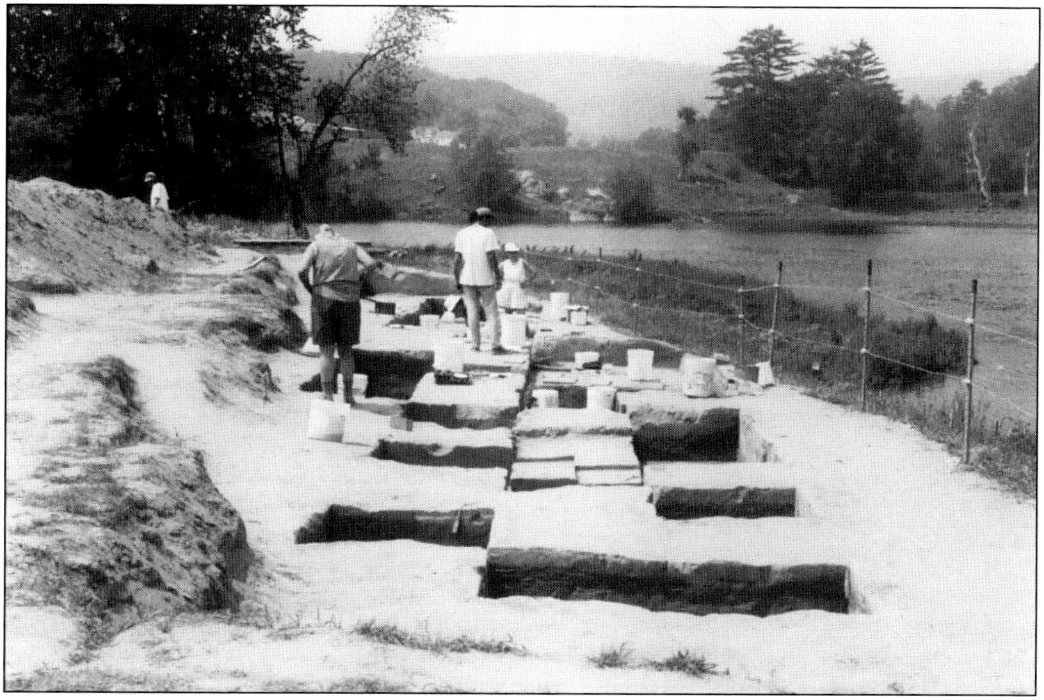

ARCHEOLOGICAL DIG ON THE LITTLE OXBOW MEADOW, 1993. "Points" (arrow and spear heads) were found, as well as pieces of Indian pottery.

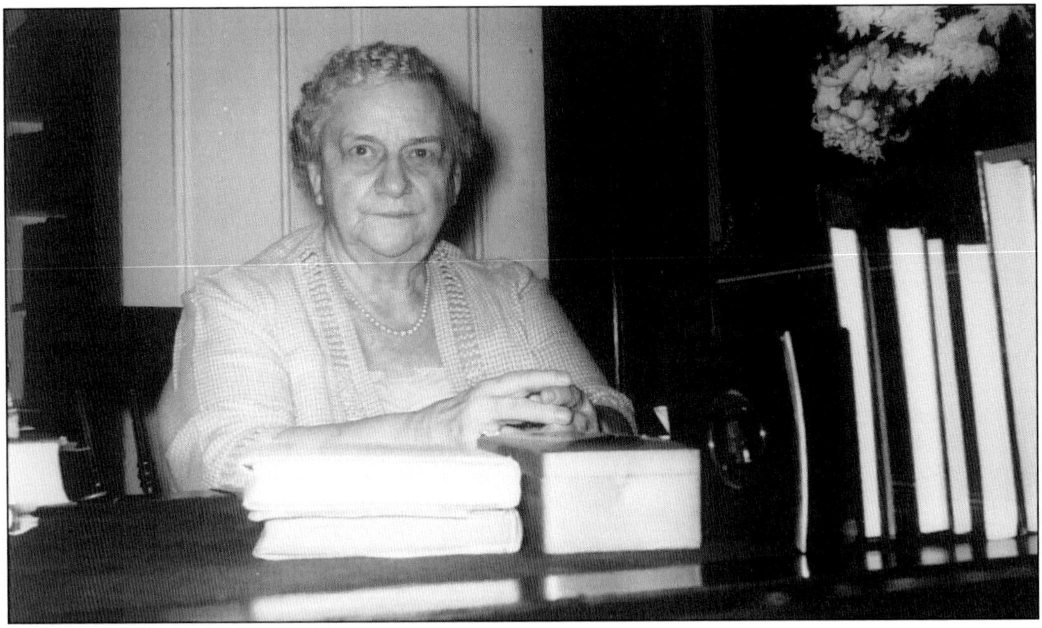

FRANCES PARKINSON KEYES, BEST-SELLING NOVELIST, 1950s. Two of her novels, *Safe Bridge* and *Also the Hills*, were set in our local area. Her husband was U.S. Senator and New Hampshire Governor Henry W. Keyes. Their home south of North Haverhill is a handsome landmark and their farm was very forward-looking in its time.

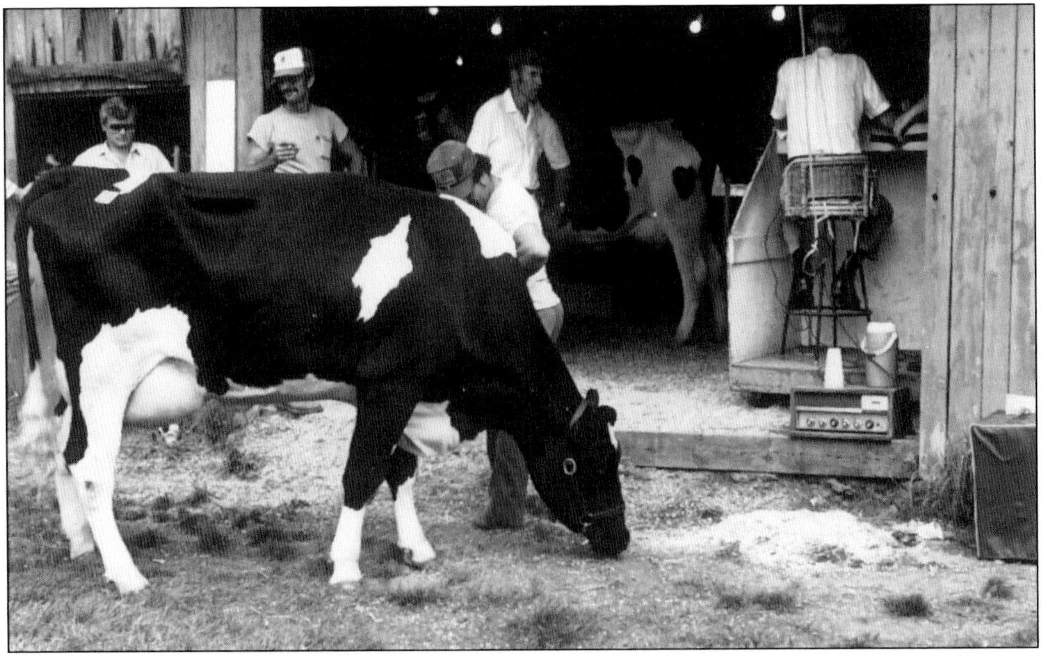

READY FOR ONE OF THE CATTLE SHOWS AT NORTH HAVERHILL FAIR. Reflecting the great importance of farming (especially dairy farming) in this town, Pink Granite Grange started this fair more than fifty years ago so that 4-H Clubs, Granges, and farmers of the area could exhibit their livestock and produce. The fair has grown to four busy days, features a great variety of events, and now has its own fairgrounds.

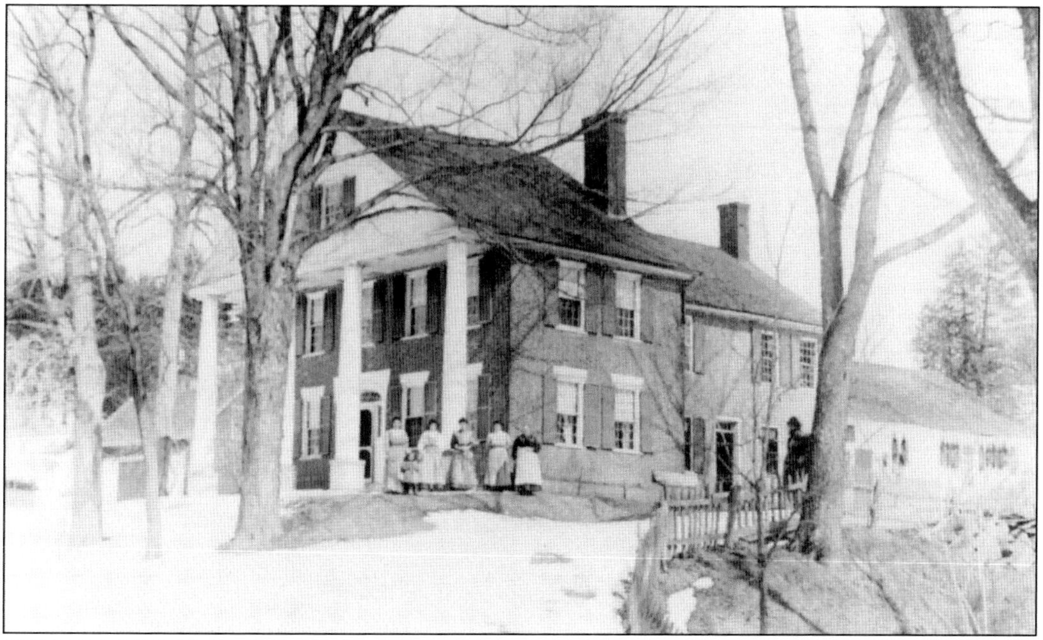

SWAN'S UNION HOUSE/BUCK'S TAVERN, C. 1900. Located across from the present North Haverhill fairgrounds, this building originated as a private residence in the late 1700s. It had numerous additions, including the portico and columns made by Phineas Swan and his son Benjamin. The early origins still show in its old fireplaces, handmade iron hinges and latches, and the extremely wide floorboards. Benjamin Swan opened it as a tavern in 1836, then sold it in 1841 to Lyman Buck.

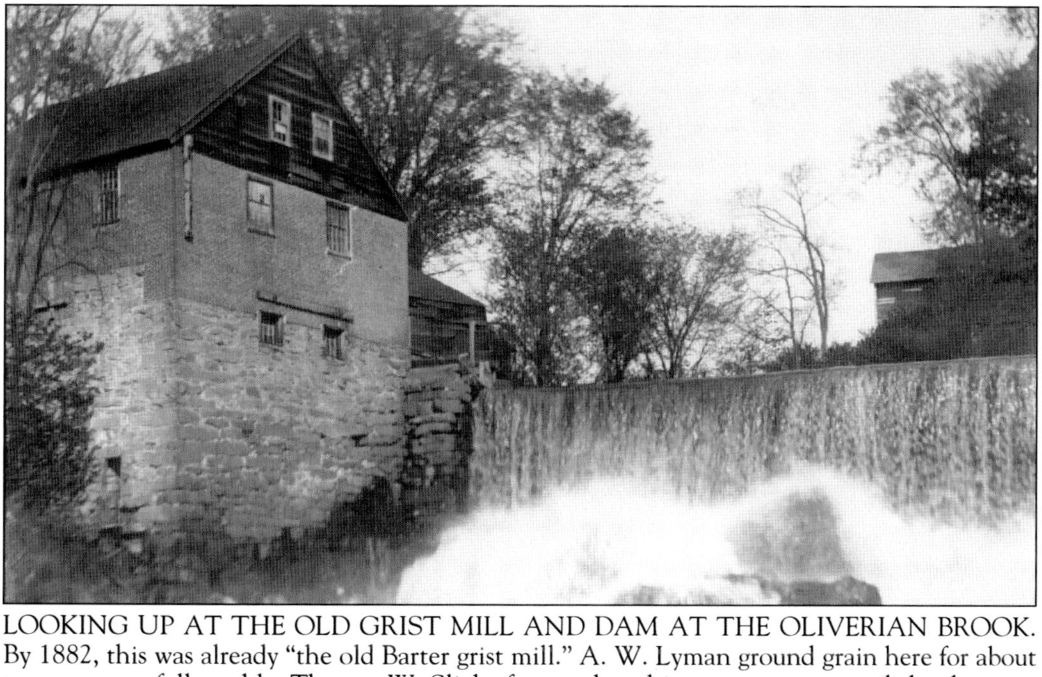

LOOKING UP AT THE OLD GRIST MILL AND DAM AT THE OLIVERIAN BROOK. By 1882, this was already "the old Barter grist mill." A. W. Lyman ground grain here for about twenty years, followed by Thomas W. Slight for another thirty years or so, until the dam was taken out by the 1927 flood.

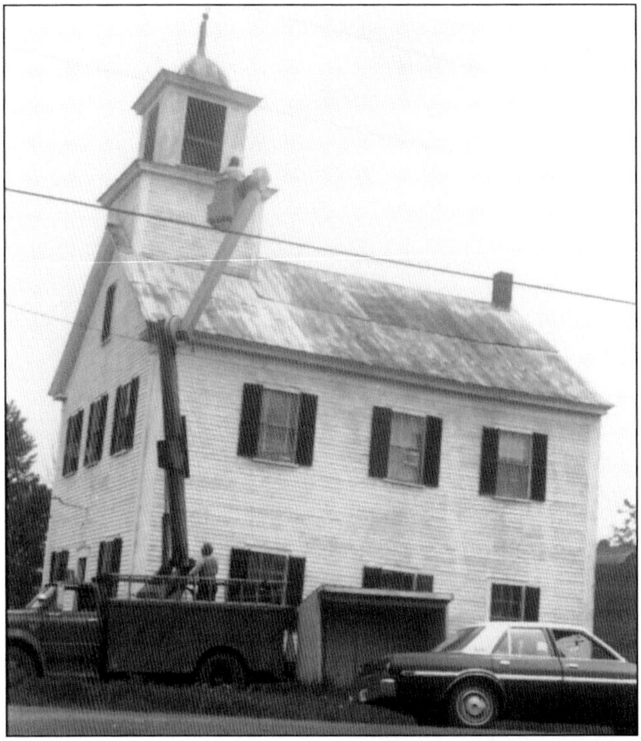

THE LADD STREET SCHOOLHOUSE. This school was built in 1849, north of Haverhill Corner. In this photograph, Gloria Poliquin of Woodsville is getting a closer view of the bell in 1976, with help from the Woodsville Water and Light truck.

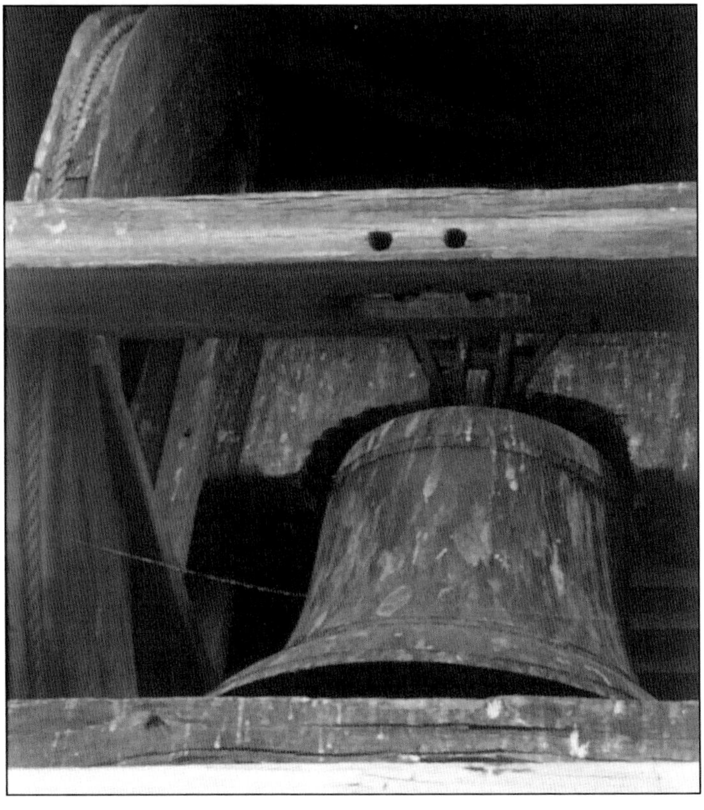

THE LADD STREET BELL, CAST IN 1802. The bell was first used in the nearby Ladd Street church, then moved when the church was dismantled and the schoolhouse was built. Pulling on the bellrope turns the vertical wooden wheel (at left) to ring the bell.

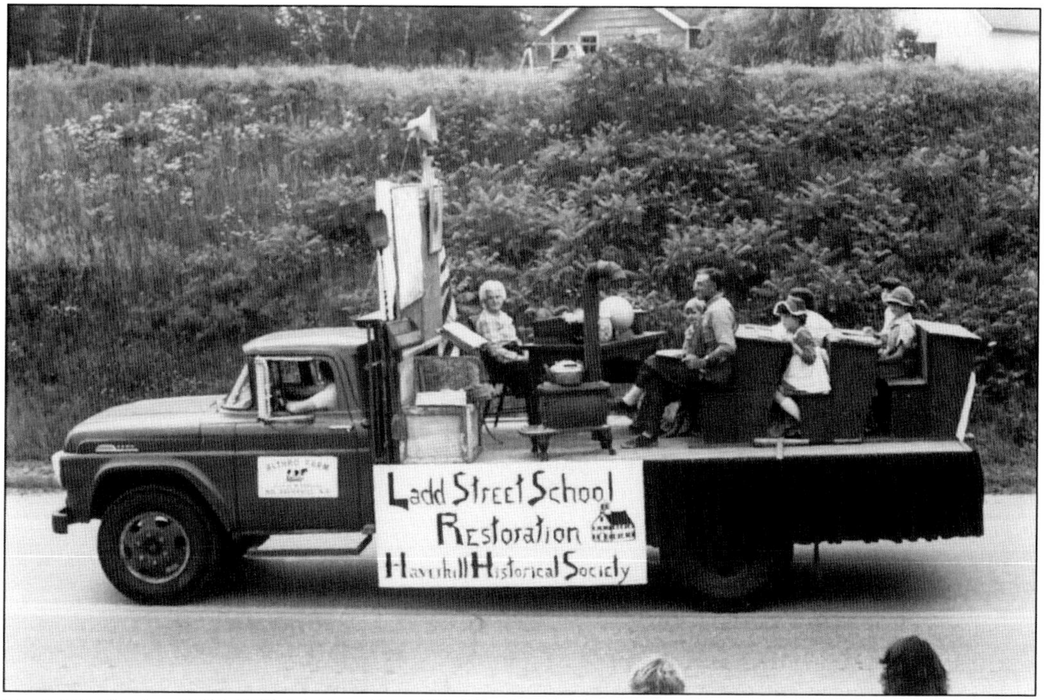

HAVERHILL HISTORICAL SOCIETY BICENTENNIAL FLOAT, JULY 4, 1976. This representation of the Ladd Street schoolroom even has an authentic teacher from the school, Frances Larty, who taught there in 1914.

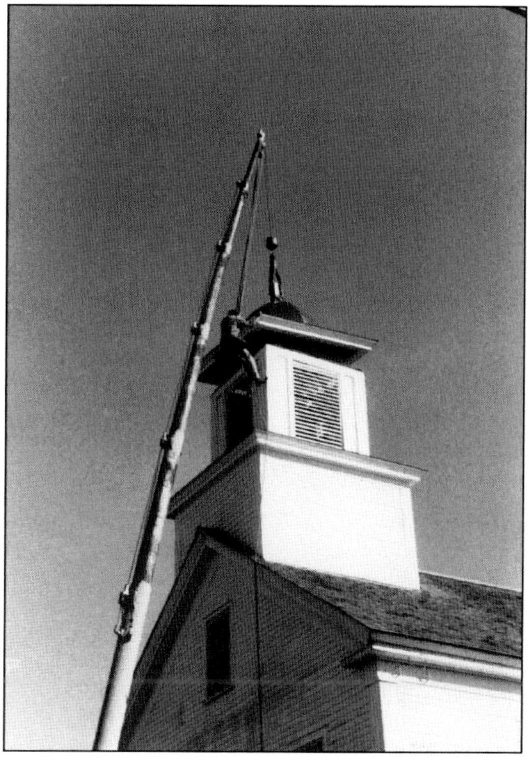

INSTALLING A NEW COPPER DOME ON THE LADD STREET SCHOOL, 1994. For many years after it closed as a school in 1927, the schoolhouse was the property and meetingplace of the Knights of Pythias and the Pythian Sisters. In 1980, the structure was deeded it to the Haverhill Historical Society, which has a long term renovation project planned for the building.

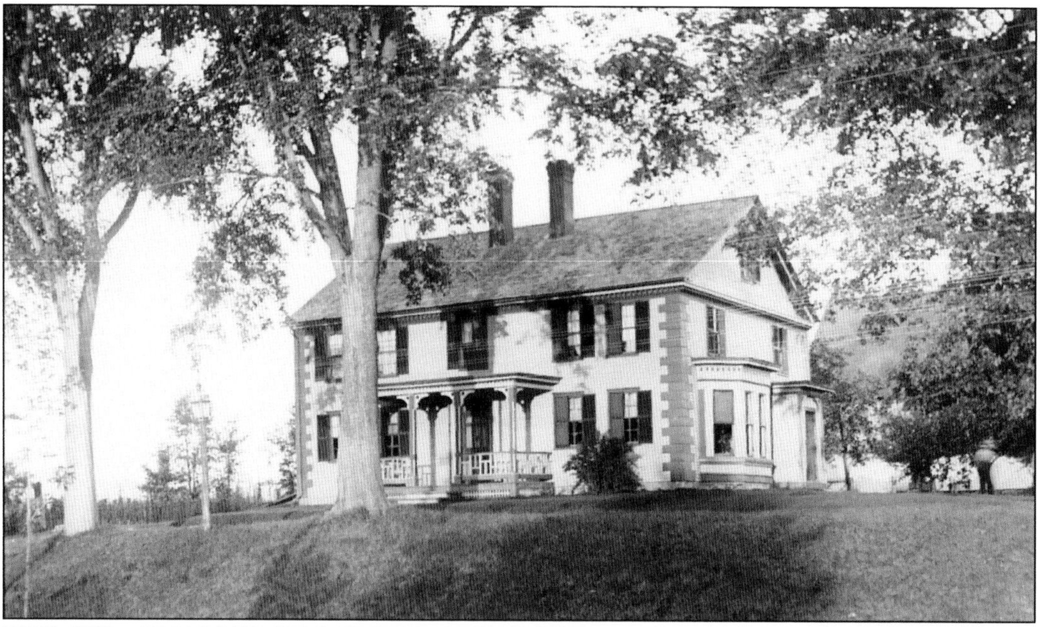

THE COL. CHARLES JOHNSTON HOUSE, BUILT SOON AFTER 1769. This was the first frame house built in Haverhill Corner, and it is the oldest still standing in the town of Haverhill. Col. Johnston was a hero of the Revolution and a great benefactor of this village.

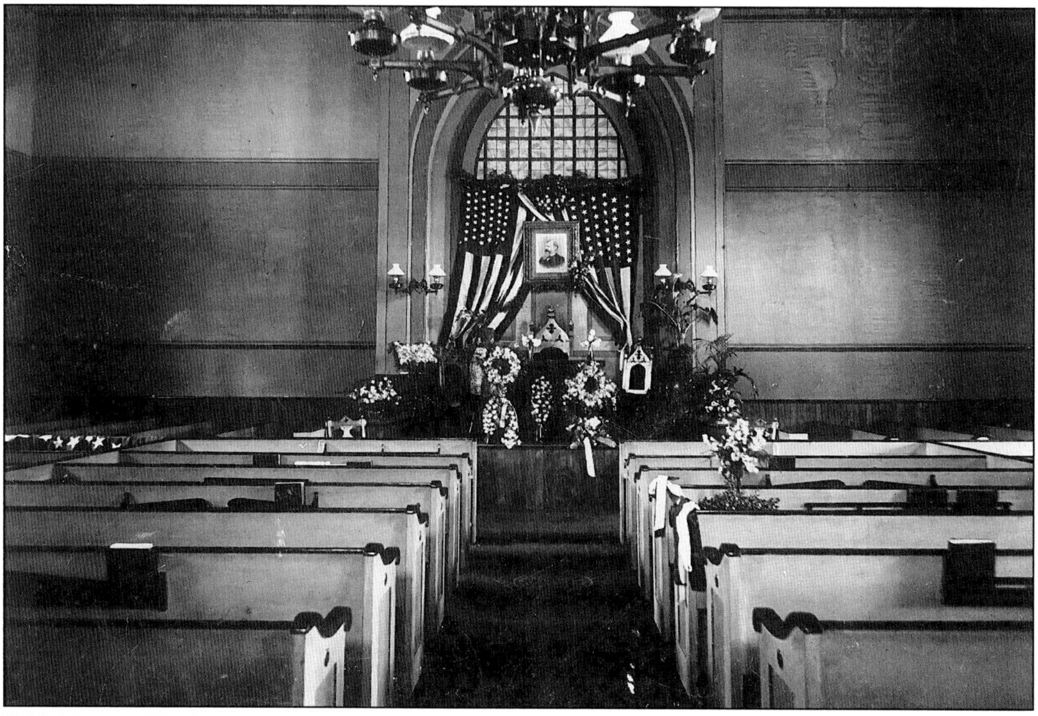

EARLY INTERIOR OF THE CONGREGATIONAL CHURCH, HAVERHILL CORNER. The chancel was added to the north end of the church in 1946. This church was originally built by the Methodist Society in Haverhill in 1827, but two years later, due to budget constraints, they sold it to the Congregationalists, who had outgrown their church at Ladd Street.

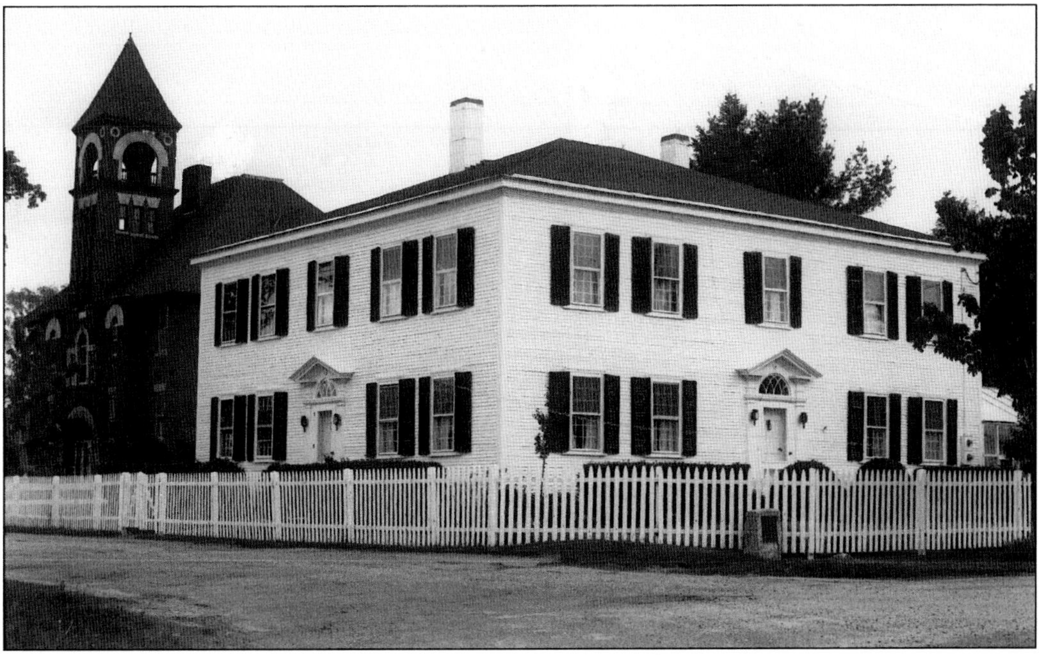

BLISS TAVERN, BUILT 1788. This was a busy place when county court sessions were in Haverhill Corner, as it traditionally was the headquarters of the judge and lawyers, including Daniel Webster. In 1795, Capt. Bliss was appointed postmaster, and this became the northernmost outpost of the federal postal system. Visible at the left is the Haverhill Academy building, built in 1897, which is now closed.

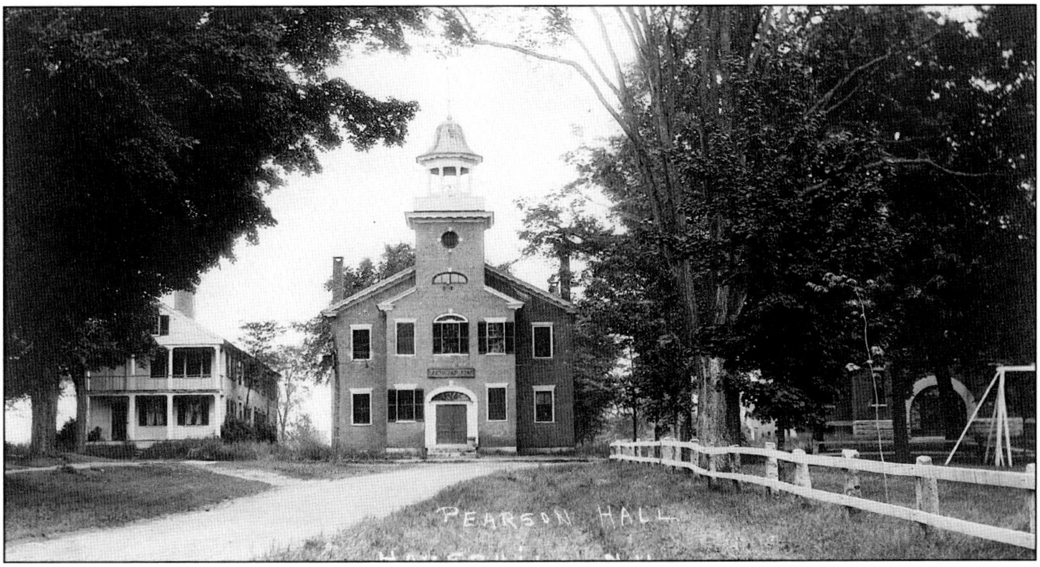

PEARSON HALL. This building was built in 1816 as the second home of Haverhill Academy. It was renovated in 1897 through the generosity of a former pupil, Henry Pearson of Chicago. In the beginning, it also served as the county courthouse until a separate one (now Alumni Hall) was built in 1846. In the early 1900s, Pearson Hall also housed the Haverhill Library. In 1969, an annex was built to connect Pearson Hall with the Academy building, so that together they served as the Haverhill Academy Junior High School.

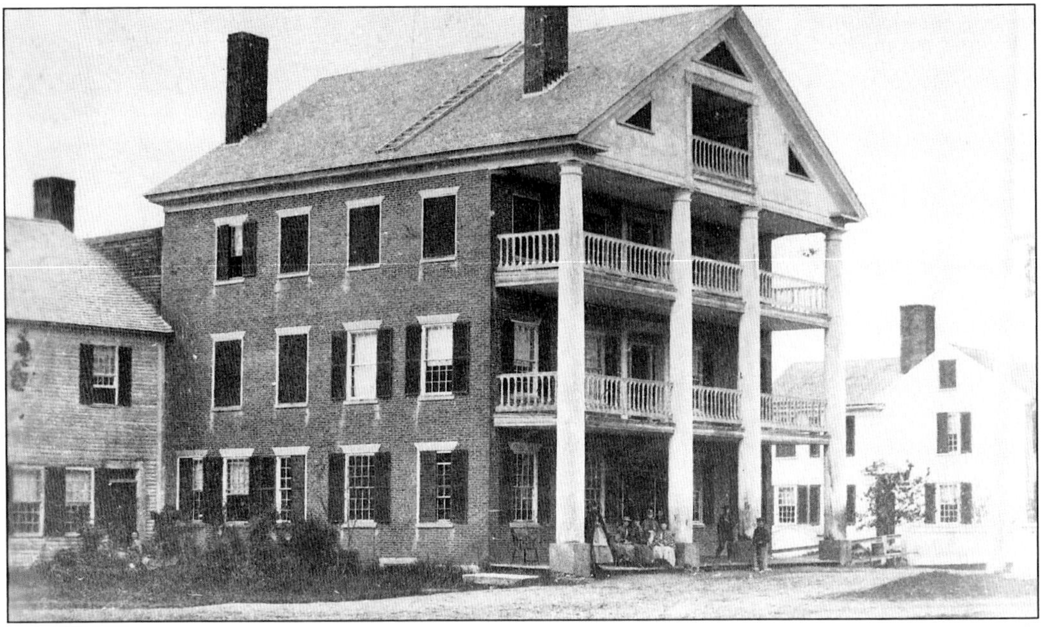

EXCHANGE HOTEL, BURNED IN 1902. Located across Main Street from the North Common, this was originally a square, two-story private residence, built soon after 1791 by Charles W. Swan. The third story, the portico, and the ell, which had a dance hall in the second story, were added later. The place was run as a tavern for nearly one hundred years. Landlords for more than forty years were the Smiths, Eleazer and then Charles, who were former stagecoach drivers.

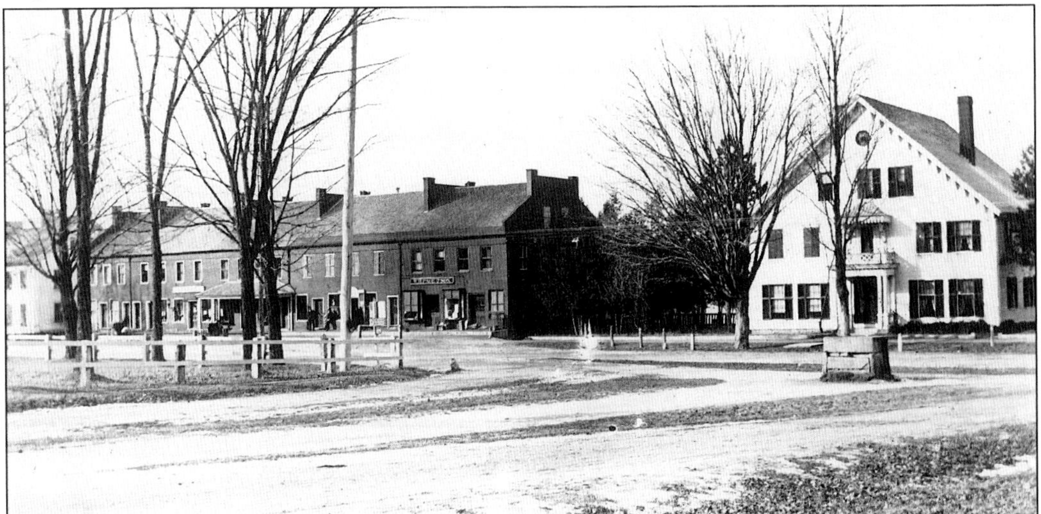

THE BRICK BLOCK AND THE TOWLE HOUSE. Both were built after the great fire of 1848. The Brick Block, also called the Phoenix Block, "rose from the ashes" opposite the South Common, replacing four business buildings lost in the fire. The Towle house replaced the Towle family's tavern, which Asa Boynton had built opposite the end of the Coos Turnpike (now Court Street) in 1797. The stone water trough is visible, where historical markers are today. The Brick Block burned in 1906 and was replaced by residences. The Towle house property lost its barn in that fire, but they saved the house, later known as the Nat Page house.

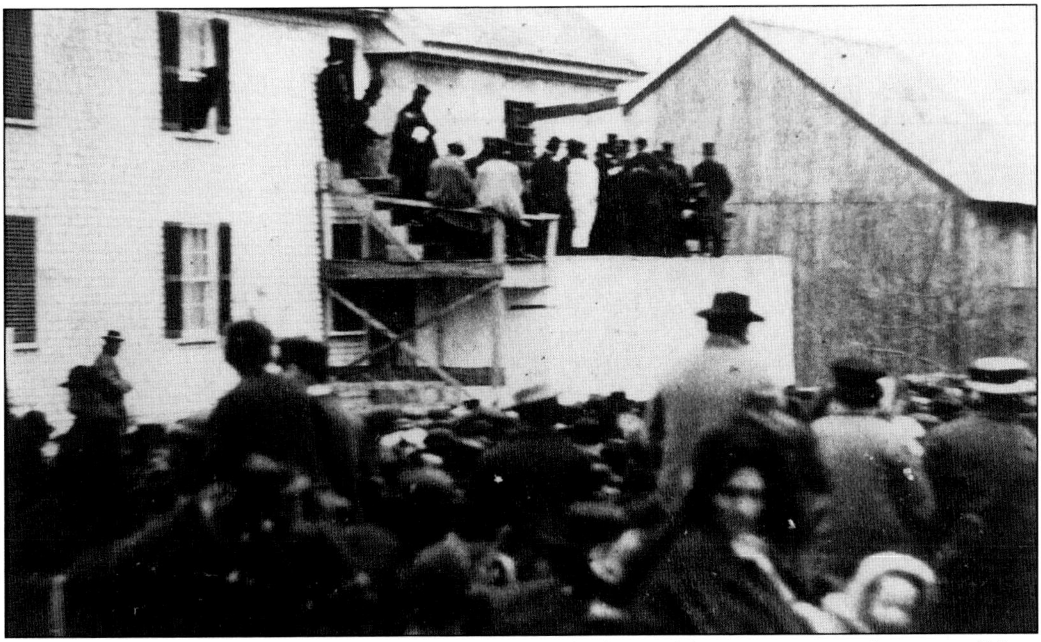

HANGING OF SAMUEL MILLS, 1868. This was the last public execution in the state of New Hampshire—and it was very public, with spectators coming from miles around in special trains. Note the woman and child in the right foreground. Mills was the white-shrouded figure at the upper center.

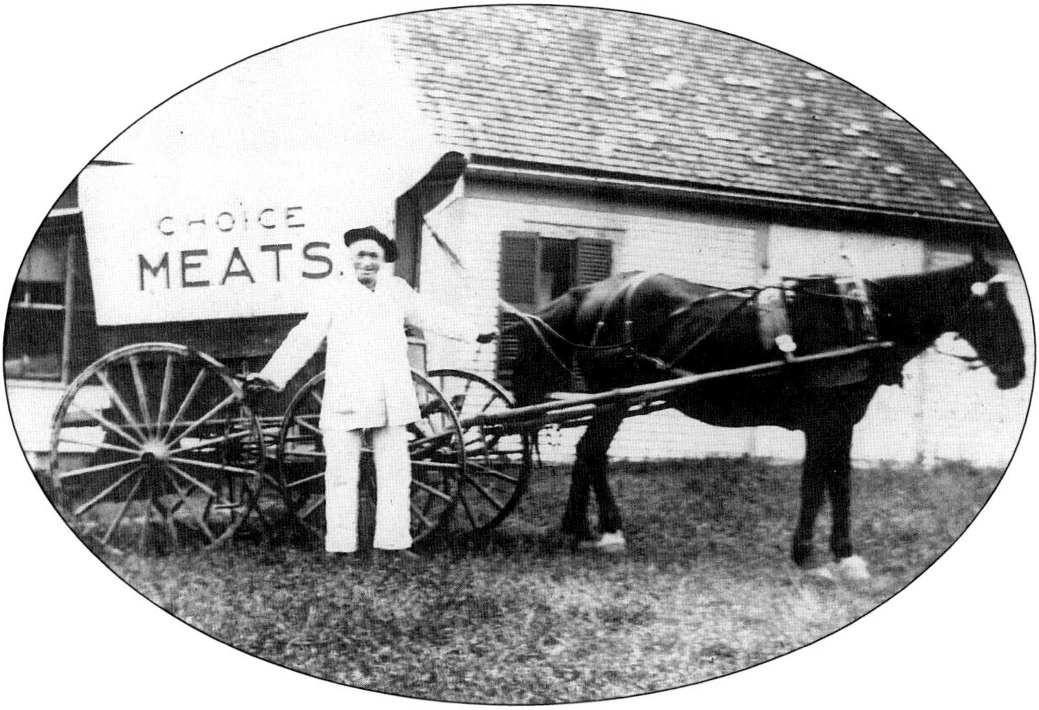

BEN COOK AND HIS MEAT CART. Mr. Cook served the Pike area, probably in the early 1900s.

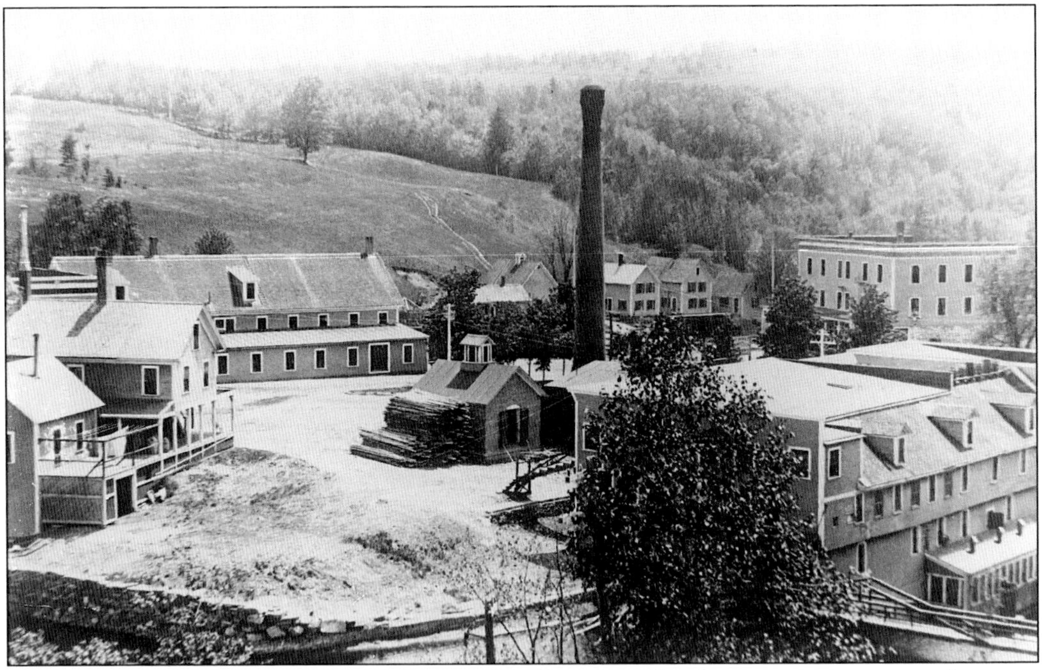

PIKE MANUFACTURING COMPANY BUILDINGS. This large company was in business from around 1830 until 1932. The village of Pike grew up around the Pike family's whetstone manufacturing empire. This became the largest such industry in the world until they were bought out by the Norton Company of Littleton, manufacturers of artificial abrasives.

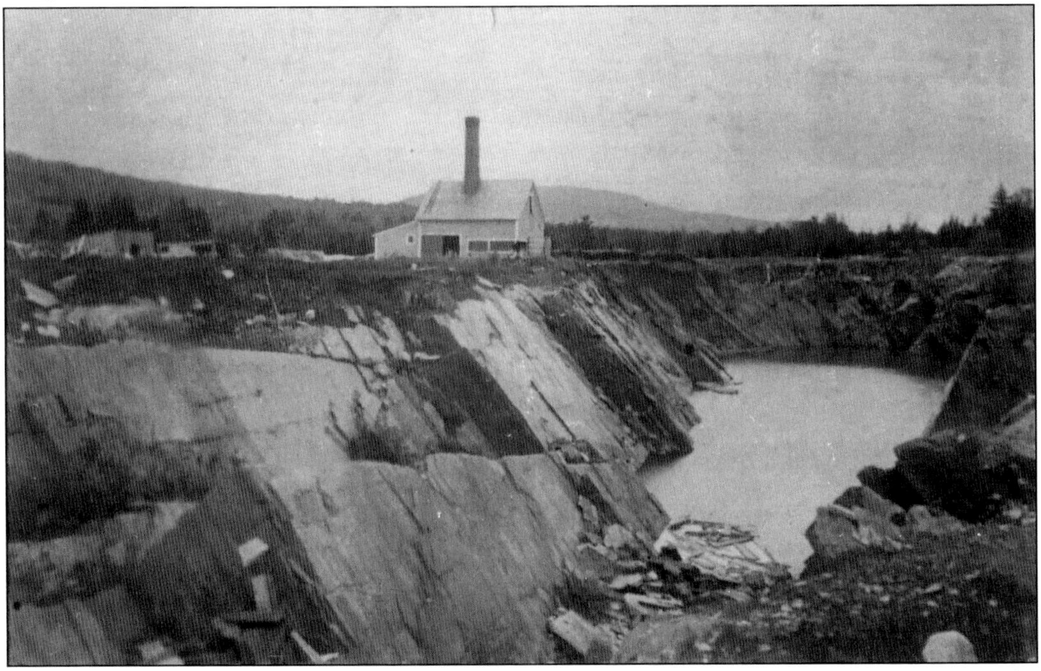

ONE OF THE WHETSTONE QUARRIES, C. 1900. Huge stone blocks were lifted out by cranes. They were then split, cut, and ground into various sizes and shapes of whetstones for sharpening scythes, razors, etc.

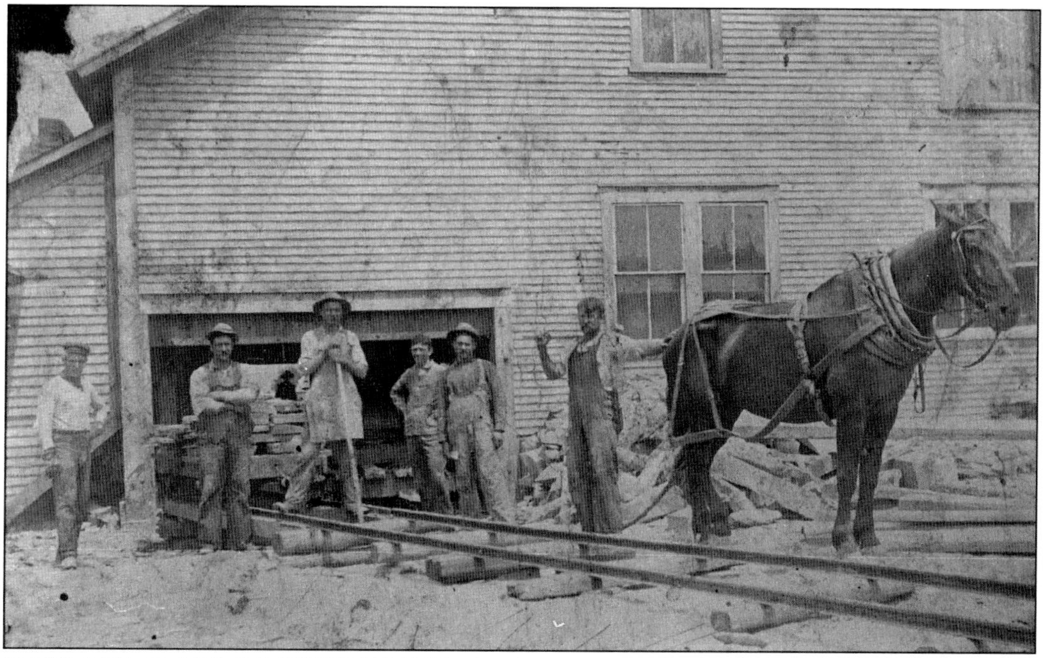

HAULING SLABS OF WHETSTONE. At the center is Fred Pike, with his hand on "Old Phoebe," whom he claimed knew more than half the men on the quarry. Next to Mr. Pike is Hiram Cross, father of Roy Cross and Esther Boutin.

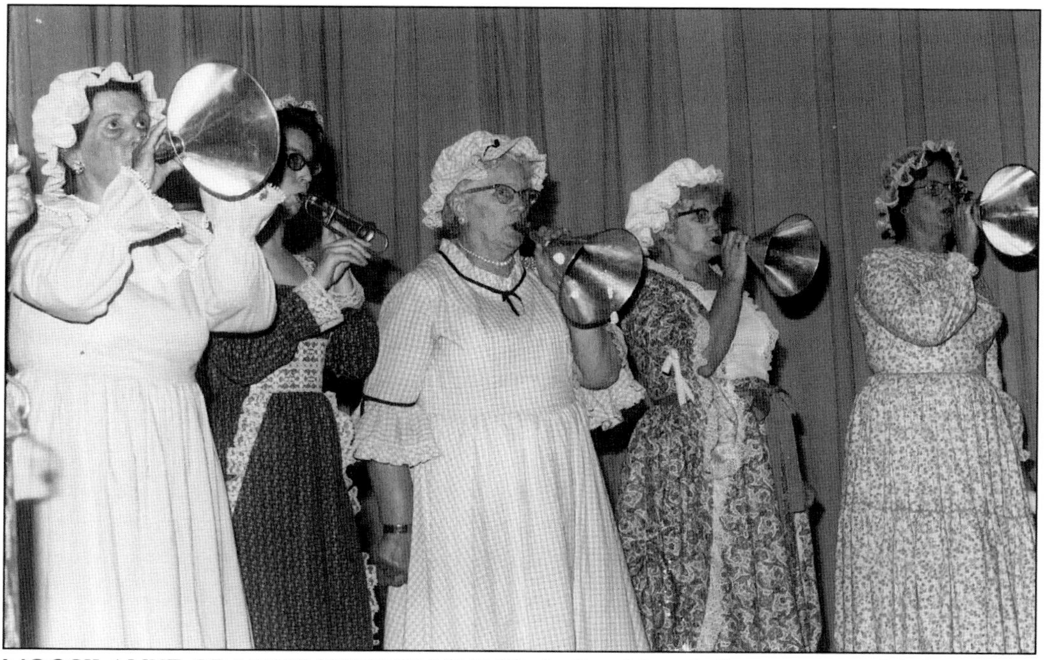

MOOSILAUKE GRANGE KITCHEN BAND. In East Haverhill, community life has always revolved around the Grange and the Methodist church. The Kitchen Band was very popular for a number of years, frequently "hitting the road" to entertain other organizations and various homes for the elderly. From left to right: Elin Chazotte, Priscilla Parker, Mildred Patten, Dorothy LaPierre, and Betty Abbott. Others also took part.

CENTER HAVERHILL CHURCH AND PASTOR CHRISTINE QUIMBY. The original church located here burned on September 4, 1931. Some of the members vowed to have a new one built "before snow flies." Snow was late that year—none fell until a veritable blizzard occurred the day after the new church was finished and dedicated on New Year's Day 1932.

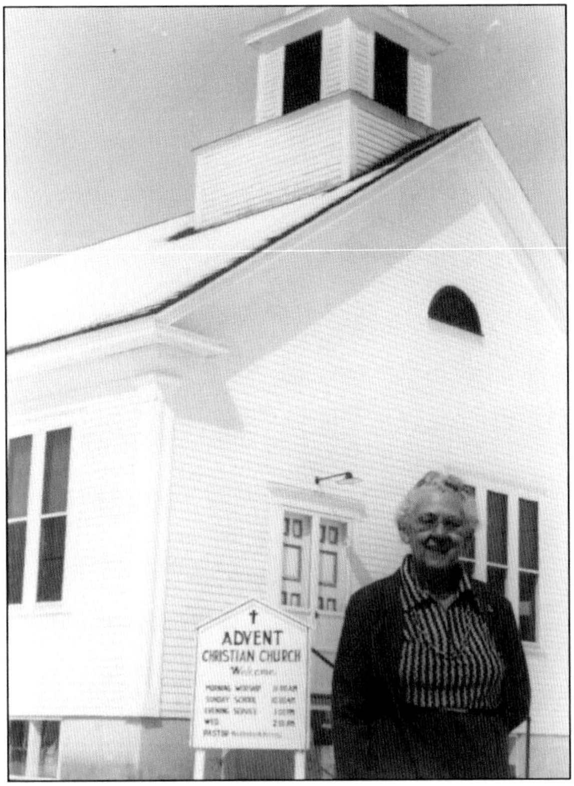

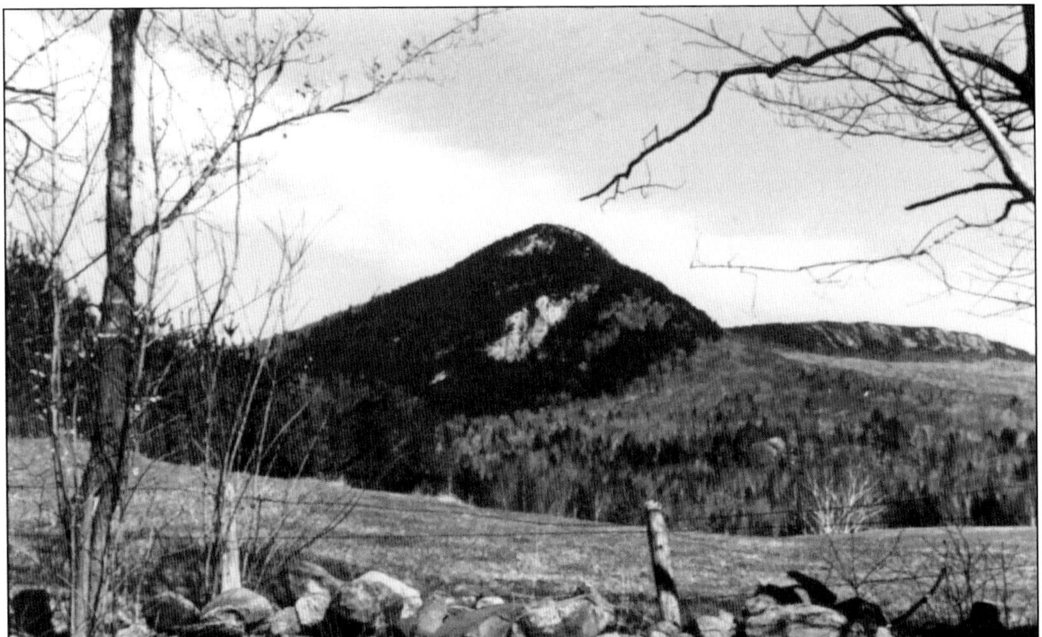

SUGAR LOAF, A NEIGHBOR OF MOUNT MOOSILAUKE. This view is from the Number Six Road. It is just a sample of this area's beautiful scenery.